THE WORKING CLASS IN BRITAIN

1850-1939

JOHN BENSON

I.B. TAURIS
LONDON · NEW YORK

Published in 2003 by I.B.Tauris & Co Ltd
6 Salem Road, London W2 4BU
175 Fifth Avenue, New York NY 10010
www.ibtauris.com

In the United States of America and in Canada distributed by
Palgrave Macmillan, a division of St Martin's Press
175 Fifth Avenue, New York NY 10010

ISBN 1 86064 902 5

A full CIP record for this book is available from the British Library
A full CIP record for this book is available from the Library of Congress

Library of Congress catalog card: available

Printed and bound in Great Britain by MPG Books Ltd, Bodmin

THE WORKING CLASS IN BRITAIN

CONTENTS

LIST OF TABLES

ACKNOWLEDGEMENTS

I have received a great deal of help in the preparation of this book. I should like to take this opportunity to acknowledge two longstanding debts: to Ken Brown, of the Queen's University of Belfast, for his help and encouragement over many years; and to my former colleague, George Bernard, of the University of Southampton, for his persistence in urging me to write a general history of the working class.

I should also like to acknowledge the many debts that I have incurred during the past three years. I am grateful for the financial support of Wolverhampton Polytechnic and the Twenty-Seven Foundation; and for the ideas, advice, information and practical assistance that I have received from Joyce Bellamy, Stella Drew, Martin Durham, Mike Haynes, Geoff Hurd, Kim McHugh, Neil Malcolm, John Rule and Harvey Woolf. I am particularly grateful to those who have taken the trouble to read, and comment upon, an earlier version of the manuscript: George Bernard of the University of Southampton; Ken Brown of the Queen's University of Belfast; Bob Cromarty of Wolverhampton Polytechnic; Eric Hopkins of the University of Birmingham; Alastair Reid of Girton College, Cambridge; John Stevenson of the University of Sheffield; and Chris Wrigley of the University of Nottingham. But once again my greatest debt is to my wife Clare, without whose support and encouragement this book would not have been written.

JOHN BENSON
November 1988

The publishers would like to thank the following for their permission to use tables in the text: Cambridge University Press, *British Economic Growth 1688–1959*, by P. Deane and W. A. Cole (Tables 1, 2 and 3); Basil Blackwell, *Profiles of Union Growth: A Comparative Statistical Portrait of Eight Countries*, by G. S. Bain and R. Price (Tables 10 and 12); and, Croom Helm, *Industrial Conflict in Modern Britain*, by J. E. Cronin (Table 13).

For Clare

INTRODUCTION

The first generation of post-war British labour historians tended to be preoccupied with working-class activism. Assuming rather too readily that the history of the labour movement was synonymous with the history of the working class, they sought to recount the struggles of activists in trade unions and left-wing political parties, organisations which, they believed, embodied the fundamental values and aspirations of ordinary working people.[1] Relying largely upon the labour movement's own records, they produced a series of committed, sometimes uncritical, and occasionally hagiographic, institutional studies – a literature that one critic has dubbed 'the boring bureaucracy of trade unions and proletarian parties'.[2]

Subsequent generations of labour (and social) historians have been concerned not merely to describe the struggles of the activists but to account for their inability to secure the support of their fellow workers, most of whom failed conspicuously to display anything remotely resembling a revolutionary class consciousness.[3] Dissatisfaction with economic explanations of working-class acquiescence and weakness led to a number of stimulating developments: the posing of new questions; the discovery (and creation) of new sources of evidence; and the adoption of some of the concerns, techniques and theories offered by the social sciences.[4] Certainly it is difficult to imagine the vitality of recent historical interest in issues such as family life, crime, popular culture and class consciousness – still less in theories such as deference, social control and hegemony – 'without at least the indirect spur of sociology and social anthropology'.[5] But whatever the impetus, labour historians began examining 'the social history of the working class and not primarily . . . the political history of militants and militancy'.[6] The result was enormously valuable: the appearance of a whole range of community and cultural studies that sought, either explicitly or implicitly, to explain both the successes and the failures of the labour movement, and to account for the persistence, alongside activism and struggle, of apathy and acquiescence.[7]

Welcome as it was, this burgeoning literature provided no cause at all for complacency. Lacunae and imbalances remained. We knew much less about some groups than about others. We knew little about what people thought (as opposed to what they did); we knew less about working people as consumers (than as producers); and we still knew far less about women and girls than we did about their brothers, husbands, sons and fathers. Our knowledge of rural workers, the unskilled and the casually employed remained sadly underdeveloped when set alongside the great deal that was known about the skilled workers, coalminers and factory hands employed in the large-scale, capital-intensive sectors of the economy. Most striking of all was the continuing discrepancy between our ignorance about the majority of the working-class population, the politically and industrially dormant, and the attention that had been lavished upon one relatively small group of workers, those who were politically active and industrially militant.

Whatever the merits or demerits of the historiography, nothing prepared labour historians for the challenges to come. When I was preparing the first edition of this book in the mid 1980s, I – along with the overwhelming majority of my colleagues – accepted that class existed, and that class was important. Such assumptions have since come in for the most scathing and contemptuous of criticism. Spurred on by the collapse of communism, the rise of Thatcherism and the dominance of the new right, labour (and social) historians began to question the significance of economic and social factors in explaining cultural and political change. Indeed, some claimed that class existed only where it was clearly and explicitly articulated in the 'texts' being consulted. 'There is a powerful sense in which class may be said to have "fallen"', explained Patrick Joyce in 1994. 'Instead of being a master category of historical explanation, it has become one term among many, sharing a rough equality with these others'.[8] Other postmodernist critics went a great deal further, claiming that historical narratives and explanations of any kind were nothing more than constructions shaped, not by the 'facts' of the past, but by the aesthetic and ideological predispositions of the historian. The 'past and history float free of each other', concluded Keith Jenkins, 'they are ages and miles apart.'[9]

Even those of us who reject the tenets of postmodernism recognise that the scale and diversity of the literature on the working class brings with it a number of difficulties. The proliferation of information, and the specialisation that it encourages, renders the task of synthesis increasingly daunting and deters all but the most ambitious (or foolhardy) from exploring the crucial, yet complex and elusive, relationships that existed between what are still often regarded as distinct aspects of working-class experience.[10] Yet the plethora of recent research into so many aspects of labour (and social) history demands that new works of synthesis should be produced as a matter of some urgency. Indeed, of all the tasks that need to be undertaken, one of the most pressing has been the re-examination of the social history of the working class in Great Britain (that is England, Wales and Scotland) between 1850 and 1939. These are the years that have been the subject of some of the most intense, and most interesting, of recent historical investigations. These are the years, it is said, that saw the establishment and consolidation of what is often regarded as 'traditional' working-class life. 'It is the working class', claims Eric Hobsbawm, 'of cup-finals, fish-and-chip shops, palais-de-danse and Labour with a capital L.'[11]

Accordingly, it is the aim of this book to reflect, and develop, the attempts that have been made to study history from below, to rewrite the history of labour from the point of view of the 'ordinary' person. The book has three broad objectives: to provide an up-to-date, read-able and wide-ranging (though by no means comprehensive) account of what is known about working-class life between 1850 and 1939; to offer a guide to some of the major issues currently under discussion in British labour and social history; and to identify, and so far as is pos-sible to rectify, some of the more obvious deficiencies in the existing literature. The book also has a number of more specific objectives. The first is to show that class existed, and that class mattered. The second is to question the accuracy of what has been described as 'one of the most commonly accepted notions in the economic and social history of late Victorian and Edwardian England . . . that the working people were slowly but assuredly being moulded into a homogeneous working class which enjoyed a common work experience and outlook'.[12] The third is to examine the extent to which material circumstances determined social and cultural aspects of working-class life, and in particular the degree to which improving economic and social conditions helped to reconcile working people to the capitalist system in which they found themselves. In fact, the material, demographic, ideological and organ-isational aspects of working-class life seem to be so intimately entwined that it has been decided to use economic differences (and particularly the division between the large-scale, capital-intensive sectors of the economy, and the smaller-scale, less mechanised 'traditional' sectors) as the most appropriate way of organising, and analysing, the evidence that is presented throughout this book.

It is surprising how few historians of the working class seek to define, and measure, their subject. Of course, it is never easy to determine the class identity of any individual or group; as Jerry White has pointed out: '"Class" is the most contested category in the whole lexicon of the social sciences. We all know class and classes exist, but it and they elude both scientific definition and enumeration.'[13] It is hard to know, for instance, whether women and children should be ascribed to the same class as their husbands and fathers.[14] It is difficult to decide whether class should be defined by economic criteria (such as occupation and income); by social and cultural criteria (such as behaviour, status, power, attitudes and relationships with other

TABLE 1. The working class in Britain, 1851–1931

Year	The working class (mills)	Other classes (mills)	Total population (mills)
1851	16.2	4.7	20.9
1861	18.0	5.2	23.2
1871	20.3	5.9	26.2
1881	23.1	6.7	29.8
1891	25.7	7.4	33.1
1901	28.8	8.3	37.1
1911	31.7	9.2	40.9
1921	33.2	9.6	42.8
1931	34.7	10.1	44.8

Source: Calculated from **P. Deane** and **W. A. Cole**, *British Economic Growth 1688–1959: Trends and Structure*, Cambridge U.P., 1969, p. 8. It is assumed that the proportion of the population engaged in, or dependent upon those engaged in, manual labour remained constant at 77.5 per cent.

groups); or by some elusive combination of them all.[15] But even those scholars who believe that class should be defined by social and cultural criteria seem forced to admit that in practice it can be measured only by means of occupation. John Burnett has pointed out that: 'Although it is unlikely that any 2 sociologists would ever agree about a definition of social class, there would be fairly widespread concurrence . . . that occupation is one of the major – perhaps the major – determinant of social class.'[16]

The dilemma is not easily solved. Yet if one accepts that social class is determined largely by occupation – and that the working class may be identified by its dependence upon manual labour – then it is perfectly possible to calculate the size of the British working class at various dates between 1850 and 1939.[17] In fact, the calculation may be made very easily because it is generally accepted that throughout this period the proportion of the population engaged in, or dependent upon, manual labour remained constant at between 75 and 80 per cent.[18] Such a calculation means, as Table 1 shows, that the size of the British working class more than doubled during this 90-year period: from just over 16 million in 1851, to more than 28 million in 1901, and almost 35 million in 1931.

It is this constantly growing working class that forms the subject of the book. Its structure is as follows. The first three chapters examine the material conditions – work, income and housing – which, it will be argued, proved such crucial determinants of other aspects of working-class existence. Chapters 4 and 5 explore family and community life, while the final two chapters consider working-class values and organisation – issues which, like family and community, can be understood, it is believed, only in the light of the material factors that are considered in the early chapters of the book.

NOTES AND REFERENCES

1. **J. Winter**, 'Introduction: Labour History and Labour Historians', in **J. Winter** (ed.), *The Working Class in Modern British History: Essays in Honour of Henry Pelling*, Cambridge U.P., 1983, p. vii; **M. Savage** and **A. Miles**, *The Remaking of the British Working Class, 1840–1940*, Routledge, 1994, pp. 2–4.

2. **H. Perkin**, 'Social History in Britain', *Journal of Social History*, 10, 1976, p. 133. Also R. Hoggart, *The Uses of Literacy: Aspects of Working-Class Life with Special Reference to Publications and Entertainments*, Penguin, 1958, p. 22. Of course, such strictures should not be applied indiscriminately, and certainly not to scholars such as Asa Briggs, Eric Hobsbawm, Sidney Pollard or John Saville.

3. **R. J. Morris**, 'Whatever Happened to the British Working Class, 1750–1850', *Bulletin of the Study for the Study of Labour History*, 41, 1980, p. 13.

4. **E. J. Hobsbawm**, 'From Social History to the History of Society', *Daedalus*, 100, 1971; **G. S. Jones**, 'From Historical Sociology to Theoretical History', *British Journal of Sociology*, 27, 1976; **D. Smith**, 'Social History and Sociology – More than Just Good Friends', *Sociological Review*, 30, 1982; **C. Kent**, 'Presence and Absence: History, Theory, and the Working Class', *Victorian Studies*, 29, 1986. It is true that historical views of the social sciences were sometimes rather naïve, with historians using the sociological literature 'as a kind of academic potting shed containing a set of handy tools'. See Smith, 'Social History', p. 287.

5. Jones, 'Historical Sociology', p. 300. Also p. 304; Hobsbawm, 'Social History', p. 12; **R. Harrison**, 'The Last Ten Years in British Labour Historiography', Canadian Historical Association, *Historical Papers*, 1980, p. 213.

6. Winter, 'Introduction', p. vii. Also **R. Johnson**, 'Culture and the Historians', in **J. Clarke, C. Critcher** and **R. Johnson**, *Working-Class Culture: Studies in History and Theory*, Hutchinson, 1979, p. 58.

7. See, for example, **P. Joyce**, *Work, Society and Politics: The Culture of the Factory in Later Victorian England*, Methuen, 1982; **R. C. Whiting**, *The View from Cowley: The Impact of Indistrialization upon Oxford 1918–1939*, Clarendon Press, 1983; **J. White**, *The Worst Street in North London: Campbell Bunk, Islington Between the Wars*, Routledge & Kegan Paul, 1986. For the History Workshop movement, see **D. Selbourne**, 'On the Methods of History Workshop', and **R. Samuel**, 'On the Methods of History Workshop: A Reply', *History Workshop*, 9, 1980.

8. **P. Joyce**, *Democratic Subjects: The Self and the Social in Nineteenth-Century England*, Cambridge U.P., 1994, p. 2. Also Savage and Miles, *Remaking*, p. 14.

9. **K. Jenkins**, *Rethinking History*, Routledge, 1991, p. 5. See also **K.**

Jenkins, *On 'What is History?': From Carr and Elton to Rorty and White*, Routledge, 1995; **A. Munslow**, *Deconstructing History*, Routledge, 1997. **P. Joyce**, 'Refabricating Labour History; or from Labour History to the History of Labour', *Labour History Review*, 62, 1997. For an accessible and trenchant criticism of such views, see **R. J. Evans**, *In Defence of History*, Granta, 1997. The debate can be followed in the pages of *Social History* between 1991 and 1996.

10.   For attempts at synthesis and interpretation, see, for example, **J. Bourke**, *Working Class Cultures in Britain 1890–1960: Gender, Class and Ethnicity*, Routledge, 1994; **K. D. Brown**, *The English Labour Movement 1700–1951*, Gill and Macmillan, 1982; **K. Burgess**, *The Challenge of Labour: Shaping British Society 1850–1930*, Croom Helm, 1980; **J. F. C. Harrison**, *The Common People: A History from the Norman Conquest to the Present*, Fontana, 1984; **E. Hopkins**, *A Social History of the English Working Classes 1815–1945*, Arnold, 1979; **E. Hopkins**, *The Rise and Decline of the English Working Classes 1918–1990: A Social History*, Weidenfeld and Nicolson, 1991; **D. Kynaston**, *King Labour: The British Working Class*, Allen and Unwin, 1976; **S. Meacham**, *A Life Apart: The English Working Class, 1890–1914*, Thames & Hudson, 1977; **R. Price**, *Labour in British Society: An Interpretative Essay*, Croom Helm, 1986.

11.   **E. J. Hobsbawm**, *Worlds of Labour: Further Studies in the History of Labour*, Weidenfeld and Nicolson, 1984, p. 194. Also **G. S. Jones**, 'Working-Class Culture and Working-Class Politics in London, 1870–1900: Notes on the Remaking of a Working Class', *Journal of Social History*, 7, 1974, p. 48.

12.   **J. A. Schmiechen**, 'State Reform and the Local Economy: An Aspect of Industrialization in Late Victorian and Edwardian London', *Economic History Review*, xxvii, 1975, p. 413.

13.   White, *Worst Street*, p. 27.

14.   **M. Glucksmann**, 'In a Class of Their Own? Women Workers in the New Industries in Inter-War Britain', *Feminist Review*, 24, 1986; **M. Glucksmann**, *Women Assemble: Women Workers and the New Industries in Inter-War Britain*, Routledge, 1990; **E. J. Yeo**, 'Gender and Class: Women's Languages of Power', *Labour History Review*, 60, 1995.

15.   For useful guides to the voluminous literature on class and class consciousness, see **T. Forester**, *The Labour Party and the Working Class*, Heinemann, 1976, pp. 8–13; **A. Marwick**, *Class: Image and Reality in Britain, France and the USA since 1930*, Fontana, 1981, pp. 18, 62–3; 3; **A. J. Reid**, *Social Classes and Social Relations in Britain, 1850–1914*, Macmillan, 1992, esp. pp. 25–36; Savage and Miles, *Remaking*, pp. 1–20.

16.   **J. Burnett**, *A History of the Cost of Living*, Penguin, 1969, p. 292.

17.   For the difficulties of using occupation as a measure of class, see Marwick, *Class*, pp. 13, 62–3.

18.   Meacham, *Life Apart*, p. 12; **G. Routh**, *Occupation and Pay in Great Britain 1906–79*, Macmillan, 1980, p. 5. Cf. **E. J. Hobsbawm**, *Industry and Empire*, Penguin, 1969, pp. 285–6.

Part One

MATERIAL CONDITIONS

Chapter 1

WORK

It would be difficult to overestimate the importance of work in working-class life. Work it was that helped to determine two crucial elements of working-class existence: the ways in which workers spent many – if not most – of their waking hours; and, of course, the amounts of money they had at their disposal. Work it was that helped to determine most other aspects of working people's lives: the standards of health they enjoyed; the types of accommodation in which they lived; the nature of their family and neighbourhood life; the ways in which they spent their leisure time; the degree of respect with which they were regarded; and even, it seems, the social, political and other values that they came to adopt.[1]

It is well known that industrialisation brought with it fundamental changes in the occupational structure of the workforce. Table 2 shows that there occurred, in particular, a sharp decline in the number (and proportion) of the population engaged in agriculture; and a corresponding increase in the number employed first in manufacturing and mining, and subsequently in transport and other service industries.[2] Not surprisingly, it is the expanding, large-scale, mechanised, heavy industries that have fascinated historians and contemporaries alike. Seduced by size and success, economic, business and labour historians have all tended to concentrate their attention upon the great nineteenth-century staples of coal, cotton and engineering, and, to a less extent, upon such 'new' twentieth-century industries as motor manufacturing.[3]

The cotton industry is commonly seen as the driving force behind Britain's industrial revolution and her emergence as the world's leading industrial power. From the middle of the nineteenth century until well into the 1920s cotton was Britain's most important manufacturing industry, employing over half a million people and producing a quarter or more of the country's exports.[4] Indeed the industry symbolises more powerfully than any other the new forms of manufacturing that have come to be associated with the development

TABLE 2. The occupational structure of the British workforce, 1851–1931

Year	Agriculture, forestry and fishing		Manufacturing, mining and building		Trade and Transport	
	No. (mills)	% of workforce	No. (mills)	% of workforce	No. (mills)	% of workforce
1851	2.1	21.7	4.1	42.9	1.5	15.8
1891	1.6	10.5	6.5	43.9	3.4	22.6
1901	1.5	8.7	7.7	46.3	3.6	21.4
1931	1.3	6.0	9.5	45.3	4.7	22.7

Year	Domestic and personal		Other	
	No. (mills)	% of workforce	No. (mills)	% of workforce
1851	1.3	13.0	0.6	6.6
1891	2.0	15.8	0.8	7.2
1901	2.3	14.1	1.3	9.5
1931	1.6	7.7	2.3	18.3

Source: **P. Deane** and **W. A. Cole**, *British Economic Growth 1688–1959: Trends and Structure*, Cambridge U.P., 1969, pp. 142–3.

of modern industrial society: the emergence of powerful employers; the growth of the factory system; the establishment of single-industry communities; and the imposition of new and more severe forms of work discipline.

The cotton industry was distinguished by its concentration both of ownership and of production. As Patrick Joyce explains: 'between 1850 and 1890 the size of the average spinning firm increased from 108 to 165 hands, that of the weaving firm from 100 to 188, and the size of the average combined firm from 310 to 429 workers'.[5] It was in Lancashire – which by 1851 had 60 per cent, and by 1910 90 per cent, of all cotton workers – that this concentration proceeded most fully and most quickly. In 1841 the typical Lancashire cotton firm had a capital of £15,000 and a workforce of almost 200.[6] In fact when Joyce wishes to 'point to the continuing importance of the small employer' in Lancashire, he claims only that 'in 1877 the average capital of 1,453 firms was £29,927, and that of 880 firms between £2,000 and £20,000'.[7] The 'small employer' in Lancashire cotton would have been a large employer in almost any other part of the economy. Concentration was particularly marked in the spinning districts of south Lancashire and Cheshire, in towns and cities such as Oldham,

Hyde, Ashton, Bolton, Stockport and Manchester.[8] Stockport was not untypical. The town's Orrell Mill, which had been opened in 1838, was a huge, six-storey building equipped with 45,000 spindles and 1,100 power looms. By 1851, it and similar, if smaller, mills employed over a third of the town's entire adult population; by 1882 Stockport's nine largest firms controlled 55 per cent of the town's looms and 61 per cent of its spindles.[9]

The cotton industry was distinguished too by the new techniques of control that its powerful employers used to compel compliance with the demands of factory production. The cotton masters were among the first to grapple with the difficulty of 'training human beings to renounce their desultory habits of work, and identify themselves with the unvarying regularity of the complex automation'.[10] They remained at the forefront of attempts to tighten supervision. This they did in several ways: by the establishment of elaborate systems of rules and procedures; by the replacement of internal subcontractors and piecemasters by directly employed foremen and later by white-collar supervisors operating from central welfare departments; by the introduction of new methods of payment, usually of course piecework, the system that Marx considered most appropriate to any capitalist system; and finally by the introduction and speeding-up of machinery and the replacement of skilled men by less skilled, less expensive and, it was hoped, less militant women and girls.[11] The combination of long hours, unpleasant conditions, increased mechanisation, closer supervision and new methods of payment was always demanding: 'You kept wiping the perspiration off,' remembers a Preston girl who started weaving in 1911, 'and you daren't stop, there was no stopping.'[12] It could also become offensive: in the same year a factory inspector discovered one firm, employing over 500 women, in which each worker had to hand a tally to a male overseer when she went to the lavatory. The time spent in the lavatory was recorded and passed to the manager and at the end of the month the worker was fined if it was found that she had spent more than four minutes in the lavatory.[13]

If the cotton industry was one of the first to display those features that are associated today with modern manufacturing industry – large-scale ownership, geographical concentration, factory production and severe work discipline – it did not stand alone for long. Spurred on by growing foreign competition, falling prices and decreasing profits, employers in other leading sectors of the economy took up the struggle to improve the efficiency of the workforce.[14] Engineering is the best-known late nineteenth- and early twentieth-century example. Although the industry included large firms such as Alfred Herbert of Coventry and Platt Brothers of Oldham, the scale of ownership generally was much smaller than in cotton; and although certain types of engineering were 'highly localized', the industry as a whole was 'scattered and no great centre of population was without some important share'.[15] Yet wherever market conditions permitted, the major engineering firms sought to tighten their management controls, extend piecework payments, increase the use of mechanisation and impose greater standardisation, interchangeability and long-run batch production. The first offensive took place between 1890 and the outbreak of the First World War. By 1914 piecework was well established, with over a third of the industry's turners and more than a half of its fitters being paid in this way.[16] Mechanisation and standardisation were equally well established: the general secretary of the United Pattern Makers claimed in 1908 that rising unemployment among his members was due both to the new machinery which was 'being introduced to an extent we would not acknowledge a decade ago' and to the standardisation which was 'playing havoc with our trade in marine centres' such as Glasgow.[17] The second, and major, offensive took place during the First World War. The growth of war-related industries such as munitions provided new opportunities for engineering employers to challenge the privileges of their skilled workers; adopting strategies of 'substitution' and 'dilution', they transferred much of their new work from skilled men to less skilled men, women and boys. During the war the number of men employed in munitions (including the metals and chemical industries) rose by almost a quarter, from 1,869,000 to 2,309,000, while the number of women increased by 345 per cent, from 212,000 to 945,000.[18] As early as 1916 the Chief Factory Inspector was able to identify some of the consequences of this extension of female employment:

> Engineering and allied trades covering munitions have, in 1915,
> not only furnished the most striking new field for women's labour,
> accounting for at least 200,000 women, but they have also offered
> the widest range of problems for adaption of processes and appliances to
> women's powers . . . In many industries, . . . remarkable figures are
> given as to output of women on processes suited to them, from which
> they were previously debarred. There is in progress a 'breaking up of
> old superstitions' as regards division of labour, and 'many a bubble has
> been pricked in regard to what constitutes skilled work'.[19]

But it was the so-called 'new' industries such as chemicals, electrical engineering and non-ferrous metal making that displayed most prominently the features characteristic of modern manufacturing industry. The inter-war years saw striking, and at times spectacular, examples of industrial rationalisation: the establishment of large factories and the amalgamation of small companies into huge combines such as ICI, EMI, Unilever and Courtaulds.[20] Indeed, just as the cotton industry stands as a symbol of the first generation of factory production, so does the motor industry as a symbol of the 'new' twentieth-century industries. Depending almost entirely upon the protected home market, the industry's output of private cars increased from just 32,000 in 1920 to 182,000 in 1929, and more than 500,000 on the eve of the Second World War. Unlike either engineering, which remained geographically dispersed, or cotton, which became concentrated in Lancashire, the motor industry (along with other 'new' industries) developed primarily in the suburbs of London and in Midland centres such as Birmingham, Coventry, Luton and Oxford.[21] A handful of giant firms came to dominate: Vauxhall in Luton; Ford and Briggs in Dagenham; Austin at Longbridge, in Birmingham; and Pressed Steel and Morris Motors at Cowley, in Oxford. In 1914 Oxford 'was still a pre-industrial town', with Morris Motors employing fewer than a hundred people. By 1939 almost a third of the city's workforce was engaged in motor car manufacture: 5,250 at Pressed Steel, 4,670 at Morris Motors and 1,190 at Morris Motors Radiators.[22]

The industry's growth was based upon the new techniques of mass production.[23] R.C. Whiting describes developments at Morris Motors:

> Before the First World War the main factory was a three-storey building in which machining and drilling were done on the ground floor, chassis assembly on the first, and the mounting of bodies on the second. The chassis was stationary on each of these floors. After the war a production line was organized with the chassis being pushed from one group of workers to the next. It was at this point that improving the organization of work by subdividing operations, by using single-purpose machines to drill the chassis frame, and by synchronising the work of various assembly lines, began to have serious effect. By 1926 each worker was engaged in a task of about 2½ minutes' duration. . . . The other major change in methods of output came in 1934 with the installation of a mechanically-driven assembly line which gave much tighter control over labour, and permitted much closer synchronization of the supply of sub-assemblies with the final production line. . . . Work at Morris's was representative of trends in the more advanced car factories, in that the typical attributes of skilled or craft labour were nowhere to be seen. . . . Workers in these conditions became mere assemblers.[24]

Neither mechanisation nor large-scale ownership and production were confined to factory-based manufacturing industry. Coalmining was not – indeed never could be – organised on a factory basis. Yet it too came to be dominated by powerful employers intent on extending their control over the workforce; already in 1914 the industry was dominated by firms like the Fife Coal Company and the Powell Duffryn Steam Coal Company, each of which had a labour force of over 10,000 and an annual output of more than two million tons. The inter-war years saw further attempts to rationalise the structure and operations of the industry; and by 1937, 77 per cent of British coal output was produced by fewer than 15 per cent of the firms active in the industry. This growing concentration of ownership was matched by a corresponding concentration of production. In 1850 only a tiny proportion of the country's miners worked in pits employing as many as 50 men; by 1913 the typical colliery employed well over 300 men, a figure that was to increase slightly during the inter-war years.[25] In certain parts of the coalfields, the industry's domination of local labour markets became quite overwhelming. In 1911 mining accounted for more than 70 per cent of the male working population in Northumberland and Durham communities like Ashington, Bedlington, Tanfield and Ryton and in small south Yorkshire towns such as Wombwell, Darfield and Royston. It was found that among the Rhondda Valley's 150,000 strong population, 'about 95 per cent belong to families engaged in, or dependent upon, the mining industry. There are few works or factories, or other employment except for the comparatively few openings for employment on the railways and in shops.'[26]

The owners tried hard to control their notoriously ill-disciplined workforce. They had long established piecework as the usual method of paying the 40 per cent or so of their employees who worked at hewing and underground haulage. They sought eventually to extend the use of coal-cutting and other types of machinery: the proportion of British coal that was cut mechanically grew from 19 per cent in 1924 to 57 per cent in 1937; the proportion that was conveyed mechanically increased from 14 per cent in 1929 to 51 per cent in 1937.[27] A South Wales miner recalls the introduction of mechanised coal-cutting.

> It was a powerful machine, and seemed immense in comparison to the limited space it had to work in. It was over ten feet long to the extent of the jib, eighteen inches high, and over two feet wide. It weighed three and a half tons. . . . It had a hundred yards of electric cable. . . .
>
> The chain had thirty-eight detachable picks screwed into it, and revolved at about three hundred revolutions a minute around the four-feet-nine-long jib. . . . It made a terrific noise when cutting, and the dust was enough to choke anyone very close by. It was a waste of effort to speak when near it – the only way to explain was to wave your lamp and make signs. . . .
>
> The drawback was in the added danger, because we could not hear the roof cracking, and with such a large under-cut there was the likelihood of it falling any second. Timber could not be set so close, either, because space had to be left for the passage of the machine. . . .
>
> The men became used to the machine to some extent, but few of them cared to be near it when it worked. In the wet places the current leaked through the damaged parts of the cable, and the air seemed to be full of electricity. We had the acid taste of it in our mouths for hours after we reached home.[28]

Despite the force of such testimony, it is important to appreciate that the working conditions of those employed in manufacturing (and to a lesser extent in mining) improved considerably during the period covered by this book. For whatever the monotony or danger of working in these industries, the time that had to be spent at work was declining very appreciably. The best evidence suggests that at the beginning of the period engineers were working a 10-hour day (and 60-hour week), and textile workers and coalminers a 12-hour day (and 72-hour week), but that in the 1870s and 1880s all three groups enjoyed a reduction to something approaching a 9-hour day (and 54-hour week). Thereafter their experiences diverged: the miners won a nominal 8-hour day in 1908, while it was not until 1937 that factory workers finally secured a basic 48-hour week.[29] It was a remarkable transition. The engineers of 1939 were working only 80 per cent as long, and the miners and textile workers only two-thirds as long, as their great-grandparents in 1850.

It was not just that there was a reduction in the hours of work. The work itself was becoming less exhausting and less dangerous. There can be no doubting the strain and monotony of modern factory work; but there can be no doubt either that in manufacturing – if not always in mining – mechanisation reduced the sheer physical effort that was required. 'You see, the machines are so adjusted that there's little for a man to do except watch them', explained a car worker in 1937. 'It's not that the job is hard work but the monotony of it gets you down.'[30] Nor can there be any doubt that in both manufacturing and mining there was a clear 'statistical trend towards safer working'.[31] Coalmining was – and is – notorious for its many dangers, but this must not be allowed to obscure the fact that work in the industry was indeed becoming safer. For although coalmining's safety record was truly terrible in 1850, and became no better between 1919 and 1939, it did improve very greatly during the second half of the nineteenth century; in the years between 1850 and 1914 the risk of ? miner being killed while at work declined by nearly three-and-half times.[32]

It is not surprising that the historiography of work should have developed in the way that it has. Economic, social and labour historians have all chosen to concentrate their attention upon one of the most arresting, and fundamental, changes that took place in the work experience of ordinary people between 1850 and 1939: the increasing likelihood that they would be employed in one or other of the large-scale, mechanised sectors of the economy. Table 3 reveals the scale of the change. It shows that between 1851 and 1931 the number of people employed in manufacturing increased from 3.2 million (33 per cent of the recorded workforce) to 7.2 million (34.1 per cent) and that the number employed in mining and quarrying rose from 0.4 million (4.1 per cent of the workforce) to 1.2 million (5.7 per cent). These were striking increases and, as will be seen in subsequent chapters, were to have manifold consequences for millions of working people.

Yet considerable caution is necessary, for the historiography can lead easily to misunderstanding. Table 3 shows not only that manu-

TABLE 3. Employment in manufacturing, mining and quarrying, 1851–1931

Year	Manufacturing		Mining and quarrying		Manufacturing, mining and quarrying	
	No. (mills)	% of workforce	No. (mills)	% of workforce	No. (mills)	% of workforce
1851	3.2	33	0.4	4.1	3.6	37.1
1891	4.8	32.7	0.8	5.4	5.6	38.1
1901	5.5	32.9	0.9	5.4	6.4	38.3
1931	7.2	34.1	1.2	5.7	8.4	39.8

Source: **P. Deane** and **W. A. Cole**, *British Economic Growth 1688–1959: Trends and Structure*, Cambridge U.P., 1969, p. 143.

facturing and mining came to employ a considerable, and growing, number of working people; it also shows that this group of workers never constituted more than a sizeable minority – between 37 and 40 per cent – of (even the low, census-based estimate of) the total working population. Moreover the historiography makes it easy to overestimate the degree of structural and other changes that took place within the heavy industrial sectors of the economy; it makes it tempting to assume that by the end of the period workers in manufacturing and mining were confronted everywhere by powerful employers, large units of production, sophisticated machinery and new, and more severe, forms of work discipline.[33]

Nothing could be further from the truth. Even in mining and manufacturing there remained a surprisingly large number of small, technologically primitive and organisationally unsophisticated enterprises. Alongside the giants of the coal industry with their scores of pits and thousands of workers, there survived hundreds of much smaller firms. It was found in 1934, for example, that 'in nearly every district there is a number of small mines, employing sometimes less than 20 or 30 men, engaged on working outcrops or drifts'.[34] A decade later it was discovered that there were more firms employing fewer than 20 men than there were employing more than 2,000.[35] Even in the late 1930s more than 40 per cent of British coal was cut, and practically 50 per cent conveyed, without the aid of machinery.[36] For a great many miners, coalmining remained what it had always been: 'a pick and shovel industry'.[37] Nor were miners without ways of retaining a degree of control over their work practices. In the old-established Northumberland and Durham coalfield they fought tenaciously to preserve 'cavilling'; this was the

> system of job control which operated for hundreds of years . . . and took the form of a kind of lottery to allocate working places. The system

16

was evolved of drawing places out of a hat along with names of men to work them. This lottery gave everyone the same chance of good and bad places, and prevented union men and agitators being victimised with bad and dangerous work places and 'crawlers' or 'gaffers' men' from getting the good places as a reward for their collaboration.[38]

In manufacturing, rising demand was met not simply by the concentration of ownership and production into fewer and fewer hands but by the proliferation of any number of small units. The owners of workshops, sweatshops and small factories proved remarkably resilient in the face of large-scale industrial development. In 1913–14 firms employing fewer than 100 workers were responsible for 97 per cent of all manufacturing business while small workshops (with fewer than 6 workers) gave employment to more than half a million people – nearly 8 per cent of all those employed in manufacturing. In fact, as late as 1935 firms employing fewer than 200 people accounted for more than a third of Britain's manufacturing output.[39] These firms were not confined to Sheffield, Birmingham and other well-known centres of small-scale production; they were common too in London, the greatest manufacturing centre in the world. In 1914 more than 97 per cent of all industrial firms in the capital employed fewer than 100 people and in 1938 the average number of workers in factories under the jurisdiction of the London County Council was just 20.1.[40]

The Staffordshire pottery is an example of an industry which completed the transition to factory-based production without adopting either large-scale ownership, systematic management or extensive mechanisation. As late as 1939 more than two-thirds of the firms in the industry employed fewer than 200 workers. This meant that large firms like Johnson's, with its clear management structure, high level of technology and specialised product range, existed alongside small undertakings such as that run by T. Price, a one-man master potter who assumed every management function with the exception of keeping the books. In small firms like this sub-contracting persisted, mechanisation remained almost unheard of, and workers were able to retain a considerable degree of independence.[41]

Nor should it be accepted too readily that employers in engineering and motor manufacturing – industries cited so often as leading exponents of the new forms of production – necessarily attempted, let alone managed, to impose upon their workers the latest techniques of management and control. It is easy to exaggerate the speed and success with which late nineteenth- and early twentieth-century engineering employers introduced mechanised methods of production and piecework systems of payment. As late as 1914, 54 per cent of the industry's fitters and 63 per cent of its turners were still being paid by time. Mechanisation proceeded at a similarly halting pace, with the bulk of work continuing to be produced, not in large runs by unskilled workers on specialised machines, but in small batches by skilled workers using general-purpose machines.[42] Despite the fact that engineering is one of the occupations chosen most often to illustrate the deleterious consequences of mechanisation, craftsmen in the industry are also 'justly famed' for their resistance to the imposition of new job controls. Well known is the apocryphal story told to James Hinton.

> There used to be a craftsman in this shop who always came to work with a piece of chalk in his pocket. When he arrived each morning he would at once draw a chalk circle on the floor around his machine. If the foreman wanted to speak to him he could do so as he wished, as long as he stayed outside the circle. But if he put one foot across that line, he was a dead man.[43]

A London engineer recalls both the disruptive impact of new technology and new discipline and also the 'passive resistance and sabotage' that 'were practised'.

> We persuaded the man in the tool room to allow us in 'just to touch this tool up, Jim', and ended by walking in and out at will. Time limits, fixed by theoretic charts, were invariably all wrong. When excessive – as they sometimes were – we ca'cannied so as not to earn too much; if insufficient, we 'went slow' just the same, and lodged a complaint to the foreman, who sent for the rate fixer. When he arrived, there ensued a wordy war between the three, then the rate-fixer timed the job with a stop-watch; but it was easy to 'swing the lead' on an inexperienced clerk by providing that the tool would not cut properly. We seldom got the increase we demanded – we didn't expect to – but we usually got enough to suit our purpose.[44]

Not even in motor manufacturing did the employers manage consistently to impose up-to-date methods of organisation and control. Despite their increasingly successful attempts to adopt mass-production techniques on the assembly line, skilled work remained essential in many other parts of the manufacturing process. Workers in the toolroom and in the machine, pattern and other specialised workshops continued to be paid by the hour and managed to retain a degree of control and discretion over the work that they performed.

> The Tool Room was the main place at [Morris] Radiators where you found regular time-served engineers – though there were also some in Sheet Metal. There were turners, shapers, jig and tool makers: they worked on their own machines, but some of them were capable of going on to other machines. It was a recognised thing that the skill of the tool makers at Radiators was very high. . . . Some of them had been through a proper apprenticeship, and had indentures, but a lot of them didn't although they were very good at the work. It was recognised throughout Oxford that if a man could get into the Tool Room he was made for life because he could go anywhere, because of the machines.[45]

It is clear then that the historiography of work is doubly misleading. It is misleading insofar as it suggests that workers in mining and manufacturing found themselves confronted everywhere by powerful employers, large-scale production, technological innovation, deskilling and severe work discipline. It is also misleading insofar as it implies that developments in mining and manufacturing were typical of changes that were taking place in the economy as a whole. As Table 3 has shown, the majority of workers were always to be found, not in mining or manufacturing, but in one of the smaller-scale, less mechanised, less regulated, less militant – and less well known – sectors of the economy.

The agricultural sector has never received the attention it deserves. It is true that the number of people engaged in agriculture (including forestry and fishing) declined sharply during this 90-year period: from 2.1 million (22 per cent of the recorded workforce) in 1851, to 1.6 million (10.5 per cent) in 1891 and 1.3 million (6 per cent) in 1931. Indeed it has been estimated that between the two world wars workers were leaving the land at the rate of 10,000 a year – nearly 200 a week.[46] But it is possible to exaggerate the impact of this contraction. The seasonal nature of farming makes it particularly impervious to census-based analysis: yet even according to the census, there were still more people employed in agriculture (including forestry and fishing) declined sharply during this 90-year textiles or in mining and quarrying; indeed, there were still nearly three times as many people engaged in agriculture as there were in all the branches of motor vehicle manufacturing put together.[47] Moreover, in many districts agriculture assumed an importance still greater than these figures suggest. The distribution of agricultural workers was such, explained the compilers of the 1931 census of England and Wales, that 'in 27 out of the 63 counties their number is the highest of all the occupational groups' with which they were compared.[48]

For the million or so workers who remained in the industry, the day-to-day experience of work changed remarkably little.[49] The majority of farms remained relatively small and investment in them relatively low. As late as 1935, 18 per cent of all agricultural holdings comprised less than 5 acres, and a further 45 per cent less than 50 acres.[50] Not surprisingly, the industry was slow to mechanise. In 1871 only a quarter of farms possessed even a reaper; 60 years later England and Wales could boast only 16,000 tractors, and those chiefly on the large farms (of over 300 acres) in the eastern counties of England. As Edith Whetham points out: 'Two conspicuous forms of farm machinery, the tractor and the milking machine, were both available before the First World War, but the majority of farms in England and Wales employed neither until a second world war showed upon the horizon.'[51] Farm work remained dirty, difficult and labour intensive, with employer–employee relationships closely personal. When Fred Kitchen returned to farm labouring in 1925 after 13 years in coalmining, he complained that he 'never had any spare time', a problem he attributed to the personality of his employer:

My hours were supposed to be from six to six, with half a day off each week on account of dairying requiring a full day on Sunday. I was lucky if I got finished by seven, including Saturday and Sunday night, and as for half-days, I gave them up as a bad job. The chief reason for being late at night lay with the boss. He couldn't keep his men, for he was the most over-bearing little wretch I ever came across; if he ever heard of the Agricultural Wages Board it was evident they had never heard of him. It was amusing really, the way he used to carry on, as though the earth was for him to walk upon, and we were bits of earth.[52]

Building is another industry that has been unduly neglected. Employment grew from 0.5 million (5.2 per cent of the recorded workforce) in 1851, to a peak of 1.3 million (7.8 per cent) in 1901, falling back slightly to 1.1 million (5.2 per cent) in 1931. For Sidney Pollard, the building boom of the 1930s 'was at once the symbol and a main carrier of British industrial recovery from the Great Depression'.[53] But, as in farming, these advances were attained without the benefit of major innovations in either the organisation or the technology of the industry. Building was always a small-scale activity. In the late nineteenth century between 70 and 90 per cent of building firms employed less than ten workers – and 50 per cent employed less than five; in 1930 more than 83 per cent of firms still employed fewer than ten men. In fact the proportion of the workforce employed in these small firms was increasing: from a fifth in 1924, to a quarter in 1930, and a third in 1935.[54] Nor is there any evidence of widespread technological change. In an industry so dominated by small firms, and so subject to cyclical and seasonal fluctuation, it is scarcely surprising that new techniques (such as standardisation and prefabrication) were introduced slowly and with considerable reluctance. In the 1930s, it has been pointed out, half the industry's workers remained 'skilled tradesmen (bricklayers, carpenters, painters, plumbers and glaziers, plasterers, masons, slaters and tilers), still practising their traditional handicrafts, especially in house-building, largely untouched by mechanization'.[55]

Such organisational and technological conservatism does not mean that building employers failed to notice, or try to emulate, the examples of strict work discipline provided by firms in other, larger-scale sectors of the economy. The late nineteenth- and early twentieth-century associations of building employers 'sought not only . . . to keep down wage levels, but also to collude on a much wider front. They sought, in fact, nothing less than the establishment of industrial order – that is, the disciplined regulation of the workforce – so that they might better stabilize a previously highly volatile industry.'[56] This regulation was not imposed without resistance. 'We are not as subservient to discipline as most workers,' explained a plasterer in 1938, 'we don't want someone, who cannot do what we can do and as well as we do it, to tell us how much we have to do and how.'[57] Indeed, it is no accident that it is upon the history of the building workers that Richard Price bases his claim that it is 'the struggle for work control' that constitutes 'the central determinant' of British labour history.[58]

If the existing historiography of work tends to neglect both agriculture and building, it fails still more signally to examine developments in the tertiary (or service) sector of the economy. In fact the service sector, so seldom the source either of organisational innovation, technological breakthrough or class confrontation, seems destined always to be overlooked. Yet the growth of a large, and increasingly sophisticated, service sector was one of the most important developments to take place in the economy between 1850 and 1939. Whereas services accounted for 3.3 million people (36 per cent of the workforce) in 1851; and 7.2 million (45 per cent) in 1901; by 1931 they gave employment to 8.6 million people (40 per cent of the working population).[59]

It is no coincidence that the one branch of services to receive systematic investigation should be transport – the one branch to undergo a significant degree of technological and organisational change. Employment in transport multiplied nearly three-fold between the mid-nineteenth century and the outbreak of the Second World War: from 0.5 million (5.2 per cent of the workforce) in 1851, to 1.1 million (7.5 per cent) in 1891, and 1.4 million (6.6 per cent) in 1931.[60] Nor is it a coincidence that attention has been directed towards those forms of transport – the railways and the buses – which became dominated, if not by huge units, then certainly by powerful firms with major investments and large numbers of workers. It is well known that the ownership of the railways became concentrated into the hands of fewer, and more powerful, firms. There was a rash of amalgamations in the 1860s and by the eve of the First World War the four largest companies (the London and North-Western Railway, the Midland Railway, the Great Western Railway and the North-Eastern Railway) accounted for a fraction under 40 per cent of the industry's £1,290 million paid-up capital and a full 40 per cent of its 54,000 miles of line. The process of consolidation was completed by the Railways Act of 1921 which provided for the merging of the industry's 123 separate companies into just four: the Southern Railway, the Great Western Railway, the London Midland and Scottish Railway and the London and North-Eastern Railway.[61]

The railway companies were among the first to grapple with the difficulties of organising and controlling large numbers of workers – 65,000 in 1851 and 174,000 in 1881.[62] 'A railway . . . is a little State,' wrote Michael Reynolds in the latter year; 'without punishment, there would be a fatal loss of power, and of salutary influence'.[63] 'Salutary influence' there was in plenty; and thanks largely to the work of ex-railwayman Frank McKenna, a good deal is now known about the ways in which the nineteenth-century companies attempted to impose military-style discipline upon their workers.

> The railway discipline stemmed partly from the needs of the work itself – obedience, literacy, and punctuality – and partly from the expectations of railway officials, many of whom were from the army and used to controlling large numbers of uniformed and obedient men. There was however, a clear difference between the military and railway ethic. Poverty was the recruiting sergeant for the nineteenth-century army: the men who enlisted were seeking escape from a life with no prospects. By contrast, the railwaymen were often drawn from literate respectable and sober families. There was more element of choice in their recruitment as railwaymen, and they were on the whole prepared to accept and internalise railway discipline, which sanctified trust as clearly as it threatened dismissal, and never involved the brutality and humiliation of an army flogging.[64]

The only other forms of transport to develop large-scale ownership – and something approaching a distinctive historiography – were those designed for road-passenger traffic: the horse bus, the tramcar and the motor bus.[65] By the late 1870s the London General Omnibus Company owned nearly 8,000 horses; by the early 1890s it ran 860 horse-drawn buses (and had 200 working in conjunction with them) while its chief rival, the recently formed London Road Car Company, ran a further 275 vehicles.[66] It is well known that the years immediately before the First World War saw the horse giving way to the (more expensive) internal combustion engine, a transition that encouraged still more the growth of large-scale ownership. By the 1930s a hundred or so local authorities operated 4,700 buses; and three large 'associated' groups, Tilling, British Electric Traction and Scottish Motor Traction, controlled (through an elaborate system of holding companies) about 40 per cent of all the buses in the country.[67] These large employers could be strict disciplinarians. A bus conductor from Bristol remembers that before the Second World War,

> . . . if you go down the office, they keep you waiting about for no reason at all. You might get reported and you'd go down on the carpet for no reason at all, they'd keep you waiting about, 'Come back tomorrow': You'd go back tomorrow they'd keep you there to about a quarter to twelve, and then you'd go and perhaps you had to be on duty at half past two.[68]

Just as the historiography of services is biased in the direction of transport, so too is the historiography of transport biased in the direction of the railways and (to a lesser extent) the buses. Such a bias is misleading because even the railways never employed more than a minority of all those engaged in transport: 21 per cent in 1851, 27 per cent in 1901 and 28 per cent in 1931.[69] The great majority of those employed in transport continued to work, as they always had, either for a small employer or, as will be seen below, on a self-employed basis. Road-passenger transport continued to provide opportunities for the small employer. A bus or coach service could be operated on a surprisingly modest basis; indeed the transition to motor transport encouraged not only the emergence of a small number of large firms, but also the proliferation of a great number of small ones. 'A large number of independent private bus firms began business shortly after the First World War. Many started with hardly any capital, except a second-hand bus or converted lorry.'[70] In 1931, the first year for which accurate statistics are available, more than 80 per cent of the industry's 6,486 operators owned fewer than five buses; and in 1937 there were still 1,850 operators with just a single vehicle each.[71] Despite the growth of large carriers such as Pickfords, road haulage too remained the domain of the small employer. Again the years after the First World War saw a flood of new entrants into the industry; and again the result was the same. When the Ministry of Transport attempted to ₔssess the nation's road haulage resources just before the outbreak of the Second World War, it discovered that even the 350 largest firms in the industry could muster no more than 10,000 vehicles between them – an average of fewer than 30 vehicles each.[72]

Domestic service was another branch of the tertiary sector to remain a major employer of working people, in this case women and teenage girls. Such a claim may come as something of a surprise for it is often assumed that domestic service was essentially a Victorian and Edwardian phenomenon that fell into decline sometime during, or immediately after, the First World War.[73] Certainly the number of people employed in domestic and personal services grew prodigiously between the middle of the nineteenth century and the outbreak of the First World War: from 1.3 million (13 per cent of the occupied population) in 1851 to 2.6 million (14 per cent) in 1911.[74] Nor can there be any doubt that during this period domestic service was the largest single employer of working-class women. 'One in every three women in Victorian England probably served as a domestic servant at some point in her life, most between the age of fifteen and twenty-five.'[75] But there was no post-war contraction. Although the number of male (and living-in) servants began to decline, the number of female servants continued to grow apace: from 1.1 million in 1920 to 1.3 million in 1931, by which date almost a quarter of the women and girls recorded in the census as working were to be found engaged in some form of domestic service.[76] Girls flocked from areas of high unemployment to more prosperous regions where they worked both for middle-class families and in hotels, boarding houses and nursing homes.[77] For a girl like Winifred Foley, who was brought up in the Forest of Dean coalfield during the 1920s,

> . . . there were only three important birthdays in your youth: the one marking your arrival into the world; the fifth, which meant you could go to school and leave a bit more room under mother's feet; and the fourteenth. This birthday meant, for a daughter, that she was old enough to get her feet under someone else's table. . . . For girls, going into service was our only future. There was no employment for us in the village, and leaving home at fourteen was common to us all.[78]

In the 1920s and 1930s, as in the nineteenth century, 'Domestic service remained a central experience for working-class women and especially for girls'.[79]

Despite the popularity in recent years of autobiographies such as Margaret Powell's *Below Stairs* and of television programmes such as 'Upstairs, Downstairs', the lives of the millions of women and girls who worked in domestic service stay stubbornly hidden from view. Yet enough is known to refute any suggestion that their lives underwent much change, let alone change for the better.[80] Their hours remained long and irregular; their work unmechanised, unpleasant and often very lonely. Their relationships with their employers remained characterised by a curious personal–impersonal quality. Evelyn Stirzaker remembers working for a Bolton millowner in the years before the First World War; the family felt that the name Evelyn was too 'fancy' and decided instead to call her 'Ellis'.[81] Winifred Foley remembers vividly the first meal that she ate as a servant in 1928.

> I was given my supper in the tiny kitchen while the family ate in the living-room. It was strange to be considered not fit to eat in the same room as other human beings. It was a good supper, a thick soup with butter beans in it, but loneliness and misery had taken away my appetite. How delicious, in comparison, seemed the remembered slice of marge-spread toast given me by Mam and eaten as a member of a family.[82]

Retailing was the other branch of services to retain, and enlarge, its role as a major employer of labour. The number of people engaged generally in trade grew from 1.0 million (10.3 per cent of the working population) in 1851 to 2.3 million (13.8 per cent) in 1901 and 3.3 million (15.6 per cent) in 1931.[83] Of course not all those employed in trade were to be found in retailing, but an increasing number were: the number of female shop assistants grew from 87,000 in 1861 to 250,000 in 1891, and by 1931 there were almost 800,000 'Sales-people and Shop Assistants' in England and Wales.[84] Nor, of course, can all these sales-people and shop assistants be defined necessarily as working class. As in the late nineteenth century, department stores started to stress quality and service, rather than just low prices, so they began to demand of their staff standards of dress and deportment that were beyond the reach of many working girls. Not surprisingly, many department store assistants developed ambiguous perceptions of their class position. A Hull shop worker remembers that:

> If you were a shop assistant you never wanted to be a factory girl. We used to look down our noses. Although they earned more money, we used to look down our noses at them. But if you had a job in a department store you were really one up and if you worked in an ordinary store and you got taken on in a department store you felt as though you'd lifted yourself a little bit.[85]

Nonetheless, there can be no doubt that between 1850 and 1939 retailing did provide employment for a large, and growing, number of shop assistants who may be defined unambiguously as working-class.

Shop assistants, like many other workers, found themselves confronted by new and more powerful employers. Department stores grew rapidly in size and importance during the final decades of the nineteenth century. Every large town and city became home to at least one: Liverpool had its Lewis's, Manchester its Kendal Milne's and Glasgow its John Anderson's. London had a whole number: Debenham's, Harrod's, Selfridge's, Whiteley's, the Army and Navy, the Civil Service Stores, Dickens and Jones', Swan and Edgar's and Marshall and Snelgrove's. In 1870 Whiteley's, the largest department store in the country, employed 2,000 people; by 1900 there were a dozen firms with a workforce of over a thousand – Whiteley's itself now employed 4,000 and Harrod's 6,000.[86] These stores were staffed by armies of young women who (at least in London and the south-east of England before the First World War) were required both to 'live in' and to submit to strict rules governing their conduct at work. In some stores girls were sacked if they sold less than their weekly quota of goods; in others they could be dismissed if 'failure to effect a sale . . . occurs three times running'.[87] More striking still was the growth of the multiple (or chain) store. 'The typical multiple shop company may own as many as 900 branches,' it was explained in 1921: 'it sells a limited number of stereotyped articles and is managed in a sterotyped fashion from a central office with a system of travelling managers.'[88] The inter-war years witnessed the emergence of household names among the furniture, footware, fashion, grocery and other chains. By 1927 Lipton's had 615 stores; by 1928 Woolworth's had 280; while Marks and Spencer opened 108 new branches between 1921 and 1939 so that by the end of the period it had a staff of over 18,000 and 'was represented in every town of any considerable size throughout the country'.[89]

But it is important to exaggerate neither the extent nor the impact of these new forms of ownership. Departmental and multiple stores never accounted for more than a minority of British retail trade: some 10 per cent in 1915 and not quite 25 per cent in 1939.[90] Consequently the great majority of shop assistants continued to work, not in well-known departmental or multiple stores, but in the hundreds of thousands of little known, privately owned shops that comprised the core of the retailing system. Of the estimated 747,000 shops that were trading in 1938, all but 90,000 remained in the hands of small firms with fewer than ten branches; the overwhelming majority were still single shops with working proprietors.[91] The great majority of shop assistants worked not for a Gordon Selfridge or a Thomas Lipton but for a man like G. Stone, a master butcher who opened a shop in Brighton in 1912: 'We had four staff and father and mother to start off with. And that went up to seven and nine staff at once, and three in the office.' The atmosphere in the shop was far removed from that of the department store. 'One of his horses ran away,' recalls Stone's son,

> he had told the man [one of his employees] to be careful with it.
> The fellow walked in here on a Friday – he said: 'Where's the horse?'
> 'It's run away Guvnor.' 'Get out the back.' He went out the back. My father went out there, he said: 'I'll give you a bloody good hiding' – he used to swear – and he knocked him down – then the other two started going for me father. He knocked them down and he came back in here – still as cool as a cucumber. 'Bang, bang' – he could use them.[92]

It is not suggested that fights between shopkeepers and their assistants were a daily, or even a common, occurrence. But testimony such as this does serve to counter any view that shop assistants – or indeed other service workers – became dependent generally upon large, impersonal employers using sophisticated techniques of control.

The historiography of work contains one further, fundamental misunderstanding. For no matter what the specific concern – whether it be the contraction of the primary sector or the expansion of the tertiary, the growth of large-scale production or the survival of small, the imposition of employer control or the success of worker resistance – one assumption seems to remain the same. It is accepted almost without question that the history of work is synonymous with the history of wage labour. Such an assumption simply cannot be sustained. Even in the most modern, mechanised sectors of the economy relatively few families were dependent solely upon the one or two types of wage labour that they described once a decade to the census enumerator. Many families continued to derive part at least of their income from a whole number of different – and easily overlooked – forms of self-employment: everything from begging, prostitution and petty crime to more respectable kinds of small-scale entrepreneurial activity.

At first sight the failure to regard begging and petty crime as forms of work appears somewhat surprising. The explanation probably lies in the fact that many of the most interesting recent studies of working-class crime have been concerned to present it not simply as a way of earning a living, but as a means by which the poor and dispossessed were able to wage the class struggle.[93] In all events, begging has been almost completely overlooked. Insofar as it has received any attention at all, it has been viewed as a form of crime rather than as a means of earning a livelihood, and has been regarded as the last resort of those on the margins of society. 'Begging' it has been claimed 'was the final makeshift of economic enterprise.'[94] Such a view is doubly misleading. For while beggars were never reluctant to parade their disabilities, tell tales of tragedy or exhibit their capacity for physical violence, this did not prevent begging from being a form of work – and often boring, distasteful and ill-paid work at that.[95] Nor can it be maintained that begging was confined to those on the margins of society. Oral and autobiographical evidence confirms that, in the towns at least, beggars were drawn from 'the great mass of ordinary working people for whom . . . poverty provided the backdrop against which they played out their lives'.[96] They took to begging for food, goods, money or credit when times were hard and there appeared to be no obvious alternative. Arthur Harding remembers that his family turned first to its immediate relatives in the east end of London, but that his father had no compunction at all about 'cadging' from complete strangers: 'the people in charge of the Mission gave him a ticket to go round the restaurants to see what they would give him in leavings.'[97] A Bristol couple remember that in the 1920s: 'Any fishmonger would give you a head of the cod, like for the cats' and that this could be mixed with potatoes in order to make inexpensive fishcakes.[98]

It is no longer possible, if indeed it ever was, to quantify the importance of an informal, casual and quasi-illegal activity such as begging. Nonetheless, it is clear that begging remained one of the many strategies of poverty: it was an expedient which, it is true, enabled a few families to avoid regular work, but which allowed many more to eke out a bare existence in times of particular distress.

Another strategy of poverty that proved equally persistent and – until recently – almost equally overlooked was petty crime. Like begging, petty crime took many forms: from prostitution to the theft of items such as food and fuel, usually for consumption but sometimes for resale. Like begging, petty crime tended to be most common among the most disadvantaged: the unskilled, the unemployed and one-parent families. So, here again, there seems little justification for seeking to identify offenders as members of a distinct (in this case criminal) group within the working class.[99] In fact every type of local economy seemed to sustain its own form of crime. On the coast there survived a deep-rooted tradition of plundering any wreckage washed in by the sea.[100] In coalmining districts 'The "picking" of coal from pit heads and slag heaps was so deeply ingrained . . . that it formed part of the daily domestic routine for many children, who were expected to salvage coal both before and after school.'[101] In the countryside children pilfered fruit and vegetables on their way home from school[102]: and, despite the risks, poaching proper remained common among rural workers, particularly those living in isolated communities or in areas close to large towns.[103] Some men lived by poaching, recalls a Kent labourer, but everybody used to do a little bit.[104] It is true that poaching suffered a significant decline during the later years of the nineteenth century, but for many workers it remained an accepted, everyday, part of rural life.[105]

The towns and cities offered their own temptations and opportunities. Oral, autobiographical and newspaper evidence confirms how common it was to rob the local shop, cheat the bookmaker, steal from the boss, and scavenge from any available gutter, market, garden, rubbish heap or empty house. An Edinburgh man remembers that in the early years of this century,

> My mother used to send Jimmy or me for a bottle of Tizer or a couple of half loaves, a tin of milk, something like that you know, well Jimmy and me would work out a plan of action and go into a shop, to see if we could skim something off it, you know. And my mother she'd said get two apples, I've seen me coming back with four, a pound of tatties, coming back with a pack, that's half a stone I think. Things like that, see, we used to nab it, steal 'em in the shop. Pretty cheap but then people must have thought they were nae stealing.[106]

Colne cotton worker Evelyn Howling remembers how she used to pilfer from the mill in which she worked: she would steal the small ends from pieces of cloth and smuggle them home in her food bag: 'I used to say to our Irene "Don't come to meet me with that frock on".'[107]

The popular press reported enthusiastically on all sorts of criminal behaviour, but in a manner that diminishes its value to the historian of the working class. The problem is that mass circulation newspapers tended to treat petty criminality in one of two ways: as salacious or as pathetic. Their approach is revealed by the most cursory of investigations. For example the *News of the World* of 5 January 1930 carried two contrasting reports: the first the case of a Leeds painter who had attempted to blackmail a fellow worker by threatening to tell his wife about an affair in which he had been involved; the second the case of a London railway porter who had stolen 4s. worth of seeds from Marylebone station so that he could fulfil the cultivation requirements of his LCC tenancy.[108]

The evidence of working-class criminality remains elusive, difficult to interpret and impossible to quantify. Nevertheless some limited generalisation is possible. There seems little doubt that certain forms of popular crime declined in importance between

1850 and 1939. Poaching became less common towards the end of the nineteenth century while prostitution diminished dramatically in the years following the First World War.[109] On the other hand, there seems little doubt that other, probably more common forms of popular crime persisted virtually unabated, with scavenging, pilfering and similar activities continuing to provide work and income for a large – though unknown – number of working-class families.[110]

Nor should it be assumed too readily that other, more respectable forms of self-employment were destroyed by urbanisation and large-scale industrialisation. Indeed it appears certain that self-employment and petty entrepreneurial (or 'penny-capitalist') activity survived among working people to an extent that has rarely been fully recognised.[111] Although it cannot be proved that such forms of work survived unscathed, it can certainly be shown that they were not destroyed during the late nineteenth and early twentieth centuries. What little statistical evidence there is suggests that at least 40 per cent of working-class families engaged in some type of penny-capitalist work between 1890 and 1914.

It has been estimated that some 10 per cent of the pre-1914 working population – chiefly middle-aged, skilled men with some savings – moved full-time into penny capitalism. It was part of their mid-life search for freedom from the increasingly severe restraints of factory and other work disciplines; they bought fishing boats, obtained smallholdings, started small building firms, ran taxis, bought horses and carts, began selling in the streets and, with their wives, opened small corner shops. Two examples must suffice. In the 1890s a Wigan joiner 'had the sense to see that there was going to be some building development in the neighbourhood, and that he would do better contracting than following his trade as a journeymen joiner'.[112] When Manchester worker Geoffrey Kershaw was made redundant in 1924, he decided to join his father in his engineering 'jobbing shop' – 'well a jobbing shop, usually consists of a person with rather clever hands, a lathe, a drilling machine, and a vice, and a file'.[113]

Full-time penny capitalism was always much less common than part-time. Reluctant to abandon wage labour completely, skilled men went into business on a part-time basis. Even in engineering workshops,

> Apprentices were encouraged to make tools, and although youths and fully rated men were not so encouraged, foremen generally winked at it when work was slack. . . . 'I haven't a job in the place!' many a foreman has said to me. 'Go and make something for yourself, and be busy when the "old man" comes round, I expect there'll be a job in tomorrow.'
>
> The material could usually be 'scrounged', but sometimes we surreptitiously extracted it from the stores. The 'heads' rarely arrived until nine o'clock, so the pre-breakfast period was spent on 'contracts', 'jobs for the king' or 'foreigners', as such jobs were colloquially called. . . .

'Contracts' were not confined to small tools. Sets of fire-irons and dogs, toasting-forks, kitchen shovels, and ornaments of novel design and ornate handles, brass, copper, bronze, and gunmetal candlesticks, photo frames and mantelpiece ornaments, door-knockers, model engines for the son, were some of the 'foreign orders' executed in the bosses' time.[114]

The vast majority of working people were not skilled and they turned to penny capitalism, as they did to begging or petty crime, to cope with the persistent, nagging poverty of underemployment and low wages. More often than not, their intention was to prevent their circumstances from deteriorating still further, rather than to make them get any better. Consequently part-time penny capitalism, like petty crime and begging, was typically the resort of women and children, the casually employed and the unskilled. Even in Barrow-in-Furness, Lancaster and Preston – at the heart of the industrial north-west – more than 40 per cent of late nineteenth- and early twentieth-century working-class mothers engaged in some form of part-time penny capitalism: they took in washing, put up boarders, sold home-made food and/or drink, and opened small parlour shops.

The working conditions of the self-employed and those employed in agriculture and services are particularly difficult to assess. But it is clear that they improved far less quickly than those of workers employed in manufacturing and mining. It has been seen above that whatever legislation was passed, inspectors appointed, or collective bargaining agreements reached, working hours remained long and/or irregular.[115] Indeed it was fortunate for the employers that the expectations of many of those employed in these sectors of the economy remained so very low. A London department store assistant spoke for many when she was interviewed by Walter Greenwood in 1937: 'Hours – oh, we really can't complain considering we are shop assistants': 'we have to be here by 8.30 and we finish at 6.30, except at sales times and at Christmas. We're allowed ten minutes for coffee in the morning, an hour for lunch and half an hour for tea.'[116] Moreover employees in agriculture and services derived few, if any, of the benefits of mechanisation. Their work remained arduous and often unexpectedly dangerous. Some statistical precision is possible. It has been found that in 1900–02, for example, building workers suffered an occupational mortality rate that was 11.5 per cent higher than that of coalminers – indeed the mortality rate of agricultural labourers was 23 per cent higher, and that of general labourers 64 per cent higher, than that of the notoriously vulnerable coalmining population.[117]

We know little of working conditions in the so-called black (intermediate or irregular) economy of scavenging, begging, theft and self-employment. Yet its survival is most important, not least for the doubt that it throws upon any lingering belief that advanced industrial societies such as Britain were able to manage without significant levels of female or juvenile employment. Even according to the census returns, a third of women (defined as those aged 10 and above in 1911, and as those aged 15 and above in 1931) were to be found engaged in paid work.[118] But any estimate based upon the census is bound to conceal the true extent of female employment. The census always tended to underrate the incidence of women's, and particularly of married women's, part-time work. In the course of her fascinating oral investigation of turn-of-the-century Barrow, Preston and Lancaster, Elizabeth Roberts discovered that

> The local census figures show that very few married women were in full-time employment outside the home . . . only four of the respondents' mothers out of 75 earned a full second income for the family. There were, however, 24 others employed on a casual part-time basis. Their occupations are not enumerated on the census returns but their financial contribution to their families could be of considerable significance.[119]

In the same way, the census always tended to underestimate the extent of child labour. Many children began to work for money long before they left school. An investigation carried out in 1908 revealed that almost 10 per cent of the country's two million school children worked outside school hours, a figure which, high though it was, excluded half-timers, street traders and no doubt beggars and petty criminals as well.[120] No such statistical precision is attainable for the decades following the First World War. Nonetheless, the oral evidence that has been collected over recent years makes it perfectly clear that in working-class families girls continued to help with washing and baby-minding; and that their brothers continued to run errands, wash windows, work on farms, serve in shops and take on milk and paper rounds. The son of a Bristol bricklayer recalls the contribution that he used to make to the family budget during the early 1930s. On Saturdays he would go to the building site where his father worked so that he could make tea and run errands; at other times he would draw pictures of local beauty spots such as Bristol cathedral and the pump room at Bath. 'As fast as I was drawing them my father was selling them, to friends' for his beer money.[121]

At last, then, there is beginning to emerge some limited awareness of the significance of working people's 'struggle for subsistence' within 'the amalgam of casual labour, economic enterprise and casual theft'.[122] Welcome as it is, this growing awareness is not without its dangers. It may well reinforce the impression that begging, petty crime, penny capitalism and other types of self-employment were confined to those inhabiting some sort of lumpen economy on the margins of established working-class society. In fact these forms of self-employment need to be set alongside wage labour and afford although not pride of place, at least a reasonably prominen in any serious study of working people's experience of work in the years between 1850 and 1939.

Recent research had done an enormous amount to deepen our understanding of nineteenth- and twentieth-century work, not least in directing attention towards the struggles between employers and employed for control of the labour process. Thanks to these studies, it is no longer possible to view work from the directors' boardroom or union head office, unaware of the changes that were taking place at the point of production; it is no longer possible to overlook the repercussions that these changes had in the lives of millions of ordinary men and women. Nonetheless, it is easy to be seduced by the insights of the new historiography into overlooking the persistent heterogeneity that lay at the centre of working people's experience of work. In seeking to reconstruct the day-to-day experiences of the millions of people who entered the labour market between 1850 and 1939, it is necessary to look beyond the struggles of the relatively few workers employed in mining, manufacturing and other heavy industries. It is essential to examine too the lives of the great mass of men, women and children engaged – whether full-time, part-time or on a casual basis – in farming, building, transport, domestic service and retailing, or in begging, crime and penny capitalism. The work of these people was affected indirectly, if at all, by the concentration of ownership, the mechanisation of production and the imposition of labour discipline that emerged so powerfully in other, better known sectors of the economy. So although it is possible to point to signs of an increasingly uniform working experience, a careful examination of the available evidence shows that the workforce remained remarkable for its diversity. What is striking is not just the growing homogeneity of work experience, but also its persistent heterogeneity.

NOTES AND REFERENCES

1. See, for example, **R. Price,** *Masters, Unions and Men: Work Control in Building and the Rise of Labour 1830–1914*, Cambridge U.P., 1980; **P. Joyce,** *Work, Society and Politics: The Culture of the Factory in Later Victorian England*, Methuen, 1982.
2. **P. Deane** and **W. A. Cole,** *British Economic Growth: Trends and Structure*, Cambridge U.P., 1969, pp. 142–3.
3. **P. L. Payne,** 'The Emergence of the Large-Scale Company in Great Britain, 1870–1914', *Economic History Review*, xx, 1967; **C. Shaw,** 'The Large Manufacturing Employers of 1907', *Business History*, xxv, 1983.
4. **A. E. Musson,** *The Growth of British Industry*, Batsford, 1978, pp. 82–3; Deane and Cole, *Economic Growth*, pp. 31, 190; **W.**

Lazonick, 'Industrial Organization and Technological Change: The Decline of the British Cotton Industry', *Business History Review*, lvii, 1983, p. 196.

5. Joyce, *Work*, p. 158. Also p. 225. Cf. Musson, *British Industry*, p. 82; **D. A. Farnie,** *The English Cotton Industry and the World Market, 1815–96*, Clarendon Press, 1979, pp. 215, 286, 316.

6. **V. A. C. Gatrell,** 'Labour, Power and the Size of Firms in Lancashire Cotton in the Second Quarter of the Nineteenth Century', *Economic History Review*, xxx, 1977, p. 127. See also **R. Lloyd-Jones** and **A. A. Le Roux,** 'The Size of Firms in the Cotton Industry; Manchester 1815–41', *Economic History Review*, xxxiii, 1980, p. 76.

7. Joyce, *Work*, pp. 158–9.

8. Musson, *British Industry*, p. 205. Also Joyce, *Work*, p. 106.

9. **R. Burr-Litchfield,** 'The Family and the Mill: Cotton Mill Work, Family Work Patterns and Fertility in Mid-Victorian Stockport', in **A. S. Wohl** (ed.), *The Victorian Family: Structure and Stresses*, Croom Helm, 1978, p. 182. Also Joyce, *Work*, p. 159.

10. Cited **S. Pollard,** *The Genesis of Modern Management: A Study of the Industrial Revolution in Great Britain*, Penguin, 1968, p. 215. See also **E. P. Thompson,** 'Time, Work Discipline and Industrial Capitalism', *Past and Present*, 38, 1967.

11. **J. Benson,** 'Work', in J. Benson, (ed.), *The Working Class in England 1875–1914*, Croom Helm, 1984, pp. 65–6. Joyce, *Work*, pp. 55, 96, 100; **D. F. Schloss,** 'Why Working-Men Dislike Piece-Work', *Economic Review*, July 1891, pp. 312–13, 323.

12. **S. Meacham,** *A Life Apart: The English Working Class 1890–1914*, Thames & Hudson, 1977, p. 110.

13. **E. Roberts,** *A Woman's Place: An Oral History of Working-Class Women 1890–1940*, Blackwell, 1984, p. 61. Also, Meacham, *Life Apart*, p. 132.

14. **C. R. Littler,** 'Understanding Taylorism', *British Journal of Sociology*, 29, 1978, pp. 91, 195; **J. Melling,** ' "Non-Commissioned Officers": British Employers and their Supervisory Workers, 1880–1920', *Social History*, 5, 1980, pp. 192–4, 196.

15. **G. C. Allen,** *British Industries and their Organization*, Longman, 1959, p. 135. Also **S. B. Saul,** 'The Market and the Development of the Mechanical Engineering Industries in Britain, 1860–1914', *Economic History Review*, xx, 1967.

16. Benson, 'Work', p. 74.

17. **J. H. Treble,** *Urban Poverty in Britain 1830–1914*, Batsford, 1979, p. 6. Also **J. Zeitlin,** 'Engineers and Compositors: A Comparison', in **R. Harrison** and **J. Zeitlin** (eds), *Divisions of Labour: Skilled Workers and Technological Change in Nineteenth Century England*, Harvester, 1985, pp. 223–34; *Club Life*, 13 January 1900.

18. **C. More,** *Skill and the English Working Class, 1870–1914*, Croom Helm, 1980, p. 28; **G. Braybon,** *Women Workers in the First World War: The British Experience*, Croom Helm, 1981, pp. 44–50; **A. Marwick,** *Women at War 1914–1918*, Fontana, 1977, pp. 51–73.

19. *Annual Report of the Chief Factory Inspector for 1915*, 1916.

20. **H. W. Richardson,** 'The New Industries Between the Wars', *Oxford Economic Papers*, 13, 1961, p. 374; **L. Hannah,** 'Managerial Innova-

tion and the Rise of the Large-Scale Company in Interwar Britain', *Economic History Review*, xxvii, 1974, p. 253.

21. Allen, *British Industries*, pp. 19–20; **R. C. Whiting,** *The View from Cowley: The Impact of Industrialization upon Oxford, 1918–1939*, Clarendon Press, 1983, p. 2

22. Whiting, *View*, pp. 5, 8–9, 30.

23. For Taylorism, see Littler, 'Understanding Taylorism', and Melling, 'Non-Commissioned Officers', p. 195.

24. Whiting, *View*, pp. 30–32. For accounts of what it felt like to be on the receiving end of the new work disciplines, see **A. Exell,** 'Morris Motors in the 1930s. Part I', *History Workshop*, 6, 1978, pp. 53, 64–5; **Television History Workshop,** *Making Cars: A History of Car Making in Cowley . . . By the People who Make the Cars*, Routledge & Kegan Paul, 1985.

25. J. Benson, 'Coalmining', in C. J. Wrigley, (ed.), *A History of British Industrial Relations 1875–1914*, Harvester, 1982, p. 187; **J. Benson,** *British Coalminers in the Nineteenth Century: A Social History*, Gill & Macmillan, 1980, pp. 6–7; Musson, *British Industry*, p. 300; **N. K. Buxton,** *The Economic Development of the British Coal Industry*, Batsford, 1978, pp. 481, 488.

26. Benson, *British Coalminers*, p. 84.

27. Buxton, *Coal Industry*, p. 183.

28. **B. L. Coombes,** *These Poor Hands: The Autobiography of a Miner Working in South Wales*, Gollancz, 1939, pp. 108–9, 117.

29. **M. A. Bienefeld,** *Working Hours in British Industry: An Economic History*, Weidenfeld & Nicolson, 1972, pp. 43–58, 118–26; **B. McCormick** and **J. E. Williams,** 'The Miners and the Eight-Hour Day, 1863–1913', *Economic History Review*, xii, 1959: *Annual Report of the Chief Inspector of Factories*, 1938, p. 87.

30. **W. Greenwood,** *How the Other Man Lives*, Labour Book Club, 1937?, p. 94.

31. **P. W. J. Bartrip** and **S. B. Burman**, *The Wounded Soldiers of Industry: Industrial Compensation Policy 1833–1897*, Clarendon Press, 1983, p. 46.

32. Benson, *British Coalminers*, p. 43; **R. Church,** *The History of the British Coal Industry Volume 3: Victorian Pre-Eminence*, Clarendon Press, 1986, pp. 582–95; **B. Supple,** *The History of the British Coal Industry Volume 4: The Political Economy of Decline*, Clarendon Press, 1987, pp. 427–8.

33. For the concentration of ownership and production, see Hannah, 'Managerial Innovation', pp. 252–3; **E. J. Hobsbawm,** *Industry and Empire*, Penguin, 1969, pp. 214–16. For the loss of control, see Littler, 'Understanding Taylorism', p. 194.

34. Cited **M. Heinemann,** *Britain's Coal: A Study of the Mining Crisis*, Gollancz, 1944, pp. 108–9.

35. **H. Wilson,** *New Deal for Coal*, Contact, 1945, p. 251.

36. **N. K. Buxton,** 'Entrepreneurial Efficiency in the British Coal Industry between the Wars', *Economic History Review*, xxiii, 1970, p. 482; Musson, *British Industry*, p. 229.

37. Cited Benson, *British Coalminers*, p. 54.

38. **D. Douglass,** *Pit Talk in County Durham: A Glossary of Miners' Talk* . . . , History Workshop, 1977, pp. 41–2.
39. Hannah, 'Managerial Innovation', p. 252; Melling, 'Non-Commissioned Officers', p. 196; **D. Bythell,** *The Sweated Trades: Outwork in Nineteenth-Century Britain*, Batsford, 1978.
40. **A. L. Bowley,** 'The Survival of Small Firms', *Economica*, 1, 1921, p. 115; **M. Haynes,** 'Capitalism in Marx's Time and Ours', *International Socialism*, 2, 1983, p. 57; **J. White,** *The Worst Street in North London: Campbell Bunk, Islington, between the Wars*, Routledge & Kegan Paul, 1986, p. 46.
41. **R. Whipp,** 'Some Aspects of Work, Home and Trade Unionism in the British Pottery Industry 1900–1920', Paper read at Anglo-Dutch Labour History Conference, Maastricht, 1982, pp. 2–6, 8, 14.
42. Benson, 'Work', p. 74.
43. **J. Hinton,** *The First Shop Stewards' Movement*, Allen & Unwin, 1973, p. 96.
44. **W. R. Watson,** *Machines and Men: An Autobiography of an Itinerant Mechanic*, Allen & Unwin, 1935, p. 92. Also pp. 12–13, 214.
45. Exell, 'Morris Motors', pp. 75–6. Also Whiting, *View*, pp. 60, 82, 102.
46. **S. Pollard,** *The Development of the British Economy 1914–1980*, Arnold, 1983, p. 87.
47. On the seasonal nature of farming, see **F. Kitchen,** *Brother to the Ox: The Autobiography of an Agricultural Labourer*, Caliban Books, 1981, p. 241; **E. H. Whetham,** *The Agrarian History of England and Wales Vol. VIII, 1914–39*, Cambridge U.P., 1978, p. 236; **A. Howkins,** *Poor Labouring Men: Rural Radicalism in Norfolk 1872–1923*, Routledge & Kegan Paul, 1985, pp. 21–6. Also Musson, *British Industry*, p. 276.
48. *Census of England & Wales*, 1921, *General Report*, p. 99. Also p. 130.
49. But cf. Howkins, *Poor Labouring Men*, pp. 8, 10–12, 14.
50. Whetham, *Agrarian History*, pp. 45, 56.
51. *Ibid.*, p. 204. Also p. 210; Howkins, *Poor Labouring Men*, p. 11.
52. Kitchen, *Brother to the Ox*, p. 201. Also Howkins, *Poor Labouring Men*, pp. 14, 17, 22–7.
53. Pollard, p. 152. Also Deane and Cole, *Economic Growth*, p. 143.
54. **J. McKenna** and **R. G. Rodger,** 'Control by Coercion: Employers' Associations and the Establishment of Industrial Order in the Building Industry of England and Wales, 1860–1914', *Business History Review*, 59, 1985, p. 207; **H. W. Richardson** and **D. H. Aldcroft,** *Building in the British Economy between the Wars*, Allen & Unwin, 1968, pp. 33–4.
55. Musson, *British Industry*, p. 335. Also Richardson and Aldcroft, *Building*, pp. 156–7; **J. Burnett,** *A Social History of Housing 1815–1970*, Methuen, 1980, pp. 252–7.
56. McKenna and Rodger, 'Coercion', p. 203. Also **W. Greenwood,** *How The Other Man Lives*, Labour Book Service, 1937?, p. 161.
57. **J. Common,** *Seven Shifts*, EP Publishing, 1978, p. 23.
58. Price, *Masters*, p. 267.
59. Deane and Cole, *Economic Growth*, p. 143; **R. M. Hartwell,** 'The Service Revolution: The Growth of Services in Modern Economy 1700–1914', in **C. M. Cipolla** (ed.), *The Fontana Economic History of Europe: The Industrial Revolution*, Fontana/Collins, 1975, p. 370. The service sector employed a disproportionately large number of unskilled

and/or female workers – groups that were often one and the same.

60. Deane and Cole, *Economic Growth*, p. 143.
61. **T. C. Barker** and **C. I. Savage,** *An Economic History of Transport in Britain*, Hutchinson, 1974, pp. 87, 109–11, 147, 158.
62. **J. Clapham,** *An Economic History of Modern Britain: Free Trade and Steel 1850–1886*, Cambridge U.P., 1952, pp. 201–2.
63. Cited **F. McKenna** 'Victorian Railway Workers', *History Workshop*, 1, 1976, p. 26.
64. *Ibid.*, p. 27. See also **F. McKenna,** *The Railway Workers 1840–1970*, Faber & Faber, 1980; **P. S. Bagwell,** *The Railwaymen: The History of the National Union of Railwaymen*, Allen & Unwin, 1963.
65. See, for example, **J. Hibbs** (ed.), *The Omnibus: Readings in the History of Road Passenger Transport*, David & Charles, 1971; **N. Owen**, *History of the British Trolleybus*, David & Charles, 1974.
66. Barker and Savage, *Transport*, pp. 127–9; Clapham, *Economic History*, p. 203.
67. Barker and Savage, *Transport*, pp. 161–2, 165–7; **P. S. Bagwell,** *The Transport Revolution from 1770*, Batsford, 1974; **J. Stevenson,** *British Society 1914–45*, Penguin, 1984, p. 27; **G. Alderman,** *Modern Britain 1700–1983: A Domestic History*, Croom Helm, 1986, p. 160; **F. M. L. Thompson,** 'Nineteenth-Century Horse Sense', *Economic History Review*, xxix, 1976.
68. Avon County Reference Library, Bristol People's Oral History Project, Transcript RO14, p. 8
69. *Census of England & Wales*, 1901, III, pp. 188–9; 1931, *Occupational Tables*, p. 9; Deane and Cole, *Economic Growth*, p. 232.
70. Barker and Savage, *Transport*, p. 169; Bagwell, *Transport Revolution*, p. 264.
71. Barker and Savage, *Transport*, pp. 174, 176–7; Bagwell, *Transport Revolution*, p. 268.
72. Bagwell, *Transport Revolution*, p. 268. Also Barker and Savage, *Transport*, pp. 174, 176–7.
73. **P. Taylor,** 'Daughters and Mothers – Maids and Mistresses: Domestic Service between the Wars', in **J. Clarke, C. Critcher** and **R. Johnson** (eds), *Working-Class Culture: Studies in History and Theory*, Hutchinson, 1979, p. 121.
74. Deane and Cole, *Economic Growth*, p. 143.
75. **T. McBride,** ' "As the Twig is Bent": The Victorian Nanny', in Wohl (ed.), *Victorian Family*, p. 53. Also **M. Anderson,** *Approaches to the History of the Western Family 1500–1914*, Macmillan, 1980, p. 27.
76. Taylor, 'Domestic Service', p. 121.
77. *Ibid.*, pp. 122–4.
78. **W. Foley,** *A Child in the Forest*, BBC, 1974, p. 141.
79. Taylor, 'Domestic Service', p. 121.
80. *Ibid.*, p. 121; Manchester Polytechnic, Manchester Studies, Transcript 20, pp. 16–17.
81. Manchester Studies, Transcript 20. p. 7
82. Foley, *Child*, p. 161. Also Taylor, 'Domestic Service', pp. 124–6; McBride, 'Nanny', pp. 51, 54.
83. Deane and Cole, *Economic Growth*, p. 143.

84. *Census of England & Wales*, 1931, *General Report*, p. 149; **B. Davorn**, 'Women and Shopwork 1875–1925 with Special Reference to Ideology, Conditions and Opportunities', M.A. Thames Polytechnic, 1986, p. 14.

85. Davorn, 'Shopwork', p. 63, Also pp. 16, 19, 73.

86. *Ibid.*, p. 15; **D. Davis**, *A History of Shopping*, Routledge & Kegan Paul, 1966, p. 289.

87. **H. R. E. Ware**, 'The Recruitment, Regulation and Role of Prostitution in Britain from the Middle of the Nineteenth Century to the Present Day', Ph.D. University of London, 1969, II, p. 390. Also pp. 386, 391; Davorn, 'Shopwork', pp. 18, 25–6, 31, 145–6.

88. **S. M. Bushell**, 'The Relative Importance of Co-operative, Multiple and Other Retail Traders', *Economica*, January 1921, p. 64.

89. **G. Rees**, *St Michael: A History of Marks and Spencer*, Weidenfeld & Nicolson, 1969, p. 79. Also **P. Mathias**, *Retailing Revolution: A History of Multiple Retailing in the Food Trades based upon the Allied Suppliers Group of Companies*, Longman, 1967, p. 120; *Daily Mail*, 9 January 1935.

90. Pollard, *British Economy*, p. 111. The co-operative societies accounted for a further 7½–9 per cent in 1915, and 10–11½ per cent in 1939.

91. *Ibid.*, pp. 111–12; Bushell,'Importance', p. 64.

92. **N. Griffiths**, *Shops Book: Brighton 1900–1930*, Queenspark Books, ND, pp. 13, 15.

93. **J. White**, *The Worst Street in North London: Campbell Bunk, Islington, Between the Wars*, Routledge & Kegan Paul, 1986, pp. 125–8; **S. Humphries**, *Hooligans or Rebels?: An Oral History of Working-Class Childhood and Youth 1889–1939*, Blackwell, 1981, p. 150–73.

94. White, *Worst Street*, p. 62. This section is based upon Benson, 'Work'.

95. **D. Jones**, *Crime, Protest, Community and Police in Nineteenth-Century Britain*, Routledge & Kegan Paul, 1982, pp. 199–200; **J. J. Tobias**, *Crime and Industrial Society in the 19th Century*, Batsford, 1967, pp. 76–7; **R. Roberts**, *The Classic Slum: Salford Life in the First Quarter of the Century*, Penguin, 1973, p. 150; **W. H. Davies**, *The Autobiography of a Super-Tramp*, Cape, 1924, pp. 203, 206, 213, 249–50.

96. **C. Bundy** and **D. Healy**, 'Aspects of Urban Poverty', *Oral History*, 6, 1978, p. 79.

97. **R. Samuel**, *East End Underworld: Chapters in the Life of Arthur Harding*, Routledge & Kegan Paul, 1981, pp. 23–4, 29–30.

98. Bristol, Transcript R056, p. 21. Also R011, p. 55: White, *Worst Street*, p. 61.

99. This section is based largely upon Benson, 'Work'; Jones, *Crime*, ch. 1, pp. 126, 135; Ware, 'Prostitution', I, pp. 67+; II, pp. 339, 366, 423–4; **D. Philips**, *Crime and Authority in Victorian England*, Croom Helm, 1977.

100. Humphries, *Hooligans*, pp. 163–4.

101. *Ibid.*, p. 27.

102. *Ibid.*, p. 28.

103. Jones, *Crime*, pp. 66–7, 69, 75–6; Humphries, *Hooligans*, pp. 28–9; Bristol R009, pp. 5–6.

104. University of Kent, Michael Winstanley, Oral History Collection, 'Life in Kent Before 1914', G2, pp. 161–2. Also B8, p. 36; B10, p. 46.

105. Jones, *Crime*, pp. 62, 67, 84; Howkins, *Poor Labouring Men*, pp. 34–5; Exell, 'Morris Motors', p. 65.

106. Humphries, *Hooligans*, p. 30. Also Bristol R007, p. 29; R009, p. 6; RO56, pp. 20–21; Bundy and Healy, 'Poverty', pp. 86, 92; **R. Samuel,** 'Industrial Crime in the 19th Century', *Bulletin of the Society for the Study of Labour History*, 25, 1972; **J. Benson,** *The Penny Capitalists: A Study of Nineteenth-Century Working-Class Entrepreneurs*, Gill & Macmillan, 1983, pp. 96, 99–100.

107. Manchester Studies, Transcript 628, p. 19.

108. *News of the World*, 5 January 1930.

109. Ware, 'Prostitution', I, p. 424; II, pp. 395, 536, 572; **J. Weeks,** *Sex, Politics and Society: The Regulation of Sexuality since 1800*, Longman, 1981, pp. 207–8.

110. For 'fiddling' after the Second World War, see **B. Jackson,** *Working Class Community: Some General Notions Raised by a Series of Studies in Northern England*, Routledge & Kegan Paul, 1968, pp. 95–7.

111. This section is based upon Benson, *Penny Capitalists*. See also **E. Ross,** 'Survival Networks: Women's Neighbourhood Sharing in London before World War One', *History Workshop*, 15, 1983, p. 7; **R. Samuel,** ' "Quarry Roughs": Life and Labour in Headington Quarry, 1860–1920: An Essay in Oral History', in **R. Samuel** (ed.), *Village Life and Labour*, Routledge & Kegan Paul, 1975.

112. Benson, *Penny Capitalists*, p. 51.

113. Manchester, Transcript 250, p. 7

114. Watson, *Machines and Men*, p. 22.

115. Benson, 'Work', p. 73: Stevenson, *British Society*, p. 192.

116. Greenwood, *Other Man*, p. 174.

117. Church, *Coal Industry*, 584. Unfortunately occupational mortality is not a direct measure of occupationally specific risk.

118. **E. Richards,** 'Women in the British Economy Since About 1700: An Interpretation', *History*, 59, 1974, p. 352; Meacham, *Life Apart*, p. 95.

119. **E. Roberts,** 'Working-Class Standards of Living in Barrow and Lancaster, 1890–1914', *Economic History Review*, xxx, 1977, p. 311. See also **E. Bridge,** 'Women's Employment: Problems of Research', *Bulletin of the Society for the Study of Labour History*, 26, 1973.

120. Meacham, *Life Apart*, p. 100; Hunt, *Labour History*, p. 9; **D. H. Morgan,** *Harvesters and Harvesting 1840–1900: A Study of the Rural Proletariat*, Croom Helm, 1982, pp. 58–73.

121. Bristol, Transcript RO59, pp. 2–3. Also RO56, p. 7; RO58, pp. 16–17; White, *Worst Street*, pp. 53–4.

122. White, *Worst Street*, p. 129, Also Samuel, 'Quarry Roughs'; Roberts, 'Standards of Living'.

Chapter 2

WAGES, INCOMES AND THE COST OF LIVING

Even more than the experience of work, it was the level of working-class purchasing power that affected the nature of everyday life. It was the interaction of wages, incomes and the cost of living that determined working-class purchasing power; and it was working-class purchasing power that, together with work, influenced virtually every aspect of working people's lives: the standards of living that they enjoyed; the pursuits in which they participated; the people with whom they spent their time; and the values and attitudes that they came to adopt. So much is well known.[1] Yet well known too are the formidable complexities of studying incomes and prices, for neither term is easy to define theoretically, let alone to measure empirically.[2]

The first section of the chapter examines the four major elements of working-class incomes: the wage earnings of the employed; the non-wage earnings of the self-employed; the insurance benefits obtained by the thrifty; and the charitable gifts received by those deemed worthy of such assistance. The second section of the chapter provides a cost-of-living index, which in the third section is combined with an index of incomes in order to produce a measure of the level and movement of real incomes. The chapter concludes with a discussion of the factors (both personal and structural) that denied a minority of working people access to the growing prosperity that was enjoyed by the majority of the population between 1850 and 1939.

The discussion of working-class incomes – the subject of the first part of this chapter – remains beset by difficulties both of definition and of evidence. It is true that wages may be defined easily enough as the remuneration (whether in cash or in kind) that employees received from their employers in return for the labour that they performed. But greater precision is required: it is essential to distinguish between wage rates (the rate of payment per unit of work done) and wage earnings (the actual payment received over a period of time). Employees' earnings never depended simply upon the prevailing wage rate; they depended upon the hours that workers were able, and willing, to work; and, in the case of pieceworkers, upon both management efficiency and the intensity with which the work was carried out.[3] Even when the distinction between wage rates and wage earnings has been made, it is easy to fall into the further error of believing that wage earnings comprised working people's sole source of income. In fact, as was seen in the previous chapter, wage earnings constituted just one, and not always the most important, of several sources of income. Wage earnings were often supplemented, and sometimes replaced, by earnings from non-wage labour such as begging, petty crime and penny capitalism; by benefits from mutual insurance schemes; as well as by grants from a range of welfare agencies, both personal and impersonal, private and public.[4]

Wage earnings were highest, and rose most quickly, in the heavy industrial sectors of the economy: in factory industries such as cotton, engineering and motor vehicle construction; and in non-factory, but large-scale, industries such as shipbuilding, transport and mining. It was in these industries that wages rose most markedly, that truck declined most completely, and that schemes of industrial welfare were introduced most successfully.[5]

The cotton mills contained some of the best paid of all nineteenth-century workers. The cotton masters led not only in the organisation of factory production and in the imposition of new forms of control, but in the payment of (relatively) high money wages and the provision of other types of benefit.[6] Table 4 shows that the 'normal' earnings of spinners, the best paid of all cotton workers, increased nearly three-and-a-half times between the middle of the nineteenth century and the mid-1920s: from 23s. a week in 1850 to 77s. a week in 1924–6. 'In 1906 three-quarters of all fine spinners earned more than 40s. a week, and half more than 45s., putting these privileged workers in the ranks of the labour aristocrats rather than the semi-skilled.'[7] Workers in some of the more successful mills enjoyed certain other benefits. As firms grew larger and the competitive environment more challenging, the traditional paternalism associated with small-scale production and the face-to-face contact of early industrialisation tended to give way to new, more bureaucratic and more broadly based schemes of industrial welfare. By the late 1930s, when employment in cotton was down to less than 400,000, over 100,000 textile workers were covered by occupational pension schemes, nearly half of which, it seems, required no contribution at all from the employee.[8]

Just as some late nineteenth-century engineering employers learned from the cotton masters about the imposition of industrial discipline, so too they saw the benefits that might be derived from the adoption of a high-wage policy. Table 4 shows that the 'normal' earnings of engineering workers more than doubled between 1880 and 1935: from 25s. a week in 1880 to 28s. in 1906, 51s. in 1924–6,

TABLE 4. 'Normal' full-time money wage earnings in selected occupations, 1850–1935

Year	Cotton spinning	Engineering	Coalmining	Agricultural labouring
1850	23		20	10
1880	19	25	21	18
1906		28	32	18
1924/6	77	51	53	32
1935		55	45	35

Sources: **A. L. Bowley**, *Wages and Income in the United Kingdom since 1860*, Cambridge U.P., 1937, pp. 8, 50–51; **E. H. Hunt**, *Regional Wage Variations in Britain 1850–1914*, Clarendon Press, 1973, pp. 39, 64; **P. H. Lindert** and **J. C. Williamson**, 'English Workers' Living Standards During the Industrial Revolution: A New Look', *Economic History Review*, xxxxvi, 1983, p. 3.

and 55s. a week in 1935. By the last date nearly 100,000 workers in engineering (metals and shipbuilding) were covered by occupational pension schemes and two years later the engineering employers agreed with the unions that all 600,000 workers in the industry should be allowed an annual holiday with pay.[9]

It is well known that high-wage policies were introduced most commonly in the 'new' industries that grew so rapidly in the years following the First World War. The motor industry is probably the prime example. Ford always paid high flat rates (2s. an hour during the 1920s) while Morris Motors tried consistently to demonstrate to its workers that their standard of living depended upon the success of the company rather than upon the spurious attractions of trade-union organisation. The firm paid high piece rates which it supplemented in the 1930s by a range of fringe benefits – pensions, holidays with pay and even, in 1936, a profit-sharing scheme.[10]

High, and rising, incomes were not confined to factory workers. Just as the railways were the only form of transport to develop large-scale forms of ownership, so too were they the only section of the industry to provide their workers with anything approaching a reasonable standard of living. The attraction of railway employment lay not just in the relatively high wages that were paid to certain grades of worker, but in the security of the job and in the range of fringe benefits to which virtually all employees were entitled. 'The companies were large enough', explains Frank McKenna, 'to keep men on even when their health began to fail.' Even in McKenna's own time on the railway, between 1946 and 1960, 'the men who swabbed the messroom tables, swept the engine sheds or acted as lavatory attendants, were workers who had once been well up in the hierarchy of the wage grades.'[11] Like the cotton masters, the railway companies saw very early the benefits to be derived from the provision of fringe benefits such as tied housing, free uniforms, cheap travel, paid holidays, subsidised friendly societies, and (later) occupational pension schemes.[12] 'The best part of my job is pay day,' explained a railwayman at the end of the period.

> I can count on an average of four pounds a week all through the year for an eight-hour day. I get a week's holiday with pay and I'm entitled to three free passes annually. Yes, they'll take me anywhere on the line. Then there's the privilege tickets. I can get these any time I want them. They cost me one-half the single rate for the return journey, but you don't get much chance to use these. You never have time to go anywhere worth while, although they're handy if the football team is playing away and you're free to go.[13]

Coalmining was another high-wage, non-factory occupation. Table 4 shows that miners' 'normal' wage earnings, already relatively good in 1850, were to rise more than two-and-a-half times by the mid-1920s. The small minority of miners working for aristocratic employers (like the Lowthers in Cumberland, the Dudleys in south Staffordshire or the Fitzwilliams in south Yorkshire) received other benefits besides. Some enjoyed what was virtually a complete system of social security. If a miner employed by the Fitzwilliam family was injured, 'his wages were continued, or more usually an allowance made, and free medical attention was provided. When the state of trade did not justify employment in his usual occupation he was often found other work to do . . . if he died his family were allowed to live on in their home and his widow was granted a pension. On retirement he was added to the list of weekly pensioners.'[14] The large minority of miners – about a fifth of the total – who were employed in Northumberland and Durham received a more restricted, though still significant, range of benefits. All workers in the coalfield were eligible for a non-contributory accident allowance known as 'smart money' while married men were also entitled to free coal and either a rent allowance or the tenancy of a colliery-owned house. These housing benefits were of considerable importance, for they were worth – according to the Samuel Commission of 1926 – 'something like 6/3 a week' to all adult workmen in the two counties.[15] Whatever the social and political disadvantages of tied accommodation, its economic value cannot be doubted. The coalowners' provision of tied housing enhanced by as much as 12 per cent the wage earnings of those miners who benefited from it. It was a provision which, although more common than in other industrial sectors of the economy, was unique only in the precision with which its value may now be calculated.

It is clear then that the years between 1850 and 1939 saw workers in manufacturing, mining and railway employment enjoy a substantial improvement – of 100 per cent and more – in the level of their 'normal' money wage earnings, an improvement that was sometimes augmented still further by their employers' provision of tied housing, paid holidays and other forms of fringe benefit. It was an improvement which, as will be made clear in subsequent chapters, was to exercise the most profound consequences upon the lives of millions of working people.

It is much more difficult to rediscover the wage earnings of those workers – always the majority – who were employed in the smaller-scale, less mechanised sectors of the economy. It was in jobs such as farm labouring and building, domestic service and retailing that regional variation persisted most strongly, that payment in kind remained most common, and that the evidence needed for detailed analysis and confident generalisation remains in the most desperately short supply. Nonetheless, a certain generalisation is possible. Table 4 suggests that although the earnings of workers in these 'traditional' occupations did rise gradually, they remained both low and significantly lower than those of employees in the industrial sectors of the economy.

Agricultural labourers remained the least known, as well as the lowest paid, of all major groups of male workers. Even the persistence of free grazing, cheap food and subsidised accommodation did not augment their money earnings sufficiently (probably by no more than 15 per cent) to lift them into the ranks of the reasonably well paid, let alone into the ranks of the comfortably off. In 1850 the earnings of farm labourers averaged just 10s. a week, half those of coalminers and barely 40 per cent of those of cotton spinners. Half a century later farm labourers still earned less than 20s. a week; indeed it was not until the establishment in 1917 of a minimum wage that their pay increased at all significantly. Yet, as Table 4 shows, the level of agricultural wages stayed stubbornly below those of workers employed in heavy industry: in 1935 farm labourers still earned only three-quarters as much as coalminers and less than two-thirds as much as engineers. Speaking to Walter Greenwood in 1937, a farm labourer explained that

His wages now were thirty-two shillings a week and 'privileges'. He lived in the village and paid five shillings a week rent out of his wage. The privileges included milk and vegetables and a small plot of ground on the farm where he could grow things and keep a pig and fowls. [16]

If agricultural labourers were among the lowest paid of all male workers, domestic servants were probably the poorest paid of all female employees. Even when the free board and lodging received by many servants is taken into account, it is clear that for the most part their earnings remained derisory. It has been estimated that at the end of the nineteenth century, for example, the average wage of a nursemaid or maid-of-all-work in London was less than £15 a year, no more than 6s. a week.[17] Indeed when Winifred Foley moved around between jobs after the First World War, she found that even at this relatively late date she had little option but to settle for a wage of 5s. a week.

> I decided to get another job to better myself. This time it was in Cheltenham, that artistocrat of towns, where in the 1920s everybody who wasn't a servant was a somebody; including the snooty little pekes and pomeranians, creatures rated much higher in their mistresses' eyes than the servants. Again I was to be the only maid, and still at five shillings a week, but I thought I was making headway into a more sophisticated and plentiful world. In fact, the only thing I found more plentiful was the work. . . . Six months was the limit of my endurance as far as the Cheltenham household was concerned. I escaped to home as soon as I reasonably could, and determined never again to look for a job where my employers were trying to keep up an appearance beyond their means.
>
> But as I couldn't stay for long to add to the burden of the little ones, I knew it could be only a brief respite. After two pinch-belly jobs, the chance to work in the house of a remote hundred-acre farm in Wales seemed a good idea. It would be no progress moneywise; the wage offered was still only a pound a month, but 'farmhouse' surely meant bowls of big brown eggs, sizzling home-cured bacon, thick creamy butter on home-baked bread, and mugs full of frothy milk still warm from the cow.[18]

For all the inadequacies of the evidence, it is clear that the years between 1850 and 1939 did see workers in 'traditional' jobs enjoy some modest improvement in their 'normal' weekly earnings. Yet it was an improvement that, in the absence of any corresponding advance in the provision of fringe benefits, left those employed in building and retailing, in domestic service and farm labouring still far worse off than their fellow workers in the industrial sectors of the economy.

The difficulties of discussing the wage earnings of those employed in the 'traditional' sectors of the economy are as nothing compared to the complexities of examining the non-wage earnings of those engaged in self-employment. Any assessment of working people's earnings from begging, petty crime or penny capitalism remains hazardous in the extreme. Indeed it must be recognised that in the discussion that follows every generalisation is tentative, and any apparent certainty potentially misleading.

It is true that the self-employed could always hope for high earnings. It has been estimated that at the beginning of the period successful prostitutes could earn two pounds a week and that throughout the nineteenth century professional poachers could make as much as five pounds in a single night.[19] Even the rawest recruit to a job such as street selling could sometimes do very well. A Brighton man recalls that:

> Well, I was out of work. 1930s was very hard. I married in 1927, lost a daughter in 1927. Had a son in 1931, another in 1933. Well, a friend who I knew was a street trader and he said, 'Well, you'll better come out and help me,' and I found it a good paying proposition. After the first day out as a street trader he said, 'That is what you've got today,' and it was £1 each, which was a hell of a lot of money in those days.[20]

Such successes were never common. Jesse Broughton's grandfather lived in Cleckheaton during the 1870s: 'Work was very short at the engineering firm where he worked, so he left and opened a greengrocer's shop. This proved to be a failure: grandma said that he was afraid of giving under-weight so he gave over-weight, and that was the main reason why he failed.'[21] In truth, the barriers to success were less personal than structural. Moreover, the barriers were becoming increasingly difficult to surmount: for the contraction of prostitution and poaching was accompanied by the expansion of large-scale industry and, in certain parts of the country, by the superimposition upon cyclical depression of all the ravages of sectorial decline.[22] Thus it was at a particularly inopportune time – the mid 1920s – that a Manchester workman and his father opened a small 'jobbing' shop to make spare parts for the motor trade: 'Well things were very bad, there's no doubt about it, things were bad, our business was flat, I just about had my keep and that was all, we'd none of us any pocket money.'[23]

Yet even the most modest earnings could prove of crucial value at times of particular need, when they were used to maintain, or even to replace, the earnings usually derived from wage labour. Students of the nineteenth- and early twentieth-century countryside are in no doubt that poaching flourished precisely in those places, and at those times, that rural wages were at their most depressed.[24] The study of penny capitalism shows that, in this form too, self-employment was always most common at times of greatest financial pressure.

> The working-class family experienced its most extreme hardship just before the eldest child left school to go to work. It was at this stage that there were young children to bring up, that the mother was tied to the home, and that expenses weighed most heavily against wages. It was at this stage that the elder boys were most likely to take to petty crime and/or street-selling. . . . It was at this stage too that the husband might well obtain an allotment; at this stage that the wife began to undertake a home-based craft or personal service which it was possible to combine with her domestic commitments.[25]

The view that self-employment constituted a strategy of last (or at least of penultimate) resort is one for which it is possible to marshal a certain amount of statistical support. The census returns confirm that disadvantaged groups such as immigrants and the elderly participated disproportionately in hawking and peddling. According to the 1901 census, 7.7 per cent of all full-time costermongers, hucksters and street sellers were foreign-born, compared to a mere 0.8 per cent of the population as a whole. Certain nationalities were represented particularly strongly: of the 15,356 male Italians enumerated in England and Wales, nearly a fifth (2,670) were working in hawking, peddling and associated forms of street selling. Still more striking is the disproportionately large number of middle-aged and elderly people working as street traders. In the census years 1881, 1901, and 1921 the proportion of full-time hawkers and pedlars aged between 45 and 64 exceeded by huge margins – 65 per cent, 44 per cent and 39 per cent – the proportion of the total population that belonged to this age group; the proportion of full-time hawkers and pedlars aged over 65 exceeded by equally large margins – 109 per cent, 26 per cent and 37 per cent – the proportion of the population that was enumerated as belonging to this, the most elderly and vulnerable of all the age groups.[26]

It was in this remedial capacity that self-employment retained much of its importance. Unfortunately it is no more possible to assess working people's earnings from this form of work than it was to gauge the extent of their participation in it. But statistical imprecision must not be allowed to descend into total neglect. Ellen Ross's comments on pre-First World War London are worthy of wider application:

> Children's and wives' wages were often required to supplement those of men. In most poor neighbourhoods, an 'intermediate' economy, constructed around neighbourhood exchange, scavenging, theft and barter, and in which wives and children were particularly active, supplemented the (mostly male) wage-based economy. At all times, wives' housekeeping skill, and their neighbourhood activity, provided the difference between mere subsistence and a reasonable level of comfort.[27]

The examination of working people's earnings from wage labour and from non-wage self-employment does not exhaust the discussion of working-class incomes. For working people did not necessarily derive the whole of their income from their earnings. The well off were often able to draw upon the insurance policies that they had taken out with friendly societies, trade unions and industrial assurance companies. Indeed the extent and impact of such self-help has become a contentious issue in recent years – the right arguing that working-class thrift was so widespread that 'the case for the wholesale expansion of state welfare is not as clear-cut as it is sometimes made out to be',[28] the left deriding such claims as unsubstantiated and ideologically based.[29]

The truth of the matter is difficult to determine. But there seems little doubt that voluntary insurance did something at least to maintain the incomes of the better off at times of particular hardship. There is a good deal of oral, autobiographical and social survey evidence attesting to the thrift of workers in cotton, engineering and shipbuilding. Lady Bell discovered that in early twentieth-century Middlesbrough, for example, out of the 700 or so workmen 'who were interrogated on the subject, 380 were in a club, 80 in two clubs, 270 in none'.[30] But as so often, much more is known about coalminers than about other groups of workers. It has been found that by the end of the nineteenth century 30 per cent of English miners were members of a trade-union accident fund, 50 per cent had joined a permanent relief fund, and 50 per cent had insured their lives with the Prudential Assurance Company. The result was that the widow of a miner killed at work in County Durham, for instance, could expect to receive three major benefits: a lump-sum payment of £10 from the Prudential; a weekly payment of 5s. (and 1s. 6d. to 2s. for each child) from the Durham Miners' Association; and the same amount again from the Northumberland and Durham Miners' Permanent Relief Fund.[31]

No matter how compelling the evidence of late nineteenth-century English coalmining thrift, it is clearly an inadequate basis from which to generalise about the incidence of self-help among industrial workers generally between 1850 and 1939. All that can be concluded with any confidence is that working-class self-help did something to maintain the incomes of heavy industrial workers at the times that they were most in need of such assistance.

Working people were also able to draw upon sources of income that derived neither from their thrift nor from their work. They turned to members of their own, and other working class, families; they appealed to middle-class charitable organisations; and they made use of various forms of statutory assistance. The benefits provided by these agencies are important not only to the study of social policy – the use that has usually been made of them – but to any full consideration of working-class incomes.

Of all the agencies that contributed towards the augmentation of working-class purchasing power, the least amenable to historical analysis is undoubtedly the informal and virtually undocumented charity of the poor themselves. Whatever the motivation behind working-class charity, and whatever the particular forms it took, there can be little doubt that it tended nearly always to help the very poorest in the community. Starting a whip-round for an injured workmate, standing him a drink in a pub, cooking a meal for a sick neighbour, or organising a treat for 'poor children' in the local working men's club all had one thing in common: they all transferred resources – to some degree at least – from the young, the healthy and the employed towards the elderly, the sick and injured, the unemployed, the battered and the bereaved. In the years before the First World War in particular the philanthropy of the poor was often of crucial – if quite unquantifiable – importance. As a perceptive London clergyman pointed out in 1908, 'the poor breathe an atmosphere of charity. They cannot understand life without it. And it is largely this kindness of the poor to the poor which stands between our present civilisation and revolution.'[32]

More amenable to historical analysis – though in fact little more studied – are the bewilderingly large number of middle-class charities, many of them nineteenth-century creations, and most of them designed specifically to direct resources towards those working people deemed to be most deserving of assistance.[33] Every bad winter, natural disaster, trade depression, and man-made catastrophe seemed to spawn its own particular form of provision: from soup kitchen to benefit concert, from 'make-work' scheme to accident relief fund. The latter often raised large sums of money and relieved, it seemed to contemporaries, a great deal of distress. For example, between 1860 and 1897 the fifty funds that were raised by public subscription following mining disasters assisted the dependants of more than 3,000 (of the nearly 4,000) men killed in the largest and most spectacular of the industry's many accidents: £81,000 was raised when 204 men were entombed at the Hartley colliery in Northumberland in 1862; £27,000 was collected after an explosion at the Clifton Hall colliery near Manchester in 1885; and £126,000 was subscribed to relieve the dependants of the 439 men killed at the Senghenydd colliery near Caerphilly in 1913.

Yet these colliery disaster funds displayed many of the weaknesses common to all forms of public appeal – and common indeed to most other forms of middle-class charity. For one thing, they were designed to deal with only a tiny proportion of total working-class distress: the 3,000 or so miners whose dependants were relieved by the funds represented no more than one-eighth of all those who were killed in the industry. Moreover, the subscriptions raised by the funds often bore little relation to the scale even of the particular need that they were intended to alleviate: 'There can be no doubt', it was explained in 1896, 'that the public heart fails to respond to oft repeated applications.' A third weakness was that, even when 'the public heart' did 'respond', fund organisers often decided to adopt remarkably miserly scales of benefit. A member of the Hartley fund committee explained in 1862 that 'they had received information to show that if persons of this class had too liberal allowance it led to idleness and neglect of their families rather than to taking advantage of matters for improving their circumstances'. Half a century later, following the Senghenydd disaster, a member of the Caerphilly District Council reported that 'he had seen the grocery bill of a person who had received a grant of 10s., and this bill included a quarter of a pound of tobacco, two pounds of bacon at 1s. 3d., butter at 1s. 3d., and jam at 10d. a pot. He did not think', he declared, that 'these were necessary things.'[34]

Much more ambitious, yet little more successful in maintaining working-class incomes, were the permanent, institutional charities, some of which survive to this day as monuments to nineteenth- and early twentieth-century philanthropic zeal. Oral testimony reveals something of the part played in working-class life by organisations such as voluntary hospitals, mayors' funds, charity schools, housing trusts, dockland settlements and the British Legion. For example, a Bristol couple remember that during the 1920s children whose parents had served in the First World War were eligible for free 'Lord Mayor's Boots' while at the Dockland Settlement anybody could buy a jug of soup for a halfpenny, and a very large one for a penny.[35]

Such anecdotal evidence is not hard to find. The difficulty is to determine the light that it throws either upon the extent of middle-class charity or upon the redistributional effects that resulted from it. 'How much actual distress was checked by private charity it is impossible to say,' admits Maurice Bruce. But, he maintains, 'active though charity was, it was, nevertheless . . . hardly more than a drop in the bucket'.[36] Such a view is scarcely credible, and certainly not when applied to the years before 1914. It has been calculated that in the early 1860s the annual expenditure of charities in London alone was very nearly equivalent to the combined expenditure of every Poor Law authority throughout England and Wales.[37] The lack of even such limited data for the years following the First World War suggests, probably correctly, that there occurred a progressive decline in the impact that middle-class charity had upon the incomes of the poor.[38]

Private charity remains largely impervious to historical analysis. It is difficult to judge the extent to which it augmented working-class incomes, let alone the degree to which it redistributed resources towards the poorest members of the community. All that can be said with any confidence is that while the charity of the working class probably retained much of its importance throughout the period, the charity of the middle class probably did not. Yet even such a tentative conclusion is sufficient to draw attention to what has been so often overlooked by labour historians: the fact that private charity, like self-employment, continued to play a significant – albeit unquantifiable and declining – role in maintaining the incomes of members of some of the most disadvantaged of all working-class groups.

Historians of labour have been more alert – though less so than students of social policy – to the significance of statutory provision. Yet still they seem reluctant to draw one fundamental conclusion about the Poor Law and the agencies that succeeded it: that for all their contemporary unpopularity and subsequent notoriety, these organisations did serve increasingly to direct resources towards, and so maintain the incomes of, some of the poorest groups within the community.

Until its collapse in the face of the mass employment of the 1920s, the Poor Law provided huge, though declining, numbers of working people with assistance at the very times that they needed it most. At the beginning of the period the Poor Law authorities were relieving over two million people a year (a figure equivalent to more than 12 per cent of the entire working-class population); in 1892 they relieved nearly one-and-a-half million people (5.8 per cent); and throughout the 1920s at least 350,000 to 450,000 of those unemployed (1.4 per cent). In fact, in 1934 there were still 1,299,233 men, women and children (3.7 per cent of the working-class population) in receipt of poor relief.[39]

The disadvantaged were helped too by the new benefits that came into existence from the turn of the century. The introduction in 1908 of non-contributory, old-age pensions (of up to 5s. a week) resulted very quickly in payments being made to over half the people aged 70 and above. In a well-known passage, Flora Thompson describes the impact that these payments had upon old people struggling to keep out of the workhouse.

> When the Old Age Pensions began, life was transformed for . . . aged cottagers. They were relieved of anxiety. They were suddenly rich. Independent for life! At first when they went to the Post Office to draw it, tears of gratitude would run down the cheeks of some, and they would say as they picked up their money, 'God bless that Lord George! (for they could not believe one so powerful and munificent could be a plain 'Mr') and God bless you, miss!', and there were flowers from their gardens and apples from their trees for the girl who merely handed them the money.[40]

At the outbreak of the First World War nearly a million pensioners were receiving, on average, just over 5s. 6d. a week – a benefit that cost the state some £14 million. By 1933 allowances had been doubled, and the cost of payment had leapt to £57 million.[41]

The National Insurance Act of 1911 also benefited some of the poorest groups in society. Under Part I of the Act workers earning less than £160 a year (£250 after 1919) were insured against one persistent scourge of working-class life: ill-health. It was a scheme which by the end of the period had more than 17 million subscribers, a figure equivalent to fractionally less than 50 per cent of the entire working population.[42] Part II of the Act insured workers against another scourge of working-class existence: unemployment. Confined initially to two-and-a-quarter million male workers (under 12 per cent of the working population) in industries such as shipbuilding, mechanical engineering, ironfounding and motor vehicle manufacturing, the scheme was subsequently extended very considerably. It was widened in 1920 to cover 12 million manual workers (62 per cent of the working population) along with their dependants; and again in 1936–7 to cover 14.5 million workers including, at last, farm labourers and domestic servants. By the end of the period 65 per cent of the working population were protected by state-organised unemployment insurance.[43]

It is possible to assess fairly precisely the extent to which these statutory benefits enhanced working-class purchasing power. Their consequences were not entirely beneficial. It must be remembered that all flat-rate taxation and insurance contributions tend to be regressive rather than redistributive; and it can scarcely be forgotten that the Poor Law, the Unemployment Assistance Board and the Public Assistance Committees all became, and have remained, bywords for statutory parsimony and bureaucratic insensitivity. Nonetheless, students of social policy have demonstrated unequivocally that during the 1920s and 1930s the Poor Law and its successors did effect some limited transfer of resources towards the less-well-off members of society. It has been estimated that whereas in the years before the First World War working people paid more in taxation and insurance contributions than they received in social welfare benefits, in the years after the war they paid substantially less: 86 per cent of the cost of their benefits in 1925; and just 79 per cent in 1935. By the end of the period the social welfare system involved the transfer of some £200–£250 million a year from those with incomes above, to those with incomes below, the £250 level. The effect was, it has been claimed, to increase the incomes of working people by somewhere between 8 and 14 per cent. This was a major benefit and one that historians have been unduly slow to recognise.[44]

It is far more difficult to assess the combined (complex and often contradictory) consequences that statutory welfare and private charity together had upon working-class incomes. Insofar as historians have considered working people's deliberate 'manipulation of dependence on state benefits or organised charity', they have assumed it to be a practice which, like petty crime, was confined to certain groups on the margins of established working-class society.[45] Insofar as historians have examined the dependence upon welfare of the ordinary 'working poor', they have concluded that, at least in the years before the First World War, 'neither private nor public welfare payments were extensive or reliable enough to alter fundamentally the needs of the poor.'[46] It has been left to students of social policy to examine properly the cumulative impact of both forms of relief. They have shown that the decline of middle-class charity (and the possible contraction of working-class charity) after the First World War was more than made up for by the extension of state provision. This is a conclusion that seems easily overlooked. Yet it is of crucial significance; for by the end of the period the effect of statutory benefits alone was to increase working people's other, better known, sources of income by anything up to 14 per cent.

It must be clear by now, if it was not at the outset, that the difficulties of determining the level and movement of working-class incomes are not easily solved. Nonetheless two major conclusions may certainly be drawn. The first conclusion concerns the nature of working-class incomes. It has been seen that working people's incomes could, and often did, comprise four elements rather than one; that to their earnings from wage labour, must be added their earnings from non-wage labour, as well as any benefits that they were able to derive from their thrift or from appeals to welfare agencies.

This quadruple definition makes it possible to draw a second conclusion, this time concerning the level and movement of working-class incomes. Although it is not known whether insurance benefits and earnings from non-wage labour increased or decreased between 1850 and 1939, it is possible to comment with some confidence upon the movement of the other two components of working-class income. Welfare benefits increased their importance, with the expansion of statutory provision more than making up for any shortfall in private benevolence; while 'normal' wage earnings rose, and rose substantially – doubling between 1850 and 1913, and doubling again between 1913 and 1938.[47]

The real problem is to determine the movement, not of the four components individually, but of the four components combined. This is a great deal more difficult. It is easy to assume that all that needs to be done in order to calculate working people's total income is to discover, and add together, their money wages, their insurance and welfare benefits and their earnings from self-employment. Such an assumption would be quite erroneous. Very often self-employment and dependence upon insurance or welfare were alternatives – not supplements – to wage labour. Often too wage labour, self-employment or the acceptance of relief from one welfare agency could result in the withdrawal of assistance by another. For example, in 1880 the Wolverhampton Poor Law Guardians turned down the application of a miner's widow for outdoor relief when they learned that she had spent more than half the £16 funeral benefit provided by an insurance club in paying for her husband's funeral. The widow and her two children were offered relief – but only in the workhouse.[48]

The difficulties of assessing the movement, and interaction, of all four components of working-class income remain formidable indeed. Accordingly, Table 5 must be approached with considerable caution and used only to provide an indication of probable changes in the level of working people's incomes. Yet for all its limitations, Table 5 represents a considerable advance upon conventional, wage-based estimates of working-class income. It suggests that working people's incomes were higher, and increased more rapidly, than is generally

TABLE 5. 'Normal' full-time incomes, all occupations, 1850–1939

Year	Money wage earnings	Earnings from self-employment	Income from insurance and welfare	Nominal total income
1850	13	1	0	14
1880	18	2	0	20
1906	23	2	0	25
1914	25	3	0	28
1924	50	5	4	59
1935	49	5	5	59
1939	53	5	6	64

Sources:
Wage earnings: **A. L. Bowley**, *Wages and Income in the United Kingdom since 1860*, Cambridge U.P., 1937, p. 30; **P. Deane** and **W. A. Cole**, *British Economic Growth 1688–1959: Trends and Structure*, Cambridge U.P., 1969, p. 25; **A. Marwick**, *Class: Images and Reality in Britain, France and the USA since 1930*, Fontana, 1981, p. 216; **G. Routh**, *Occupation and Pay in Great Britain 1906–79*, Macmillan, 1980, p. 110.

Self-employment: See Notes and References; **E. Roberts**, *A Woman's Place: An Oral History of Working-Class Women 1890–1940*, Blackwell, 1984, pp. 135–48; **J. Benson**, *The Penny Capitalists: A Study of Nineteenth-Century Working-Class Entrepreneurs*, Gill and Macmillan, 1983. Earnings from self-employment are assumed to equal 10 per cent of money wage earnings.

Self-help and Welfare: See Notes and References.

supposed: that the 'normal' full-time income of the 'average' working person was 14s. (rather than 13s.) a week in 1850; 28s. (rather than 25s.) a week in 1914; and 64s. (rather than 53s.) a week in 1939.[49]

Unfortunately the fact that working-class incomes rose so much does not of itself reveal whether, let alone to what extent, there occurred a similar improvement in levels of real incomes – in the amount, that is, of the goods and services that these rising incomes would buy. What is needed is a cost of living index against which to set the index of working-class incomes. It is the construction of this cost of living index that forms the subject of this, the second and much shorter, section of the present chapter. The complexities of compiling such an index are well known.

The major difficulty for any student of the history of the cost of living is the paucity of data on past prices. Although scattered references to prices are to be found in almost any contemporary source – from household books and accounts to diaries, journals, letters and autobiographies – they usually relate to a particular place at a particular time only. . . . Again, there is an obvious difference between wholesale and retail prices, but all too often in contemporary records it is not clear which is being quoted. What the historian would like are long series of retail prices of goods of a known and standard description, bought at various places at frequent and regular intervals, but these are almost non-existent. . . .[50]

Certainly it is considerably easier to plot the changing cost of individual items such as rent, food, fuel and clothing (that will be examined in subsequent chapters) than it is to compile the index of all retail prices that is required for the present purpose. Nonetheless, Table 6 provides a serviceable enough guide to changes in the general level of retail prices between 1850 and 1939. However it is an index that, like Table 5, needs to be approached with considerable caution. When this is done, it can be used to provide a reasonable indication of both the direction and the magnitude of the most significant changes to occur in the prices that working people had to pay for the goods and services they needed. Table 6 shows quite clearly that over the period as a whole the cost of living increased by approximately one third.

What Table 6 cannot show are the shorter-run, and much sharper, fluctuations with which working people were forced to contend. Prices rose by some 20 per cent between 1850 and 1880, especially in the boom years of 1854–5 and 1871–3. But fortunately for working people the prices that rose most were those of raw materials, while the prices that 'rose considerably less than the average or fell absolutely' were those of foodstuffs. Thereafter prices fell fairly consistently until almost the end of the century. These were the years of the so-called 'Great Depression', the years that saw the spread of the steamship, the invention of refrigeration, the importation of grain and meat from all over the world – and a reduction of approximately one-third in the prices that working people in Britain had to pay for their food. It is true that between 1896 and 1913 there occurred an inflation of about 20 per cent, with the price of mutton rising by 20 per cent, the price of bacon by 29 per cent, and that of coal by 30 per cent.[51] Nonetheless, as Table 6 shows, the cost of living had changed remarkably little

TABLE 6. Cost of living index, 1850–1939

Year	Index	Year	Index	Year	Index
1850	100	1913	105	1935	119
1880	121	1924	180	1939	131
1906	105				

since the beginning of the period, with prices in 1913 only slightly higher than they had been in 1850.

After 1913 price movements assumed 'an altogether new order of severity'.[52] The years during and immediately following the First World War witnessed rampant inflation: within six years the cost of living increased by well over 100 per cent. As the Special Commissioners of Enquiry into Industrial Unrest in the North-east of England reported in 1917:

> The high prices of staple commodities have undoubtedly laid severe strain upon the majority of the working classes, and in some instances have resulted in hardship and actual privation. It is no doubt true that in some industries wages have risen to such an extent as largely to compensate for the increased cost of living, but there are workers whose wages have been raised very slightly, if at all, and some whose earnings have actually diminished.[53]

From their peak in 1920, prices fell rapidly for two years, and moderately for well over ten. Indeed even the rises that followed the trough of 1933–4 were insufficient to wipe out the gains from this decade and a half of falling prices.[54] The result was that the inter-war years saw prices fall by about 25 per cent, with the cost of living ending the 1930s only a quarter higher than it had been in 1913, and no more than a third higher than it had been in 1850, at the very beginning of the period.

Armed with this cost of living index, it is possible to proceed to the third, very brief, yet probably most important, section of this chapter: the construction of an index of real working-class incomes over the 90-year period that forms the subject of the book. The results that are revealed in Table 7 will probably come as no very great surprise. For of course it is no accident that the long-running and bitter debate over working-class standards of living refers to the century before 1850, rather than the century after it. Table 7 confirms the dramatic

TABLE 7. 'Normal' real incomes, all occupations, 1850–1939

Year	'Normal' full-time incomes	Cost of living	'Normal' real incomes
1850	100	100	100
1880	143	121	118
1906	179	105	170
1913–14	200	105	190
1924	421	180	234
1935	421	119	354
1939	457	131	349

improvement that took place in the value of working-class incomes between 1850 and 1939. 'Normal' real incomes rose by 90 per cent in the years before the First World War, and by practically 250 per cent between 1850 and 1939. These were changes of the greatest possible importance. That mythical beast, the 'typical' British worker, was three-and-a-half times better off at the end of the period than at the beginning.[55] Unfortunately, for the real working person – as opposed to 'the "typical" British worker' – this growing prosperity proved neither as straightforward nor as beneficial as the figures above would suggest. The improvement in working-class purchasing power could be, and frequently was, checked by a wide range of social and economic factors: some of them personal, self-inflicted and short-lived; others impersonal, structural and deep-rooted; yet many of them it seems, mutually reinforcing.

Personal failings should not be discounted.[56] Naturally working-class frailty is not the stuff of which most labour histories are made. Yet there is no reason to suppose that during the period covered by this book working people were any less lazy or any less likely to indulge in unwise expenditure than their predecessors and descendants in earlier and later generations. Oral and autobiographical evidence confirms the existence of idle, shiftless and irresponsible parents, not all of whom can be the figments of filial animosity.[57] So too does the contemporary social survey evidence. Indeed it was 'Drink, betting, and gambling ignorant and careless housekeeping, and other improvident expenditure' that constituted the immediate cause of what Seebohm Rowntree called 'secondary' (or avoidable) poverty.[58] When he and Bruno Lasker conducted their 1910 survey of unemployment in York, they decided that just over 8 per cent of those out of work in the city could be described as 'work-shy'. They were perplexed by the attitudes of many of those whom they placed in this category. One 40-year-old man 'was originally apprenticed to a trade, but left after only two and a half years work, owing, as he says, to trade depression. He has done no work since, apart from occasional odd jobs at the railway station and in the streets. He has undergone a term of imprisonment for theft, and is said to have become completely reckless, having drifted to the lowest possible stage at which he can maintain himself.'[59] In many households, concludes James Treble, of the years before 1914, 'imprudent budgeting and heavy drinking were the twin foundations upon which working-class poverty was built'.[60]

Nor should it be forgotten that, in the view of some commentators, industrial disputes constituted another self-inflicted cause of working-class poverty.[61] They can point to the fact that in the decades between 1893 (when official statistics were first collected) and the outbreak of the Second World War industrial disputes resulted in the loss of over 600 million working days – an average each year of more than 13 million days.[62] They can point to the fact that in a strike-prone industry such as coalmining (which accounted for almost half of all the time lost) the burden of poverty and suffering could be heavy indeed. As dispute followed dispute, it was the plight of the children that aroused the greatest concern. Two south Yorkshire examples must suffice. A local clergyman paid a Christmas visit to Denaby Main at the end of 1902, two-thirds of the way through a bitter nine-month strike.

> My band of willing workers were all impressed with the same fact, namely that the children were desperately hungry. They arrived at this conclusion through the eagerness of the little ones for plain bread. We thought that it being the festive season they would plunge into some sweet cake, but the children asked for bread and butter.[63]

During the General Strike and Miners' Lockout of 1926 the *Sheffield Independent* inaugurated a 'Feed the Children Fund':

> You may sympathise with the miner
> And think his cause is just
> You may feel sorry for the owner
> Whose profits may go 'bust'
> You may weep for the poor old dealer
> Who's got no coal to deal
> You may pity the hard-hit taxpayer
> Who's got some cause to squeal
> But think of the innocent kiddies
> Whose laughter is turned to a sob
> They're hungry, ill clad, starving
> For them – we want a 'bob'.[64]

The number of working days lost appears enormous, their consequences horrendous. Yet it is easy to be misled. Industrial disputes were virtually unknown in retailing, farming, domestic service and all the other traditional sectors of the economy. Even the 13 million days lost in a typical year represented the loss of less than one day's pay from the income of each member of (even the low, census-based estimate of) the working population.[65] Moreover, the poverty brought about by industrial disputes was counterbalanced – to some extent at least – by the alternative sources of income that were considered earlier in this chapter. There is ample evidence to show how strikers and their families took other jobs, turned to begging, petty crime and penny capitalism, and applied for whatever charitable or statutory assistance was available. 'Somehow we could not believe that the lock-out in 1921 would happen,' explains a South Wales miner, 'and when it did we felt stunned.'

> We had some money in the bank, and my wife had caught the
> craze for shopkeeping, so I made a counter and shelves, and our
> front room was a shop – it was well stocked too. We had reared two

bacon pigs and we were selling the bacon, and had pens and poultry out in the garden. . . . We paid the wholesaler's bills, used the rest of our money, then did as almost all the workers were compelled to do – went to get parish relief. . . . We hunted for wood on the mountains, and opened levels so that we could have coal for our use. This was not permitted but we took the risk.[66]

The view that strikes and lockouts constituted a major impediment to the growth of working-class prosperity is one that seems to retain a considerable hold. Yet it is a view that needs to be resisted. For while it is true that certain workers in certain industries did suffer greatly from industrial disputes, the same cannot be said of the great mass of the working population. For most members of the working class strikes and lockouts were never more than a minor cause of the poverty and uncertainty with which they had to contend.

Prosperity was checked, and poverty dispersed, much more widely than the discussion of personal failings and industrial disputes would lead one to suppose. Working people's inability to enjoy a rising standard of living resulted not so much from self-inflicted wounds as from impersonal, structural factors over which they could exercise virtually no control whatsoever.

One small, but highly visible, group denied access to the growing prosperity enjoyed by other members of the working class were those belonging to the country's various immigrant communities. It was seen above that foreign-born workers (such as Italians) tended to be employed disproportionately in low-status, low-income occupations such as hawking and peddling. Similarly disadvantaged were those belonging to the largest immigrant communities: the Irish, who made up some 5 per cent of the late nineteenth- and early twentieth-century workforce; and the Jews, who from the 1880s onwards accounted for nearly 1 per cent of the country's working population. Both groups were concentrated in London and northern cities such as Leeds, Liverpool, Manchester and Glasgow; and both groups remained confined to a narrow range of poorly paid occupations. The Jews sold in the streets or sweated in clothing, footwear and furniture workshops. The Irish took on labouring jobs in farming, in the docks, in building and construction, or in any other industry that was at hand.[67] 'The Irish seldom get any better,' claimed a Birmingham employer in 1834. 'They are born bricklayers' labourers and die bricklayers' labourers.' Fifty years later the *Dundee Catholic Herald* saw no reason to challenge this view: 'Among our Catholic boys and girls', it regretted, there was still 'a great dearth of social and education ladder-climbing.'[68]

Still better known are the disadvantages suffered by women workers. Like immigrants, women remained confined largely to a limited range of low-wage jobs – in this case in retailing, clothing, domestic service and (later) light engineering.[69] Even when women did manage to find work in high-wage industries such as cotton, pottery or motor manufacturing, it did them very little good. For even when wage rates were nominally equal, there remained all sorts of ways of depressing female earnings. In the north Staffordshire pottery industry, for example, it was an unwritten rule that women were not allowed to earn more than their male colleagues, with the result that they were forced to stop work if it seemed to the men in their shops that they were increasing their pay to unacceptable levels.[70] But most often wage rates were not even nominally equal. In the motor industry – that flagship of the twentieth-century high-wage economy – women were paid only half as much as men. In the press shop at Morris Radiators 'there were 60 presses . . . and lots of these little ones. And these little ones, you know, these girls used to do. There was a *big* difference in the rates paid for women and for men: in the press shop and in any part of the factory. The women worked for, I think it was, 10 pence an hour, on the same work as a man was getting 1/9 an hour for.'[71] Clementina Black's condemnation of married women's work may be extended to virtually all female employment: 'The grave drawback of much of the work done for money . . . is not that it is injurious in itself but that it is scandalously ill-paid.'[72]

Even the claim that the ill-paid nature of women's work afforded them some protection against the ravages of unemployment stands in need of modification. It is true that at times of depression many employers probably preferred to keep on their poorly paid married women at the expense of their better paid male workers: in 1931, according to the official statistics, the female unemployment rate stood at 8.9 per cent compared to a male rate of 13.3 per cent. Yet the comparison cannot be made with any great confidence for, as Booth and Glynn have pointed out, 'It is impossible to obtain any realistic assessment of female unemployment since there is no way of knowing how many unoccupied women would have been willing to seek paid employment at prevailing wage rates, had it been available.'[73]

Working-class women ended the period as they had begun it: confined overwhelmingly to a narrow range of low-paid jobs (in both old and 'new' industries) that made it hard for them to earn as much as the male members of their families, let alone to support themselves independently or to maintain any dependants for whom they might be responsible. Widowhood and desertion remained disasters from which many women were never able to recover.[74]

Less well known is the poverty brought about by poor health. For despite the many improvements that occurred during this period (and will be examined in a later chapter), physical and mental incapacity continued to plague working people's attempts to attain a better standard of living. As that pioneer social investigator, Lady Bell, pointed out in 1907,

> The question of health, so important a factor in the existence of all
> of us, assumes still greater importance in the lives of the workmen, to
> whom even a passing ailment means either a diminution of the weekly
> income, or else a continuance of work under conditions which may turn
> the slight indisposition into something more serious.[75]

The study of working-class health remains inherently elusive. Yet
some precision is possible in the discussion of occupational safety. It
can be shown that in an industry such as coalmining that was notorious
both for the bitterness of its industrial relations and for the severity of
its industrial accidents, the latter proved a far more serious cause of
poverty than the former. In years such as 1896 or 1897 (when there
occurred neither great dispute nor devastating disaster) fewer than
two million days were lost in strikes and lockouts, yet more than
three million days were lost as a result of the 100,000 non-fatal
accidents that occurred in the industry.[76]

Even such limited generalisation cannot be extended very far.
It is difficult to assess the incidence of occupational injury in other
industrial sectors of the economy, let alone in traditional sectors such
as retailing, farming and domestic service that were famed neither
for their disputes nor for their accidents.[77] It is even more difficult
to quantify the burden of occupational disease: the nystagmus that
blinded so many miners: the anthrax that threatened anybody working
with cattle and sheep; or the rheumatism that afflicted such large
numbers of outdoor workers. It remains completely impossible to
measure the incidence and consequences of everyday illnesses such as
influenza or migraine, still less of chronic complaints such as arthritis,
sciatica or the proverbial 'bad back'. The more common the illness,
the more difficult it seems is its measurement.[78]

Moreover, it is never easy to discern the precise nature of the
relationship between poor health and poverty. It is not always clear to
what extent it was poverty that led to poor health or, as will be argued
here, that it was poor health that led to poverty. In all events, there
is incontrovertible evidence that low-paid labourers were frequently
of poor physique; and compelling evidence that it was their poor
physique that diminished their earning capacity, and so prevented
them from sharing in the prosperity that more and more working
people were beginning to enjoy. While those with physical or mental
handicaps might be able to obtain jobs at times of full employment,
they always found it hard to earn as much as their workmates; in
times of depression they were likely to find themselves, along with
married women, among the first to be laid off and the last to be
re-employed.[79]

Poor Law statistics attest to the correlation between ill-health
and poverty. They show that between 1842 and 1866 more than 40
per cent of those receiving outdoor relief were sickness or accident
cases and that during the opening decade of the twentieth century

nearly one-third of all paupers were in receipt of medical treatment.[80] The relationship between poor health and poverty is confirmed by the contemporary social survey evidence. Charles Booth claimed that 10 per cent of the 'submerged one-tenth' in the east end of London had been impoverished by sickness and infirmity[81]; Rowntree and Lasker reported that probably 10 per cent of the 'regular workers' in their sample of the unemployed in York were 'in some way physically disqualified' from obtaining work[82]; while in its classic 1938 study of *Men Without Work*, the Pilgrim Trust concluded that 18 per cent of the long-term unemployed in Blackburn, Crook, Deptford, Leicester, Liverpool and the Rhondda could be described either as 'unfit' or as suffering from 'obvious physical defects'.[83] So although there is no doubt that working-class health improved very greatly between 1850 and 1939, there is no doubt either that the ill-health which did persist was associated with, and helped to cause, the low pay and poverty that continued to frustrate so many hopes of self-improvement.

There was one further socially determined cause of low pay and poverty that posed a recurring threat to almost every family – no matter how healthy, hard working, acquiescent and 'British' its members. This was the working-class life cycle that was first identified by Seebohm Rowntree.

> The life of a labourer is marked by five alternating periods of want and comparative plenty. During early childhood, unless his father is a skilled worker, he probably will be in poverty; this will last until he, or some of his brothers or sisters, begin to earn money and thus augment their father's wage sufficiently to raise the family above the poverty line. Then follows the period during which he is earning money and living under his parents' roof; for some portion of this period he will be earning more money than is required for lodging, food, and clothes. This is his chance to save money. If he has saved enough to pay for furnishing a cottage, this period of comparative prosperity may continue after marriage until he has two or three children, when poverty will again overtake him. This period of poverty will last perhaps for ten years, *i.e.* until the first child is fourteen years old and begins to earn wages; but if there are more than three children it may last longer. While the children are earning, and before they leave home to marry, the man enjoys another period of prosperity – possibly, however, only to sink back again into poverty when his children have married and left him, and he himself is too old to work, for his income has never permitted his saving enough for him and his wife to live upon for more than a very short time.

The implication was clear. 'The proportion of the community who at one period or other of their lives suffer from poverty to the point of physical privation is therefore much greater, and the injurious effects of such a condition are much more widespread than would appear from a consideration of the number who can be shown to be below the poverty line at any given moment.'[84] This cycle of deprivation, the so-called working-class life cycle, has proved of considerable value in the study of the standard of living. For together with the other social factors that have been considered above, it created a formidable set of barriers to working people's hopes of escaping from poverty and attaining a reasonable level of well being.

Even if working people did somehow manage to evade these social barriers to their prosperity, they faced an equally formidable set of economic difficulties. For those employed in the traditional sectors of the economy, casual work was always a major cause of low and uncertain earnings. It is true that the years after the First World War saw some decasualisation of labour in dock work, road haulage and local authority employment. But the country's ports and building sites remained bastions of casual employment, with workers continuing to be hired, not by the week or the month, but by the day or part of the day.[85] In Bristol, recalls one woman, 'nearly everybody where I lived, their fathers were dockers. Well, they may go to work one day and they may not go to work for another week.'[86] In the building industry, claimed the *Glasgow Herald*, 'a large number of men . . . are not employed; they are always underemployed, loitering in a stagnant pool about certain large centres of employment, and doing an odd day's work now and again'.[87]

It is no easy matter to isolate casual labour, and assess its role in the creation of working-class poverty. Yet its significance cannot be doubted. Gareth Stedman Jones suggests that casual workers and their families comprised about 10 per cent of the late nineteenth-century population in the east end of London.[88] Rowntree and Lasker discovered that even in a city such as York, which had no great industry run on casual lines, casual work still accounted for more than a third of all unemployment in the early years of the twentieth century.[89] Moreover, the correlation between casual employment and poverty had not disappeared by the end of the period; for even in 1937 dock labourers and building workers were suffering from unemployment rates ranging from 10 to 27 per cent, well above the national average.[90]

Workers in all sectors of the economy encountered difficulties brought about by seasonal and cyclical fluctuation. Seasonality of employment reduced the earning capacity of all outdoor workers. Farming was one industry badly affected: each year after the harvest hours were shortened and wages reduced; in a really severe winter, like that of 1911–12, labourers could be out of work for three or even four months.[91] Building was another vulnerable industry, and not just its outdoor trades. 'My father was a painter and decorator,' recalls an Accrington man, 'and he used to be out of work several weeks every winter because people didn't want workmen in the house in the winter when it was cold and wet.'[92] But seasonal fluctuation was not confined to the traditional sectors of the economy. Coalmining was affected by the weather, the car industry by the motor show.

In '30 or '31, work at [Morris] Radiators went very, very slack; we were only doing three or four days, down to two days, and then there was hardly any at all, and they made the decision to shut down until the following September or October, when they expected a lot of orders for the Motorshow. During that time I went back home to Wales, but there was no work there. . . . After the Motorshow she [my future wife] wrote to say that things weren't too bad and they were going to start people. I came back. As soon as ever I got back I went to Radiators and they said, 'OK can you start Monday morning?'[93]

This seasonal volatility was of considerable significance. 'It can be safely concluded', as James Treble says of urban poverty before 1914, 'that for all but an artisan elite, seasonality of employment represented yet another route to social deprivation and poverty.'[94]

Seasonal fluctuation was at least reasonably predictable. The depredations of the trade cycle appeared far less so. In the years before the First World War in particular the troughs of the cycle seemed to follow the peaks with bewildering rapidity. Among the worst years were 1857–8, 1862–4, 1866–7, 1878–9, 1884–7, 1892–3, 1903–5, 1907–9, 1921–2 and 1931–2.[95] Building was affected extremely severely: in the late nineteenth century production at the peak of the cycle was probably ten to fifteen times as great as it was in the trough.[96] But also affected were industries throughout the manufacturing sectors of the economy. 'There was a proper slump,' recalls a Gloucestershire paper mill worker of the 1930s. 'And although we officially didn't have the sack, I think we did work about two thirds of the week. And all the rest was short time.'[97] Even the motor industry was not immune. 'It was only a matter of working while they had those orders in,' explains the daughter of a pattern-maker at Vulcan Motors near Southport. 'They wouldn't keep anybody on working to stock or anything. He would probably have about six months a year, then he had to finish again.'[98]

Such cyclical and seasonal fluctuation meant that the incomes of even the best paid and most regularly employed workers were far less secure than the discussion of their 'normal' wage earnings would lead one to suppose. The prosperity that they enjoyed in the years following the First World War remained halting and uncertain, and could never be taken for granted.

Best known of all the groups denied access to the growing prosperity of the twentieth century were those dependent directly or indirectly upon the great staple industries of coal, cotton, engineering and iron and steel. For it was the industries that had grown so prodigiously during the nineteenth century that collapsed so ignominiously during the twentieth. Moreover, the geographical concentration that had served these industries so well during the years of expansion, tended merely to aggravate the difficulties of their workers during the years of contraction. Nobody could fail to notice 'the contrast between the high rate of unemployment in the heavy industries upon which the Special Areas have in the past been so largely dependent, and the lower rate of unemployment in the South and Midlands where industry is more varied.'[99]

Just as the nineteenth-century cotton industry had stood as a symbol of enterprise and success, so in the twentieth century cotton became a monument to the inability of a pioneering industry to cope with changing market conditions. Production plummeted and employment shrank from a peak of 621,000 in 1912 to 288,000 in 1938. In 1931–2 unemployment among cotton workers stood at over 28 per cent; in Blackburn nearly half the workforce was without work.[100] Even those fortunate enough to keep their jobs were probably put on short time, and this meant of course a reduction in their earnings: 'You only got what you produced you see.'[101]

Coalmining experienced a similar sequence of rapid expansion followed by seemingly irreversible decline. Employment in the industry collapsed from a peak of 1,248,000 in 1920 to 766,000 in 1939. As in cotton, even those who remained in work faced a reduction in their earnings. In 1924 the average miner worked 260 shifts and took home £138; a decade later he worked 239 shifts and took home £110.[102] In the isolated, single-industry communities that were to be found in part of Scotland, Yorkshire, Northumberland and Durham, and South Wales the consequences were catastrophic: in 1934, for example, almost three-quarters of the insured populations of Greenock, Motherwell, Jarrow, Gateshead, Dowlais and Brynmawr were out of work.[103] For Eric Hobsbawm,

It was the concentration of permanent, hopeless unemployment in certain derelict areas, politely renamed 'special areas' by a mealy-mouthed government, which gave the depression its particular character. South Wales, central Scotland, the Northeast, parts of Lancashire, parts of Northern Ireland and Cumberland, not to mention smaller enclaves elsewhere, resisted even the modest recovery of the later 1930s. The grimy, roaring, bleak industrial areas of the nineteenth century – in Northern England, Scotland and Wales – had never been very beautiful or comfortable, but they had been active and prosperous. Now all that remained was the grime, the bleakness, and the terrible silence of the factories and mines which did not work, the shipyards which were closed.[104]

The historical study of wages, incomes and the cost of living has advanced less rapidly than the study of work. Yet the advances that have been made all confirm the need to incorporate non-wage sources of income into the analysis of working-class standards of living. From this analysis, three major conclusions emerge. First, it is important to recognise that during the years covered by this book most members of the working class enjoyed a striking improvement in the value of their incomes. Not only does this improvement provide the period with a certain unity; it also proved, as will be seen in subsequent chapters, of crucial significance in determining every other aspect of working-class life. Second, it must be recognised that because the social and economic roots of poverty were not eradicated during this period, a small minority of the working class continued to live below even the stringent primary poverty line laid down by Seebohm Rowntree – probably 15 per cent of the working population in 1900, and up to 10 per cent during the 1930s.[105] The final conclusion derives from the second. Although the number of working people living in primary (unavoidable) poverty was always relatively small, the number living in secondary poverty was probably as large again; while those living with the fear of poverty was far larger still. The fear of poverty, like the enjoyment of prosperity, proved of the greatest significance. 'Economic uncertainty', concludes Standish Meacham, was 'the final arbiter of working-class existence'.[106]

NOTES AND REFERENCES

1. **J. Stevenson,** *British Society 1914–45*, Penguin, 1984, p. 182; **P. Johnson,** 'Credit and Thrift and the British Working Class, 1870–1939', in **J. Winter** (ed.), *The Working Class in Modern British History: Essays in Honour of Henry Pelling*, Cambridge U.P., 1983, p. 147.

2. **J. Burnett,** *A History of the Cost of Living*, Penguin, 1969, pp. 9–14.

3. **E. H. Phelps Brown** with **M. H. Browne,** *A Century of Pay: The Course of Pay and Production in France, Germany, Sweden, the United Kingdom and the United States of America 1860–1960*, Macmillan, 1968, p.41.

4. **A. L. Webb** and **J. E. B. Sieve,** *Income Redistribution and the Welfare State*, Bell, 1971, p. 16; **P. Townsend,** *Poverty in the United Kingdom: A Survey of Household Resources and Standards of Living*, Penguin, 1979, pp. 45, 175, 180.

5. **G. W. Hilton,** *The Truck System: Including a History of the British Truck Acts, 1465–1960*, Cambridge U.P., 1960; **A. Russell,** 'The Quest for Security: The Changing Working Conditions and Status of the British Working Class in the Twentieth Century', Ph.D. University of Lancaster, 1982; **H. Jones,** 'Employers' Welfare Schemes and Industrial Relations in Inter-War Britain', *Business History*, xxv, 1983.

6. **S. Pollard,** *The Genesis of Modern Management: A Study of the Industrial Revolution in Great Britain*, Penguin, 1965, pp. 204–5; **P. Deane** and **W. A. Cole,** *British Economic Growth 1688–1959: Trends and Structure*, Cambridge U.P., 1969, p. 26.

7. Burnett, *Cost of Living*, p. 252. Also **J. W. F. Rowe,** *Wages in Practice and Theory*, Routledge & Kegan Paul, 1928, p. 33.

8. **P. Joyce,** *Work, Society and Politics: The Culture of the Factory in Later Victorian England*, Methuen, 1982, pp. 146, 170; Jones, 'Employers' Welfare', pp. 61–2; Russell, 'Quest', pp. 60, 166, 193,

290, 588. Cf. **D. Roberts,** *Paternalism in Early Victorian England,* Croom Helm, 1979; **J. Wiseman,** 'Occupational Pension Schemes', in **G. L. Reid** and **D. J. Robertson** (eds), *Fringe Benefits, Labour Costs and Social Security,* Allen & Unwin, 1965, pp. 172–3.

9. Russell, 'Quest', p. 193; **G. C. Cameron,** 'The Growth of Holidays with Pay in Britain', in Reid and Robertson, *Fringe Benefits,* p. 279.

10. **R. C. Whiting,** *The View from Cowley: The Impact of Industrialization upon Oxford, 1918–1939,* Clarendon Press, 1983, pp. 85–6, 101–2; Jones, 'Employers' Welfare', pp. 62–3.

11. **F. McKenna,** 'Victorian Railway Workers', *History Workshop,* 1, 1976, p. 32.

12. *Ibid.,* pp. 35–7; Cameron, 'Holidays', p. 275; Russell, 'Quest', pp. 70, 165, 193.

13. **W. Greenwood,** *How the Other Man Lives,* Labour Book Club, 1937?, p. 46.

14. **J. Benson,** *British Coalminers in the Nineteenth Century: A Social History,* Gill & Macmillan, 1980, pp. 177–8. **R. J. Waller,** *The Dukeries Transformed: The Social and Political Development of a Twentieth Century Coalfield,* Clarendon Press, 1983, ch. 4.

15. Rowe, *Wages,* p. 30. Also **J. Benson,** 'The Compensation of English Coal Miners and their Dependants for Industrial Accidents, 1860–97', Ph.D. University of Leeds, 1974, pp. 227–8.

16. Greenwood, *Other Man,* p. 73. Also Burnett, *Cost of Living,* p. 250; **S. Pollard,** *The Development of the British Economy 1914–1980,* Arnold, 1983, p. 87.

17. **T. McBride,** ' "As the Twig is Bent": the Victorian Nanny', in **A. S. Wohl** (ed.), *The Victorian Family: Structure and Stresses,* Croom Helm, 1978, p. 50. Also **S. Meacham,** *A Life Apart: The English Working Class 1890–1914,* Thames & Hudson, 1977, p. 183; **P. Taylor,** 'Daughters and Mothers – Maids and Mistresses: Domestic Service Between the Wars', in **J. Clarke, C. Critcher** and **R. Johnson** (eds), *Working-Class Culture: Studies in History and Theory,* Hutchinson, 1979, p. 129.

18. **W. Foley,** *A Child in the Forest,* BBC, 1974, pp. 184, 190. Also Manchester Polytechnic, Manchester Studies, Transcript 20, pp. 5, 9.

19. **H. R. E. Ware,** 'The Recruitment, Regulation and Role of Prostitution in Britain from the Middle of the Nineteenth Century to the Present Day', Ph.D. University of London, 1969, I, p. 92; **D. J. V. Jones,** 'The Poacher: A Study in Victorian Crime and Protest', *Historical Journal,* 22, 1979, p. 842. **F. Finnegan,** *Poverty and Prostitution: A Study of Victorian Prostitutes in York,* Cambridge U.P., 1979; **J. R. Walkowitz,** *Prostitution and Victorian Society: Women, Class and the State,* Cambridge U.P., 1980.

20. **N. Griffiths,** *Shops Book: Brighton 1900–1930,* Queenspark Books, ND, p. 35. Also Manchester Studies, Transcript 250, p. 11.

21. **J. B. Broughton,** 'A Record of his Early Life', Manchester Studies, Transcript 924, p. 1.

22. **J. Benson,** *The Penny Capitalists: A Study of Nineteenth-Century Working-Class Entrepreneurs,* Gill & Macmillan, 1983, p. 133.

23. Manchester Studies, Transcript 250, p. 8.

24. Jones, 'Poacher', pp. 836–8; **A. Howkins,** *Poor Labouring Men: Rural Radicalism in Norfolk 1872–1923*, Routledge & Kegan Paul, 1985, pp. 34–5; **P. Horn,** *Labouring Life in the Victorian Countryside*, Gill & Macmillan, 1976, pp. 228–34.

25. Benson, *Penny Capitalists*, p. 130. Also **E. Ross,** 'Survival Networks: Women's Neighbourhood Sharing in London before World War One', *History Workshop*, 15, 1983, p. 7.

26. **J. Benson,** 'Hawking and Peddling in England and Wales, 1850–1939', unpublished manuscript.

27. Ross, 'Survival Networks', p. 7.

28. **C. G. Hanson,** 'Welfare before the Welfare State', in **R. M. Hartwell** (ed.), *The Long Debate on Poverty*, Institute of Economic Affairs, 1972, p. 113.

29. **J. L. Halstead,** 'Ideology in History', *Bulletin of the Society for the Study of Labour History*, 26, 1973, pp. 61–2.

30. **Lady Bell,** *At the Works: A Study of a Manufacturing Town*, Arnold, 1907, p. 113. See also **E. Roberts,** *A Woman's Place: An Oral History of Working-Class Women*, Blackwell, 1984, pp. 163–4.

31. Benson, 'Compensation', table xiii, pp. 404, 475; **J. Benson,** 'The Thrift of English Coal-Miners, 1860–95', *Economic History Review*, xxxi, 1978.

32. **F. K. Prochaska,** *Women and Philanthropy in Nineteenth–Century England*, Oxford U.P., 1980, p. viii. See also Ross, 'Survival Networks', pp. 6–8, 11; Benson, 'Compensation', pp. 136–214; *Club Life*, 6 January 1900; Manchester Studies, Transcript 630, p. 14; Transcript 664, p. 13; Avon County Reference Library, Bristol People's Oral History Project, Transcript R007, p. 20.

33. **D. Owen,** *English Philanthropy 1660–1960*, Harvard U.P., 1964; **D. Fraser,** *The Evolution of the British Welfare State: A History of Social Policy since the Industrial Revolution*, Macmillan, 1973, pp. 116–17; **N. McCord,** 'The Poor Law and Philanthropy', in **D. Fraser** (ed.), *The New Poor Law in the Nineteenth Century*, Macmillan 1976; **E. H. Hunt,** *British Labour History 1815–1914*, Weidenfeld & Nicolson, 1981, pp. 126–30.

34. **J. Benson,** 'Colliery Disaster Funds, 1860–1897', *International Review of Social History*, xix, 1974, p. 80; Benson, *British Coalminers*, p. 177. Also pp. 37–8, 176.

35. Bristol, Transcript RO56, pp. 7–8. Also RO11, pp. 9, 19–20, 34; McCord, 'Poor Law'; **N. J. Chamard,** 'Medicine and the Working Class: The Dispensary Movement in London, 1867–1911', Ph.D. University of Toronto, 1984, pp. 129d, 392.

36. **M. Bruce,** *The Coming of the Welfare State*, Batsford, 1968, p. 124.

37. Hunt, *Labour History*, p. 126. In 1911 the private charities of Edinburgh were still distributing more than twice as much as the city's poor law authorities.

38. Hunt, *Labour History*, p. 128. But see **E. Wilkinson,** *The Town that was Murdered: The Life-Story of Jarrow*, Gollancz 1939, pp. 226–35; **R. H. C. Hayburn,** 'The Voluntary Occupational Movement, 1932–39', *Journal of Contemporary History*, 6, 1971, p. 136.

39. Hanson, 'Welfare', p. 116; **M. E. Rose,** *The Relief of Poverty, 1834–1914*, Macmillan, 1972, p. 53; **S. Pollard,** *The Development of*

the British Economy 1914–1980*, Arnold, 1983, p. 160; *Daily Mail*, 2 January 1935.

40.　Bruce, *Welfare State*, p. 180. Also Manchester Studies, Transcript 628, p. 4. But cf. Transcript 20, p. 15.

41.　Wiseman, 'Occupational Pension Schemes', pp. 176–7; Rose, *Relief*, p. 50; Bruce, *Welfare State*, pp. 179, 246.

42.　*Twentieth Annual Report of the Ministry of Health 1938–39*, p. 138; Bruce, *Welfare State*, p. 244; Fraser, *Evolution*, pp. 154–5.

43.　Fraser, *Evolution*, pp. 161, 170–1, 181–2; Bruce, *Welfare State*, p. 199; **J. Stevenson,** *British Society 1914–45*, Penguin, 1984, pp. 274, 297. For the view that 'the prolonged high unemployment was due to the operation of an unemployment insurance scheme that paid benefits that were high relative to wages and available subject to few restrictions' see **D. K. Benjamin** and **L. A. Kochin,** 'Searching for an Explanation of Unemployment in Interwar Britain', *Journal of Political Economy*, 87, 1979, p. 441.

44.　Bruce, *Welfare State*, p. 252; Webb and Sieve, *Income Redistribution*, p. 18.

45.　**J. White,** *The Worst Street in North London: Campbell Bunk, Islington, Between the Wars*, Routledge & Kegan Paul, 1986, p. 130.

46.　Ross, 'Survival Networks', p. 20. Also pp. 5, 18–19.

47.　For money-wages, see Deane and Cole, *Economic Growth*, p. 25; Stevenson, *British Society*, p. 117.

48.　Benson, *British Coalminers*, p. 174. Also Benson, 'Compensation', pp. 39–62.

49.　This rise in working-class incomes does not imply any significant redistribution of wealth. See, for example, **E. J. Hobsbawm,** *Industry and Empire*, Penguin, 1969, p. 274.

50.　Burnett, *Cost of Living*, pp. 11–13. Also **E. H. Hunt,** *Regional Wage Variations in Britain 1850–1914*, Clarendon Press, 1973, pp. 77–105; A. L. Bowley, *Wages and Income in the United Kingdom since 1860*, Cambridge U.P., 1937. pp. 114–26.

51.　Burnett, *Cost of Living*, pp. 203–5. Also **R. A. Church,** *The Great Victorian Boom 1850–1873*, Macmillan, 1975, pp. 13–16; **W. H. B. Court,** *A Concise Economic History of Britain from 1750 to Recent Times*, Cambridge U.P., 1958, pp. 200–1.

52.　Burnett, *Cost of Living*, p. 321.

53.　**A. Marwick,** *Britain in the Century of Total War: War, Peace and Social Change 1900–1967*, Bodley Head, 1968, p. 98.

54.　Burnett, *Cost of Living*, p. 307; **J. Stevenson** and **C. Cook,** *The Slump*, Quartet Books, 1979, p. 18.

55.　In fact, the improvement tended to occur in a series of fits and starts: first in the early 1870s; then during and immediately following the First World War; and finally during the 1930s. See Burnett, *Cost of Living*, p. 254; Bowley, *Wages*, p. 30.

56.　**J. H. Treble,** *Urban Poverty in Britain 1830–1914*, Batsford, 1979, pp. 110–20: **B. Eichengreen,** 'Unemployment in Interwar Britain: New Evidence for London', *Journal of Interdisciplinary History*, xvii, 1986, p. 356.

57.　Bristol, Transcript RO11, p. 75; **R. Samuel,** *East End Underworld:*

Chapters in the Life of Arthur Harding, Routledge & Kegan Paul, 1981, p. 15.

58. **B. S. Rowntree**, *Poverty: A Study of Town Life*, Macmillan, 1902, pp. 141–2.

59. **B. S. Rowntree** and **B. Lasker**, *Unemployment: A Social Study*, Macmillan, 1910, p. 191. Also pp. 173–83, 302.

60. Treble, *Urban Poverty*, p. 120.

61. See, for example, Hunt, *Labour History*, pp. 335–6.

62. **B. J. McCormick,** *Industrial Relations in the Coal Industry*, Macmillan, 1979, p. 155.

63. Benson, *British Coalminers*, p. 204.

64. **J. A. Peck,** *The Miners' Strike in South Yorkshire 1926*, University of Sheffield Institute of Education, 1970, p. 19. See also **C. Wrigley,** '1926, Social Costs of the Mining Dispute', *History Today*, November 1984, pp. 9–10.

65. Deane and Cole, *Economic Growth*, p. 143. Even the 162 million working days lost in 1926 as a result of the General Strike and Miners' Lockout was equivalent to the loss of only eight days pay per worker.

66. **B. L. Coombes**, *These Poor Hands: The Autobiography of a Miner Working in South Wales*, Gollancz, 1939, pp. 142, 144. See also Benson, *British Coalminers*, p. 204; **K. Howarth,** *Dark Days: Memories and Reminiscences of the Lancashire and Cheshire Coalmining Industry up to Nationalisation*, K. Howarth, 1978, pp. 81–9; **C. Foreman,** *Industrial Town: Self Portrait of St Helens in the 1920s*, Paladin Books, 1979, pp. 205–52.

67. For the Jews, see Hunt, *Labour History*, pp. 176–7; **G. S. Jones,** *Outcast London: A Study in the Relationship between Classes in Victorian Society*, Clarendon Press, 1971, pp. 109–10; **C. Holmes,** *Anti-Semitism in British Society 1876–1939*, Arnold, 1979. For the Irish, see **J. A. Jackson,** *The Irish in Britain*, Routledge & Kegan Paul, 1963, pp. 73–86; Jones, *Outcast London*, pp. 62, 89, 91, 115, 148–9; Hunt, *Labour History*, pp. 159–60. For other groups, see **K. Little,** *Negroes in Britain: A Study of Racial Relations in English Society*, Routledge & Kegan Paul, 1972; **C. Holmes** (ed.), *Immigrants and Minorities in British Society*, Allen & Unwin, 1978.

68. Hunt, *Labour History*, p. 165.

69. **G. Braybon**, *Women Workers in the First World War: The British Experience*, Croom Helm, 1981, pp. 216–17; **D. Bythell,** *The Sweated Trades: Outwork in Nineteenth-Century Britain*, Batsford, 1978.

70. **J. Benson,** 'Work', in **J. Benson** (ed.), *The Working Class in England 1875–1914*, Croom Helm, 1984, p. 75.

71. **A. Exell,** 'Morris Motors in the 1930s. Part I', *History Workshop*, 6, 1978, p. 58. Also Meacham, *Life Apart*, p. 100.

72. **C. Black** (ed.), *Married Women's Work: Being the Report of an Enquiry Undertaken by the Women's Industrial Council*, Bell, 1915, p. 11.

73. **A. E. Booth** and **S. Glynn**, 'Unemployment in the Interwar Period: A Multiple Problem', *Journal of Contemporary History*, 10, 1975, p. 615. Also **D. Martin,** 'Women without Work: Textile Weavers in North-East Lancashire 1919–1939', M.A. University of Lancaster,

1985, p. 7; Eichengreen, 'Unemployment', p. 342; **S. Constantine,** *Unemployment in Britain between the Wars*, Longman, 1980, p. 23.

74. Rose, *Poverty*, p. 19; Treble, *Urban Poverty*, pp. 95–102.
75. Bell, *At the Works*, p. 85. Also Treble, *Urban Poverty*, pp. 91–5.
76. Benson, *British Coalminers*, pp. 40–1.
77. But see **P. W. J. Bartrip** and **S. B. Burman**, *The Wounded Soldiers of Industry: Industrial Compensation Policy 1833–1897*, Clarendon Press, 1983.
78. See, for example, Benson, *British Coalminers*, pp. 44–6.
79. Constantine, *Unemployment*, p. 5.
80. Rose, *Relief*, pp. 18–19.
81. Hunt, *Labour History*, pp. 120–2.
82. Rowntree and Lasker, *Unemployment*, pp. 54–5.
83. **Pilgrim Trust,** *Men Without Work*, Cambridge U.P., 1938, p. 424.
84. Rowntree, *Poverty*, pp. 136–8. Also **H. Tout,** *The Standard of Living in Bristol: A Preliminary Report of the Work of the University of Bristol Social Survey*, Arrowsmith, 1938, pp. 35–6.
85. Treble, *Urban Poverty*, pp. 55–71: White, *Worst Street*, pp. 42, 220; **N. Whiteside,** 'Welfare Insurance and Casual Labour: A Study of Administrative Intervention in Industrial Employment, 1906–21', *Economic History Review*, XXXII, 1979; **G. Phillips** and **N. Whiteside,** *Casual Labour: The Unemployment Question in the Port Transport Industry 1880–1970*, Clarendon Press, 1985.
86. Bristol, Transcript RO11, p. 10.
87. Treble, *Urban Poverty*, p. 63.
88. Jones, *Outcast London*, p. 56.
89. Rowntree and Lasker, *Unemployment*, pp. 302–5.
90. Constantine, *Unemployment*, p. 24.
91. Howkins, *Poor Labouring Men*, p. 24.
92. Broughton, 'Record', p. 2. Also Treble, *Urban Poverty*, pp. 72–3.
93. **A. Exell,** 'Morris Motors in the 1930s: Part II', *History Workshop*, 7, 1979, p. 48. Also Whiting, *Cowley*, pp. 88–9; **J. M. Mogey,** *Family and Neighbourhood: Two Studies in Oxford*, Oxford U.P., 1956, p. 5.
94. Treble, *Urban Poverty*, p. 90. Also Jones, *Outcast London*, pp. 33–51.
95. Treble, *Urban Poverty*, p. 86–90; Constantine, *Unemployment*, pp. 2–3, 17–18.
96. **J. McKenna** and **R. G. Rodger,** 'Control by Coercion: Employers' Associations and the Establishment of Industrial Order in the Building Industry of England and Wales, 1860–1914', *Business History Review*, 59, 1985, pp. 205, 207.
97. Bristol, Transcript R008, p. 33.
98. University of Lancaster, 'The Quality of Life in Two Lancashire Towns, 1880–1930': 'Social and Family Life in Preston, 1890–1940', Transcript Mrs A1P, p. 5. Also Whiting, *Cowley*, pp. 78, 81.
99. *Report . . . Special Areas*, 1938, p. 31.
100. Constantine, *Unemployment*, p. 19; Pollard, *British Economy*, p. 156.
101. Manchester Studies, Transcript 786, p. 16.
102. Benson, *British Coalminers*, pp. 7, 217; **N. K. Buxton,** *The Economic Development of the British Coal Industry: From Industrial Revolution to the Present Day*, Batsford, p. 202; **M. W. Kirby,** *The British Coalmining Industry, 1870–1946: A Political and Economic History*,

Macmillan, 1977, pp. 115, 139, 172; **G. L. Allen,** *British Industries and their Organization*, Longman, 1959, p. 50.
103. Stevenson and Cook, *The Slump*, p. 5.
104. Hobsbawm, *Industry and Empire*, p. 208.
105. Hunt, *Labour History*, pp. 117–20; Tout, *Standard of Living*, pp. 25, 51.
106. Meacham, *Life Apart*, p. 103.

Chapter 3

HOUSING

There can be no doubt as to the importance of housing in working-class life. Historians of labour have pointed out time and again that the nature of a family's accommodation affected not only its comfort, its health and its status, but also the efficiency with which its members performed at work and the manner in which they conducted their industrial relations.[1] Indeed, for historians such as David Englander and Mark Swenarton the landlord–tenant relationship constituted a vital element of broader class relations, and the state housing campaign of 1919–21 'the central element in the government's programme of social reconstruction and the major weapon in its propaganda battle to stave off revolution'.[2]

These are large claims. But their validity is difficult to test because the study of working-class housing remains beset by two major difficulties: the one empirical, the other conceptual. The empirical difficulty is that, as with so many other aspects of working-class history, the evidence that survives is both patchy and partial. The sources reveal a good deal more about the provision of accommodation than about its occupation; and a great deal more about the minority of accommodation provided by employers and charitable organisations than about the majority of accommodation provided by private landlords. The conceptual difficulty is more intractable still. It is no easy matter to agree upon a definition of what constitutes 'good' accommodation. Cost must always be set against quality; convenience against status; and the fabric of the building against the nature of the surrounding environment. Moreover, it is impossible to bridge the ideological gap between those who view housing (and other) reform as a means of improving the workers' lot and those who regard it as a method of maintaining the social cohesion of an unjust capitalist society.[3]

It will be argued here that just as working people gained (at least in the short term) from any reduction in their working hours or from any increase in their take-home pay, so too they benefited from any improvement that was made to their standard of accommodation. Accordingly in this chapter attention will be directed towards three of the most important, and most accessible, indicators of the standard of working-class accommodation: its cost; the freedom of action that it allowed; and the quality of its construction.

In the high-wage sectors of the economy a growing minority of workers and their families began to purchase their own homes. It is not always clear whether they did so from choice or from necessity; whether the impetus came from the husband or the wife; and whether their aspirations were primarily material or non-material.[4] Nonetheless, it is clear that over the period covered by this book home ownership did become increasingly common among the working-class population (see Table 8). Although there is no way of knowing the extent and distribution of working-class owner-occupation during the early years of the period, there are signs of its popularity in what would appear to be most unpropitious economic and social circumstances. A Cannock Chase miner recalls that during the depression of the 1880s, he

> stayed at Colliery work, got a better job (if I could I didn't mind what), so that I got a bit more money to save. I settled down to hard work, and saved a bit of money towards getting married, but first I had a house built. I had to borrow nearly all the money (£150). I did a lot of the work myself, and altogether it cost about £175. Then I looked round for a wife to put in it. . . .[5]

As this passage suggests, it would be a mistake to assume that the cost of home ownership was such as to confine it to

TABLE 8. Working-class accommodation, 1850–1939

	Form of Tenure (as % of all accommodation)		
Year	*Owner-occupied*	*Local authority owned*	*Privately rented*
1850	c. 5	0	c.95
1918	c.10	c. 0.5	c.90
1939	c.19	c. 10	c.71

Sources: **S. Merrett**, *State Housing in Britain*, Routledge & Kegan Paul, 1979, p. 26; **Department of the Environment**, *Housing Policy. Technical Volume Part 1*, HMSO, 1977, p. 38; **M. Swenarton** and **S. Taylor**, 'The Scale and Nature of the Growth of Owner-Occupation in Britain Between the Wars', *Economic History Review*, xxxviii, 1985, p. 391; **M. J. Daunton** 'Introduction', in **M. J. Daunton** (ed.), *Councillors and Tenants: Local Authority Housing in English Cities, 1919–1939*, Leicester U.P., 1984, pp. 32-3.

the middle and upper classes. The early building societies were working-class institutions designed specifically to facilitate house purchase by ordinary people. Indeed once the initial deposit had been paid, it sometimes seemed as cheap to buy a house as it was to rent it. The Barrow-in-Furness Trades Council claimed in 1904 that if a worker could only raise the £10 deposit needed to purchase a small terraced house, it would cost him no more than 3s. a week to meet his mortgage repayments – much less than the 5s. or more that he would have to pay to rent similar accommodation.[6] But the need to put down a deposit was a major stumbling block that long confined working-class home ownership to the minority of workers who were employed in the heavy industrial sectors of the economy. In the early years of the twentieth century, explain the leading authorities on the history of home ownership, the 'Areas noted for their high level of working-class owner-occupation were the Lancashire cotton towns, the mining regions of South Wales, shipbuilding towns such as Jarrow, and to a lesser extent the Yorkshire wool districts and some isolated working-class suburbs of south-east London'.[7]

Certainly working-class owner-occupation was common in the cotton towns. It was said that in early twentieth-century Oldham, for example, nearly a third of the town's 33,000 houses were either owned or in the process of being acquired by 'artisan proprietors'.[8] Working-class owner-occupation was common too in the towns and villages of the South Wales coalfield: by 1913, it seems, there were 46,000 South Wales miners – almost 20 per cent of the workforce – living in homes of their own. Nor was owner-occupation unknown in other, less prosperous coalfields. Indeed, the most recent study suggests that in 1913 there were probably 80,000 British miners – some 7 per cent of all those employed in the industry – living, not in the tied accommodation of popular imagination, but in homes that they themselves owned.[9] It is clear that in the coalfields, and in other parts of the country too, working-class home-ownership was becoming increasingly common among those employed in the expanding, high-wage sectors of the nineteenth- and early twentieth-century economy.

In the years following the First World War home ownership became both more common and more widely diffused. 'Towns with a tradition of working-class owner-occupation in the nineteenth century carried this legacy into the twentieth century.'[10] They were joined by towns based upon the so-called 'new' industries; by 1939 37 per cent of houses in Coventry, and 44 per cent of those in Oxford, were owner-occupied. In Oxford, for instance, building societies did most of their business at the lower end of the market, many of their borrowers working in the city's new car factories.[11] Towards the end of the period owner-occupiers from cotton, coal and motor manufacturing were joined by a small number of workers employed in other, normally less well paid jobs. Walter Greenwood met one young married couple. The

> husband, a joiner, earned three pounds eighteen shillings a week, of which she received three pounds five shillings which had to pay for all their household and living expenses.
> They were buying the house in which they lived (a semi-detached) on mortgage . . . His job was more constant than is customary in his trade; he never yet had experienced unemployment, so they can be said to be representative of the more comfortably circumstanced in the working-class community.[12]

There is no doubt that working-class owner-occupation became increasingly common between 1850 and 1939, and that the process accelerated after the First World War. Table 8, which incorporates the results of the most recent research, shows that whereas in 1850 some 5 per cent, and in 1914 some 10 per cent of all working-class accommodation was owner-occupied, by 1939 the figure stood at almost 20 per cent.

However, it is important not to exaggerate the growth or the significance of working-class owner-occupation. 'The conclusion seems to be that in general only the élite of the working class could afford home ownership – and even then at the cost of self-sacrifice and thrift.'[13] Yet for those who could afford it, the purchase of a house meant, if not financial gain, nearly always greater comfort and increased freedom of action. House purchase signalled progress, then, in two of the three indicators of accommodation standards that were identified at the beginning of the chapter.

The cost of home ownership remained a considerable financial burden. All but the most highly paid families found the repayment of their loans a difficulty. The joiner's wife interviewed by Walter Greenwood complained that:

> Nobody, to my way of thinking, can live a reasonably comfortable life on an income of less than five pounds a week. For my part, I find that living on my three pounds five shillings means too much worry; too much energy has to be spent struggling and scheming to make ends meet and keep respectable.[14]

Even the most highly paid families found the repayment of their loans a recurring anxiety. Their anxiety was fuelled less by the level of repayment than by the unpredictability of their earnings. For, as was seen in the previous chapter, the earning capacity of even the most highly paid workers was at constant risk from ill-health and industrial dispute, from the working-class life cycle, from seasonal and cyclical fluctuation and, in the long term, from the threat of structural decline. The anxiety was difficult to avoid. Even Oxford car workers earning as much as £5 or £6 a week could not be sanguine about their ability to maintain the mortgage repayments of a pound or more a week that were required to buy a good quality house in the city in the 1930s. The danger, confirmed a social survey carried out at the very end of the period, lay in the irregular nature of the car worker's earnings. Home ownership, the survey concluded, 'is attended with too great a risk, as prolonged ill-health, or unemployment, or an ever-increasing family, may prevent him fulfilling his obligations'.[15]

That such well-meaning financial advice so often went unheeded is explained by the many non-financial benefits that owner-occupation seemed to confer. One advantage was that home ownership changed, and nearly always extended, the purchaser's freedom of action. Of course it would be hard to deny that buying a house curtailed the purchaser's freedom to move home quickly and easily. Yet it would be equally difficult to deny the fact that home ownership enhanced most other aspects of the purchaser's freedom of action. With this in mind, trade-union leaders in industries where tied accommodation was common often urged their members to buy their own homes. During the boom of the early 1870s, for example, one Scottish miners' agent encouraged men living in colliery-owned property to form co-operative building societies 'so that they might be independent of their employers for houses'.[16] However, the independence that lay at the heart of working-class home-ownership was more profound than this. Home-ownership became a symbol – increasingly important as time went by – of working-class respectability, pride and independence: the independence to invest, both financially and emotionally, in a home of one's own. The 'fact of the working man obtaining a house', claimed a south-east London fitter in 1887, 'makes them more thoughtful and more law-abiding citizens, in every form and shape'.[17]

The other great advantage of home ownership was that it nearly always improved the quality and comfort of everyday life. It is true that some families could meet the cost of house buying only by taking in lodgers – a practice which, as will be seen in the next chapter, eased their financial difficulties at the expense of disrupting their domestic arrangements. It is also true that some families were able to afford only the oldest and cheapest property on the market. Thus it has been found that in towns such as Burnley and Merthyr Tydfil, which had a long tradition of working-class home-ownership, the vast majority of owner-occupied houses in 1939 were 'prewar properties of the cheapest class'.[18]

Even the oldest properties were improved by the adoption of late nineteenth-century advances in domestic technology. By 1914 nearly every house in the country had its own supply of piped water; and most houses in the larger English towns also had their own water closets. 'By the First World War, the sanitation of working-class districts in English towns had been largely transformed. The demise of the night-soil man was one case of technological unemployment which no one had cause to regret.'[19] Even the oldest properties were improved by the enthusiasm of their owners. A Barrow-in-Furness boilermaker bought a new terraced house about 1902. 'It didn't have a bathroom,' recalls his daughter, 'so my dad put one in.'[20] As Ross McKibbin points out in his pioneering investigation of work and hobbies, 'How much time was spent on "home-hobbies", repairing, making, decorating, tinkering, is . . . not known, except that it was extensive.'[21]

Any family able to afford a new house, especially one built after the First World War, benefited enormously from the comfort, space and other amenities that it offered. In Wolverhampton, £365 (a £25 deposit and mortgage repayments of 9s. 8d. a week) would buy a three bedroomed house with a living room, a sitting room, a kitchen-cum-bathroom, a garage space and a large garden. In Nottingham in 1932, £450 would secure a detached bungalow with three bedrooms, a living room, a scullery and a separate bathroom. At Kenton, in the northern suburbs of London, £825 (a deposit of £45 and repayments of 25s. 4d. a week) was needed to obtain one of the semi-detached houses advertised in 1937 as 'The Best in the North West'. With three bedrooms, a drawing room, a dining room, a kitchen and bathroom, each house boasted 'Concrete foundations. Double slate damp course. All lead flashings. No zinc used. Crittall steel windows. Close boarded roof. English tiles. Kitchenette large and modern, tiled and fitted with Ideal Boiler, gas copper and Easiwork dresser, Delfast sink, chromium plated taps. Tiled bathroom, pedestal wash basin. Decorations to choice.'[22]

High London prices serve as a timely reminder that during this period working-class house buying never was, and never could be, anything more than a minority activity. Yet by 1939 almost 20 per cent of the working population – some seven million people in all – were living in homes that they had either bought or were in the process of buying. Indeed, for the large minority of families dependent upon employment in the high-wage sectors of the economy, home ownership represented a considerable material and psychological advance. Buying a house normally proved a good financial investment; it usually engendered feelings of pride and independence; and it nearly always improved the comfort and convenience of everyday life.

For all its benefits, home ownership was an ideal to which most working people could scarcely begin to aspire. Forced to look elsewhere for improvement, they discovered that their best hope lay, not in dreaming of owner-occupation or in looking for a better landlord, but in renting a council house from their local authority. It was a choice that really became available only after the First World War. For although the Artisans' and Labourers' Dwellings Improvement Act of 1875 and the Housing of the Working Classes Act of 1890 both empowered local authorities to provide housing for rent, virtually nothing was done. By 1914 even the most active authorities, like London, Glasgow and Liverpool, had managed to house fewer than 2 per cent of the populations for whom they were responsible. Over the country as a whole, the 24,000 houses owned by local authorities at the outbreak of war accounted for less than 0.5 per cent of the total housing stock.[23]

The situation changed dramatically during the inter-war years, a period that saw the local authorities emerge as one of the major suppliers of working-class housing. However cynical the motivation behind Lloyd George's 'homes fit for heroes' campaign of 1919–21, there is no doubt that it marked a turning point in the provision of working-class accommodation.[24] Of the four million new houses built in England and Wales between 1919 and 1939, one-and-a-half million were erected by local authorities. The large authorities were by far the most active: the largest authority of all, the London County Council, built over 100,000 houses; and five of the largest midland and northern authorities, Birmingham, Liverpool, Manchester, Sheffield and Leeds, erected a further 215,000. The houses built by these six authorities alone accounted for over 20 per cent of all the council housing erected in England and Wales between 1919 and 1939. The result was, as Table 8 shows, that by the end of the period 10 per cent of all working-class accommodation was owned by local authorities.[25]

The benefits of living in one of these new council houses were obtained only at a certain cost, for the rents charged were relatively high and the cost of travelling and shopping considerably increased.[26] In fact, in the early years of the inter-war period rents were fixed at levels that were likely to deter – and often exclude – many of those most in need of improved accommodation. The rent of a standard, three-bedroomed council house (without a parlour) seems to have stabilised at around 14s. a week.[27] Although less than the cost of buying a house, this was still a considerable commitment for most families to undertake: it was equivalent to almost 25 per cent of a normal weekly income, and to more than 40 per cent of the earnings of an agricultural labourer. In Birmingham, complained one councillor, 'Not even a Corporation employee with three children could afford to pay the rents asked without depriving his family of necessities.'[28] In nearby Wolverhampton, the town clerk admitted that those most in need of the authority's new council houses were ex-servicemen and those living in unhealthy or overcrowded accommodation. But, he explained, the new houses were expensive to build and

> generally speaking, the class of tenants who inhabit overcrowded or insanitary houses is not the class to which it will be desirable to let the new houses being built. . . . It might be desirable to require some evidence of character and reserve the right to refuse unsatisfactory tenants. . . . This question, however, will probably settle itself on economic grounds since the rents of the new houses are bound to be high and the class of tenant I have in mind will usually be the least able to pay high rents.[29]

It was not until the late 1920s that a combination of lower rents and somewhat higher incomes allowed the less well paid to start to join the better off families already living on the new council estates.

The high-rent policy was supplemented by a number of other devices designed to ensure the respectability of council tenants. There was no lack of central information and advice. 'It cannot . . . be too strongly impressed upon local authorities', claimed the Housing Department of the Ministry of Health in 1920, 'that direct management is essential to success. . .'

> Whatever system is adopted arrangements will have to be made
> for carrying out the following objects:
> (1) The careful selection of tenants;
> (2) The elimination of unsatisfactory tenants;
> (3) Constant supervision of the property and its occupants by officials
>   directly employed and paid by the owners;
> (4) Systematic and punctual collection of rents.[30]

It is clear that tenants were carefully selected, and not always by purely financial criteria. In Oldham, for example, priority was given officially to ex-soldiers, and unofficially to teachers, civil servants and – so it was claimed – to those who had friends or relatives on the council.[31] It is clear that tenants were also closely supervised. In 1938 the Central Housing Advisory Committee discussed once again the 'problems of housing management'. Good management, it explained, might involve anything from the provision of adequate furniture to the prevention of bed-bugs; but good management, insisted the committee, should always involve 'teaching a new and inexperienced community to be housing minded'.[32] By the time this advice was offered, the London County Council was responsible for over 92,000 properties and a rent roll of more than £3 million a year.

> The general experience of the Council is that tenants on the whole
> respond well to the new surroundings, that houses and gardens are
> generally well kept and neighbourly behaviour maintained. There are,
> of course, occasional black sheep, but these are few; and the Council is
> in a strong position to enforce a good standard because a dismissed tenant
> is scarcely likely to obtain comparable quarters at so low a rent.[33]

It is no easy matter to assess tenant reaction to such forms of selection and supervision. However, it may very well be that those best able to satisfy the councils' selection procedures were also those most likely to resent their attempts at supervision and control.[34]

Whatever the irritations, moving into council-owned property offered one very great advantage: a vastly improved physical standard of accommodation. Naturally the improvement was most striking in the case of the slum-dwellers whom councils rehoused in such large numbers during the 1930s. But it was an improvement that benefited virtually all those who moved from rented premises into the new council accommodation that was erected during the inter-war years.

Least popular were the small number of city-centre flats built by some of the larger local authorities. In 1927, for example, Birmingham City Council erected 180 flats, in three-storey blocks, on a vacant site in Garrison Lane close to the Birmingham City football ground; and a decade later Leeds City Council demolished 2,000 slum houses and replaced them with the 938 high-rise flats known as the Quarry Hill development. Although these and other council flats were generally conveniently situated and built to high standards of space, comfort and privacy, they were never popular. When the Garrison Lane flats were first built, they were known locally as 'The Mansions', a name that their tenants soon changed to 'The Barracks'.[35]

Of course the great majority of council tenants were housed on the large, suburban estates that have become synonymous with municipal housing: developments such as Kirby (near Liverpool), Wythenshawe (near Manchester), Longbridge (outside Birmingham), Knowle and Bedminster (to the south of Bristol) and Becontree (on the eastern outskirts of London). However unimaginatively designed and lacking in amenities, these 'mass suburbs' of 'two-storey cottages, built in groups of four or six, with medium or low-pitched roofs and little exterior decoration, set amongst gardens, trees, privet hedges and grass verges, and often laid out in cul-de-sacs or around greens', constituted a vast improvement on the working-class housing that had gone before.[36] It was an improvement that virtually all tenants seem to have appreciated. 'The council were very good,' recalls a St Helens joiner, 'they built good houses . . . The queues for the houses were miles long – everyone put their names on the council list. They were made and jumped for joy if they got a council house.'[37] A Lancaster man remembers moving into a council house during the 1920s: 'It had a bathroom that was another luxury . . . and what my mother particularly enjoyed was hot water from the boiler, just open the tap and that was it, smashing. And there was an open space at the back and a garden to sit in. You could see some green grass instead of flags and cobbles.'[38]

For the 10 per cent or so of the working population that managed to secure the tenancy of a council house, the consequences could be far-reaching. In London, it has been claimed, 'the LCC cottage estates made flesh an idyllic ideal of the family house with a garden and all mod. cons. And they put that dream within the potential grasp of large sections of the London working class.'[39] But this is to exaggerate. The dream of a 'family house with a garden and all mod. cons.' remained way beyond the reach of most working people – whether they lived in London or in any other part of the country.

It is important to remember that throughout the period covered by this book, the vast majority of the working population lived neither in council property nor in their own homes, but in accommodation that they rented from one of the country's many private landlords. Whether they rented a city-centre tenement, an urban terrace, a country cottage or a suburban semi-detached, private tenants shared only slowly and uncertainly in the improvements enjoyed by council tenants and owner-occupiers.

Naturally, it is a good deal more difficult to discover the rents paid for privately owned property than it is those paid for the accommodation belonging to the local authorities. Nonetheless, some generalisation is possible; it is clear above all else that the real cost of renting declined very considerably between 1850 and 1939. This may seem somewhat surprising for, as is well known, rents were the one item of basic working-class expenditure whose cost did not fall significantly during the late nineteenth and early twentieth centuries. Indeed, Table 9 shows that the cost of renting a 'typical' working-class house probably increased by about 14 per cent between 1880 and 1912–14, and (despite the introduction of rent controls) by a further 50 per cent between 1912–14 and 1935–6. The key to the apparent paradox lies, of course, in the fact that incomes were rising at a still faster rate. It was seen in the previous chapter that 'normal', full-time, working-class incomes rose by 60 per cent between 1880 and 1914, and by 80 per cent between 1914 and 1935. The result was the real cost of renting declined very markedly: by 30 per cent between 1880 and 1914; and by over 36 per cent between 1914 and the mid 1930s. So whereas in 1880 the payment of the rent probably took 17.5 per cent of a 'typical' tenant's 'normal', full-time

TABLE 9. The rent (excluding rates) of a 'typical' working-class house in the private sector, 1850–1939

Year	Rent (shillings and pence)	Rent as % of a 'normal' full-time income
1850	c.2s.6d.	
1880	3s.6d.	17.5
1906		
1912–14	4s.0d.	14
1924		
1935–6	6s.0d.	10

Sources: **Department of the Environment**, *Housing Policy. Technical Volume Part 1*, HMSO, 1977, p. 43; **M. J. Daunton**, *House and Home in the Victorian City: Working-Class Housing 1850–1914*, Arnold, 1983, p. 36; **J. F. C. Harrison**, *The Common People: A History from the Norman Conquest to the Present*, Fontana, 1984, p. 374; **J. Burnett**, *A Social History of Housing 1815–1915*, Methuen, 1986, p. 150.

income, in 1914 it took only 14 per cent, and by 1935–6 no more than about 10 per cent.

The improvement did not benefit all those living in rented accommodation. This was because the two components of real rents – income and rent – varied so very widely. While it was shown in the previous chapter that 'normal' full-time incomes rose greatly between 1850 and 1939, it was also made clear that by no means all workers shared in the general advance. The rents that working people had to pay also varied very greatly. Rural rents remained low.[40] Urban rents often climbed high above the average – it has been estimated, for instance, that urban rents generally rose by 85 per cent between 1845 and 1910.[41] They rose steeply in London, in Scotland and in the larger provincial cities – anywhere in fact where the demand for accommodation outstripped the supply. For example, the expansion of the South Wales coalfield placed landlords in such a favourable position that they were able both to demand key-money and to insist that their tenants purchase goods from the shops that they owned. Indeed, it is striking that one of the main targets of rioters active during the Cambrian coalmining dispute of 1911 were local landlords who were accused of charging inflated rents for their property.[42] London rents were always among the highest in the country. Already in the 1890s a single room near the centre of the city cost more than 4s. a week and by the end of the period two 'unfurnished rooms of mediocre character' could fetch as much as £1 a week.[43]

The combination of high rents and low incomes was catastrophic for the urban poor. Indeed, the poorer the family, the larger the proportion of its income that it was likely to spend on rent. Maud Pember Reeves outlined the general nature of the problem in her 1913 study of working-class Lambeth:

A middle-class well-to-do man with income of £2,000	might pay in rent, rates, and taxes, £250 –	a proportion of his income which is equal to *one-eighth*.
A middle-class comfortable man, with income of £500	might pay in rent, rates, and taxes, £85 –	a proportion of his income which is equal to about *one-sixth*.
A poor man with 24s. a week, or £62 8s. a year	might pay in rent, rates, and taxes, 8s. a week, or £20 16s. a year –	a proportion of his income which is equal to *one-third*.[44]

In his 1902 study of York, Seebohm Rowntree explained in more detail how the burden fell most heavily upon those least able to afford it. His conclusion was that 'while rent only absorbs 9 per cent of the total income of the few exceptionally well-to-do working-class families earning as much as, or more than, 60s. a week, it absorbs no less than *29 per cent of the total income of the very poor,* whose family earnings are under 18s. weekly'.[45]

Nonetheless, the real cost of renting from a private landlord did decline decisively between 1850 and 1939. For the 70 per cent and more of the working population that continued to live in rented accommodation, the diminishing cost of housing represented a significant, and most welcome, improvement in their standard of living.

Nor was this all. For there seems little doubt that during the course of the twentieth century a combination of structural changes and legal reforms enabled tenants to deal on somewhat more equal terms with even the most insensitive, obstructive and unscrupulous of private landlords. Structurally, the tenants' bargaining position was strengthened by the decline of those forms of property ownership (by philanthropic organisations and by industrial employers) that were associated most closely with tight supervision and control. Still well known today are nineteenth-century philanthropic bodies such as the Peabody Trust and the Four Per Cent Industrial Dwellings Company – organisations that sought to exercise close supervision over respectable tenants in good quality accommodation. But the importance of these organisations has been much exaggerated: the fact that their activities touched only a tiny minority of working people meant that their decline affected only marginally the overall balance of power between landlord and tenant.[46]

Much more significant was the employers' involvement in, and subsequent withdrawal from, the provision of working-class housing. It was not uncommon in agriculture and in the great nineteenth-century industries of cotton, coal, shipbuilding and railway transport for employers to seek to use their ownership of housing as a means of reinforcing the other means of control that they had at their disposal.[47] By the beginning of the twentieth century, for instance, approximately 15 per cent of all coalminers lived in tied accommodation; their lives controlled, to some extent at least, by their landlords-cum-employers. 'There was no reason', insisted one Derbyshire coalowner, 'why they should not have a village where three things could exist successfully . . . the absence of drunkenness, the absence of gambling, and the absence of bad language.'[48] Tied accommodation remained common in agriculture but declined in the industrial sectors of the economy[49] where it helped workers to live their lives rather more as they wished. It also signalled the beginnings of a wider change: because industrial employers had been so much more active than philanthropists in the provision of accommodation, their withdrawal did something at least to alter the balance of power generally between landlord and tenant.

If the decline of tied accommodation was of immediate advantage to only a small minority of tenants, the legal reforms that were introduced from the turn of the century were designed to benefit all those living in privately rented property. The turning point came during the First World War: 'The position of the private landlord was transformed by the war-time policy of rent control and security of tenure, which fundamentally changed the pre-war pattern of landlord–tenant relations.'[50] The landlord's power to seize goods in order to recoup arrears of rent was restricted by early twentieth-century amendments to the law of distress.[51] The landlord's power of eviction was curtailed by legislation passed in 1915 and 1923.

> The Act of 1923 laid down that landlords could recover property only by obtaining a court order. The landlord had to prove failure to pay rent; show that the tenant was causing a nuisance or allowing the property to deteriorate; or satisfy the court that alternative accommodation was available where the house was required by the landlord as the residence of himself, a dependant or employee. The tenant could, for his part, apply for a court order to withold rent if the house was not in a reasonable state of repair.[52]

Even the landlord's power to decide how much rent to charge was not immune from attack. The legislation of 1915 fixed the rent of all houses below a certain rateable value at the level that had been in force at the outbreak of the war. It is true that the legislation passed in 1923 decontrolled the rent whenever a new landlord came into possession, but in 1931 almost 90 per cent of all working-class houses remained subject to some form of rent control. As Martin Daunton concludes, the change was enormous: 'The ability of the landlord to control his own property had been curtailed, and the protection of the tenant increased.'[53]

Of course neither legal reform nor structural change could resolve the conflicting interests that lay at the heart of the landlord–tenant relationship. Indeed, as will be seen in subsequent chapters, tenants and landlords continued to fight out their differences, sometimes publicly and collectively, more often privately and individually. Yet there can be no doubt that during the course of the twentieth century the balance of power between landlord and tenant did change – and that it changed decisively in favour of the latter.

This was all to the good. Yet in practice the lot of the private tenant changed far less than the discussion of rents and landlord–tenant relations might lead one to suppose. This was because the physical quality, comfort and convenience of privately rented accommodation always remained markedly inferior to that of owner-occupied or council-owned property. It is difficult to convey an adequate impression of the conditions in which many private tenants were forced to live. A correspondent to *The Builder* complained in 1848 that 'Whilst we are exhausting our ingenuity to supply villas with "every possible convenience" we are leaving our working classes to the enjoyment of every possible inconvenience, in wretched shells to which men of substance would not consign their beasts of burden.'[54] When the Royal Commission on Scottish Housing reported in 1917, it described:

> unspeakably filthy privy-middens in many of the mining areas, badly constructed, incurably damp labourers' cottages on farms, whole townships unfit for human occupation in the crofting counties and islands . . . gross overcrowding and huddling of the sexes together in the congested industrial villages and towns, occupation of one-room houses by large families, groups of lightless and unventilated houses in the older burghs[55]

and 20 years later George Orwell found that

> As you walk through the industrial towns you lose yourself in labyrinths of little brick houses blackened by smoke, festering in planless chaos round miry alleys and little cindered yards where there are stinking dust-bins and lines of grimy washing and half-ruinous w.c.s . . . At the back [of each house] there is the yard, or part of a yard shared by a number of houses, just big enough for the dustbin and the w.c. Not a single one has hot water laid on.[56]

Such improvements as did take place occurred in one of three ways: by slum clearance; by the provision of new accommodation; and by the improvement of the property that already existed. It is easy to measure the speed and extent of inter-war slum clearance: during the 1920s 11,000 houses were demolished, a figure that leapt, in the 1930s, to more than 270,000.[57] It is less easy to measure the provision (and quality) of new accommodation. However it does seem, between 1850 and 1914: that 'new housing was provided at a slightly faster rate than population increase'[58]; that most of it was built for rent; and that the majority of it was built to higher standards than had been common earlier in the century. The Public Health Act of 1875 marked a turning point in the regulation of private house building. It allowed sanitary authorities in the provinces to pass bye-laws for the control of building standards: the model bye-laws issued by the Local Government Board required that all new streets over 100 feet long should be at least 36 feet wide; and that every new house should have an open space at the rear and windows whose area equalled at least 10 per cent of the floor space. The regulations began to transform the material conditions of rented working-class housing.

> . . . nothing else made so much difference to the physical appearance and condition of British towns. Large parts of them were built under this regime and still survive. They seem a grim and depressing legacy, yet they represent a considerable advance on what came immediately before. The streets of this time were monotonous, but the monotony of order was an advance on the earlier monotony of chaos. They were devoid of all inspiration but at least they were sanitary, exposed

adequately to air and moderately to light, and this was a result achieved widely and by deliberate provision, instead of occasionally and more or less by chance.[59]

There was much less building for rent in the years following the First World War, although nearly 100,000 new homes did become available during the mid-1930s. A Nottingham engineer and his family moved into one of them.

By 1936 the financial situation seemed to improve. My brother was earning enough to keep himself and pay my Mother a few shillings, and when I got a job at fourteen, it was decided that we could afford a better house in a 'nicer' neighbourhood. We moved a couple of miles out of Nottingham to a detached modern house with a garden. We rented it for £1 per week. We were all thrilled with it and took on a new lease of life. The joy of a bathroom can only be appreciated when you've lived without one. The ritual of lighting the copper, dragging the zinc bath up the cellar steps, emptying the dirty water every time anyone had a bath, was at last over.[60]

It is more difficult to gauge the effectiveness of the various attempts that were made to improve the quality of existing stocks of rented accommodation. Municipal, commercial and individual effort all played a part. It was during the 1890s that local authorities like Birmingham began to adopt limited policies of renovation. It was during the same decade that working-class tenants generally began to enjoy the benefits of commercially supplied gas and water; by 1914, it has been claimed, 'it was the rare house which did not have a piped water supply'.[61] Even such limited precision is impossible when assessing the improvements that working people themselves made to the property that they rented. But increasingly, it seems, improvements were made, and especially in those houses rented by better-off families: woodwork was painted, walls decorated, partitions erected and extensions built. A Durham miner recalls the

row after row of colliery houses containing one large living-room. . . . Over the living-room there was one large bedroom. Sizes of families were regarded immaterially, so father, at his own expense, partitioned the upstairs to make two bedrooms. In addition the stairs had no handrail and this had to be erected at one's own cost. Wash-day was a total upheaval of the living-room until father had a lean-to built adjoining the pantry which eventually became a wash-house-cum-storeroom.[62]

Little, it seems, could stand in the way of the dedicated home-improver.

Yet much remained to be done. Neither slum clearance, nor house building, nor home improvement really had very much effect upon the conditions in which millions of private tenants continued to live out their lives. For all the publicity it has received, slum clearance did little to alter the fundamental quality of the housing stock. Even the 284,000 houses that were demolished during the 1920s and 1930s represented less than 3 per cent of all the houses in England and Wales.[63] Indeed in the short term slum clearance possibly aggravated, rather than relieved, the problem of unfit housing. It has been suggested, for example, that of the 70,000 working-class houses that were demolished in London between 1902 and 1913, no more than 15,000 were actually replaced.[64]

Moreover, the majority of privately rented accommodation remained unimproved by either landlord or tenant. On the one hand, the introduction of rent controls reinforced the reluctance of many landlords to invest in the maintenance, let alone the improvement, of their property. On the other hand, the very nature of rented accommodation presumably discouraged most tenants from spending much time or money on property that did not belong to them.[65] Whatever the explanation, the result was the same: the survival of a large stock of poor-quality housing for rent; as late as 1939 86 per cent of all privately owned housing had been built before the First World War and there remained – even according to official estimates – nearly half a million slum houses that needed to be demolished.[66]

The privately rented sector always housed the least well-off in the poorest-quality accommodation. Rural housing remained particularly bad. The daughter of a Norfolk gamekeeper recalls the cottage in which she was brought up during the 1930s: a 'dark, damp and dismal house that could only have been designed by a member of the opposite sex. Tiny little windows deliberately closing their eyes to the fairy-tale view outside, with a puny north-facing kitchen with at least eight doors each letting in its separate gale to our frozen feet. Drinking water was drawn twice-daily by Father from a sixty foot well, which was still the mode used by most of the villagers.'[67] Indeed, according to the Ministry of Health, 'The lack of cottages supplied with modern amenities, is one of the main factors which accounts for the desertion of the land, especially by the younger generation, for industrial employment in towns.'[68] Of course, urban housing could be just as bad. Every town and city had its own black spots. London had some of the very worst. In Islington, Jerry White has pointed out, 'Campbell Road was not bad enough to be classed as a slum.' Yet

All the houses were in more or less severe disrepair, through bad building and subsequent neglect. There was rising damp, leaking roofs and rotting woodwork; staircase balustrades had frequently been removed for fire wood even though stairs and passages were badly lit; the WC in the yard was sometimes shared by 30 people, the seat and pan fouled with 'Mr Brown'; one tap only was usually provided for the shared use of up to eight households; there was no gas for the vast majority of houses until about 1938, forty years after it had become the commonest fuel for cooking and lighting among the London working class.[69]

Yet 'Campbell Road was not bad enough to be classed as a slum.'

Housing stood, with work and income, at the very centre of working-class life. Although 'good' housing is notoriously difficult to define and measure, it is clear that as the period progressed, so there emerged a substantial minority of workers who, by buying a house or renting from their local council, managed to enjoy a significantly improved standard of accommodation. It is equally clear that the great majority of workers, who lived in rented property, shared only slowly and uncertainly in the benefits of 'good' housing. Accommodation standards remained scandalously low in the urban slums and nearly as poor in parts of the countryside. But this was not the core of the housing failure. The problem was not so much that some working-class housing remained scandalously bad, but that so much of it remained depressingly mediocre: cramped, noisy, dirty, uncomfortable, inconvenient and either too hot or too cold. It would be difficult to better W. G. Hoskins's description of working-class housing in nineteenth-century Preston; it was, he said, 'neither good enough to promote happiness nor bad enough to produce hopelessness'.[70] It is a judgement that may be applied to the majority of working-class housing in Britain between 1850 and 1939.

NOTES AND REFERENCES

1. **D. Englander**, *Landlord and Tenant in Urban Britain 1838–1918,* Clarendon Press, 1983, pp. 43, 126, 210, 241; **M. J. Daunton**, *House and Home in the Victorian City: Working-Class Housing 1850–1914,* Arnold, 1983, pp. 132, 138–9, 179.

2. **M. Swenarton**, *Homes Fit for Heroes: The Politics and Architecture of Early State Housing in Britain,* Heinemann, 1981, p. 136. Also Englander, *Landlord and Tenant,* pp. v, 194, 303.

3. **Daunton**, *House and Home,* p. 37; Swenarton, *Homes,* p. 7; **M. Swenarton** and **S. Taylor,** 'The Scale and Nature of the Growth of Owner-Occupation in Britain between the Wars', *Economic History Review,* xxxviii, 1985, p. 373.

4. **G. Crossick,** *An Artisan Elite in Victorian Society: Kentish London 1840–1880,* Croom Helm, 1978, p. 149; **E. Roberts,** *A Woman's Place: An Oral History of Working-Class Women 1890–1940,* Blackwell, 1984, pp. 111–12.

5. **J. Benson,** 'The Autobiography of Albert Edward Foster, 1866–1949', *West Midlands Studies,* 11, 1978, p. 35. Also **J. Benson,** 'Staffordshire Miners and their Houses 1800–1914', *West Midlands Studies,* 12, 1979; **J. Benson,** *British Coalminers in the Nineteenth Century: A Social History,* Gill & Macmillan, 1980, pp. 107–10.

6. **E. Roberts,** 'Working-Class Standards of Living in Barrow and Lancaster, 1890–1914', *Economic History Review,* xxx, 1977, pp. 307, 318.

7. Swenarton and Taylor, 'Owner-Occupation', p. 378.

8. *Ibid.,* p. 379. Also Manchester Polytechnic, Manchester Studies, Transcript 924.

9. **R. Church,** *The History of the British Coal Industry, Volume 3, 1830–1913: Victorian Pre-eminence,* Clarendon Press, 1986, p. 600. Also Benson, *British Coalminers,* pp. 107–10.

10. Swenarton and Taylor, 'Owner-Occupation', pp. 387–8.

11. *Ibid.,* pp. 387–8; **R. C. Whiting,** *The View from Cowley: The Impact of Industrialization upon Oxford, 1918–1939,* Clarendon Press, 1983, p. 165.

12. **W. Greenwood,** *How the Other Man Lives,* Labour Book Service, 1937?, p. 122. Also **H. Tout,** *The Standard of Living in Bristol: A Preliminary Report of the Work of the University of Bristol Social Survey,* Arrowsmith, 1938, p. 29.

13. Swenarton and Taylor, 'Owner-Occupation', p. 385.

14. Greenwood, *Other Man,* p. 129.

15. Whiting, *Cowley,* p. 165.

16. Benson, *British Coalminers,* p. 109.

17. Crossick, *Artisan Elite,* p. 149. Also Roberts, *Woman's Place,* p. 128.

18. Swenarton and Taylor, 'Owner-Occupation', p. 388.

19. Daunton, *House and Home,* p. 260. Also pp. 246, 258.

20. Roberts, *Woman's Place,* pp. 131–2.

21. **R. McKibbin,** 'Work and Hobbies in Britain, 1880–1950', in **J. Winter** (ed.), *The Working Class in Modern British History: Essays in Honour of Henry Pelling,* Cambridge U.P., 1983, p. 132. Also Greenwood, *Other Man,* p. 122.

22. **J. Burnett,** *A Social History of Housing 1815–1985,* Methuen, 1986, p. 257. Also pp. 212, 272; **G. J. Barnsby,** *A History of Housing in Wolverhampton 1750 to 1975,* Integrated Publishing Services, ND, p. 49.

23. Swenarton, *Homes,* p. 28; **E. H. Hunt,** *British Labour History 1815–1914,* Weidenfeld & Nicolson, 1981, p. 98; Daunton, *House and Home,* p. 3; **S. Merrett,** *State Housing in Britain,* Routledge & Kegan Paul, 1979, p. 26; **C. G. Pooley,** 'Housing for the Poorest Poor: Slum Clearance and Rehousing in Liverpool, 1890–1918', *Journal of Historical Geography,* 11, 1985.

24. See Swenarton, *Homes,* e.g. pp. 86–7, 194–5.

25. **J. B. Cullingworth,** *Housing and Local Government in England and Wales,* Allen & Unwin, 1966, p. 28.

26. **R. Jevons** and **J. Madge,** *Housing Estates: A Study of Bristol Corporation Policy and Practice between the Wars,* University of Bristol, 1946, p. 35; **T. Young,** *Becontree and Dagenham: A Report Made for the Pilgrim Trust by Terence Young,* Becontree Social Survey Committee, 1934, p. 79.

27. *News of the World,* 5 January 1930; Burnett, *Social History,* pp. 238–9; **Benwell Community Project,** *Private Housing and the Working Class,* Benwell Community Project, 1978, p. 48; Barnsby, *Housing,* p. 31; **D. Englander,** 'Tenants and Politics: The Birmingham Tenants'

Federation During and After the First World War', *Midland History*, vi, 1981, p. 133; **C. Bedale,** 'Property Relations and Housing Policy: Oldham in the Late Nineteenth and Early Twentieth Centuries', in **J. Melling** (ed.), *Housing, Social Policy and the State,* Croom Helm, 1980, p. 67.

28. Englander, 'Birmingham', p. 134. Also **M. D. Summerbell,** 'Bristol's Housing Policy 1919–30', M.Sc.(Econ) University of Bristol, 1980, p. 177.

29. Barnsby, *Housing,* p. 29. Also Jevons and Madge, *Housing Estates,* p. 44; Young, *Becontree,* pp. 84, 120.

30. Merrett, *State Housing,* pp. 210–11.

31. Bedale, 'Property Relations', p. 67.

32. Cullingworth, *Housing and Local Government,* pp. 74–5.

33. **G. Gibbon** and **R. W. Bell,** *History of the London County Council 1889–1939,* Macmillan, 1939, pp. 395–6.

34. **G. W. Jones,** *Borough Politics: A Study of the Wolverhampton Town Council, 1888–1964,* Macmillan, 1969, pp. 312–18.

35. **A. Sutcliffe,** 'A Century of Flats in Birmingham 1875–1973', in **A. Sutcliffe** (ed.), *Multi-Storey Living: The British Working-Class Experience,* Croom Helm, 1974, p. 192. Also **A. Ravetz,** 'From Working-Class Tenement to Modern Flat: Local Authorities and Multi-Storey Living between the Wars', in *ibid.,* pp. 122–4, 131–2.

36. Swenarton, *Homes,* p. 1.

37. **C. Forman,** *Industrial Town: Self Portrait of St Helens in the 1920s,* Granada, 1979, p. 139.

38. **E. Roberts,** *Working Class Barrow and Lancaster 1890 to 1930,* University of Lancaster, 1976, p. 35. Also **P. Willmott,** *The Evolution of a Community: A Study of Dagenham after Forty Years,* Routledge & Kegan Paul, 1963, pp. 6–7.

39. **J. White,** *The Worst Street in North London: Campbell Bunk, Islington, Between the Wars,* Routledge & Kegan Paul, 1986, p. 223.

40. Burnett, *Social History,* p. 277; Hunt, *Labour History,* p. 95.

41. **G. H. Wood,** 'Real Wages and the Standard of Comfort since 1850', *Journal of the Royal Statistical Society,* lxxii, 1909, p. 95; Hunt, *Labour History,* p. 95.

42. Benson, *British Coalminers,* p. 106.

43. *Report of the Unemployment Assistance Board, 1938,* p. 77. Also Hunt, *Labour History,* p. 96; **A. S. Wohl,** 'The Housing of the Working Classes in London, 1815–1914', in **S. D. Chapman** (ed.), *The History of Working-Class Housing: A Symposium,* David & Charles, 1971.

44. **M. P. Reeves,** *Round About A Pound A Week,* Bell, 1913, p. 23. Also Burnett, *Social History,* pp. 147–9.

45. **B. S. Rowntree,** *Poverty: A Study of Town Life,* Macmillan, 1902, p. 165.

46. **J. N. Tarn,** *Five Per Cent Philanthropy: An Account of Housing in Urban Areas between 1840 and 1914,* Cambridge U.P., 1973; **J. White,** *Rothschild Buildings: Life in an East End Tenement Block 1887–1920,* Routledge & Kegan Paul, 1980; Daunton, *House and Home,* pp. 192–3; Burnett, *Social History,* pp. 153, 176–9.

47. **S. Pollard,** *The Genesis of Modern Management: A Study of the*

Industrial Revolution in Great Britain, Penguin, 1968, pp. 234–6; Daunton, *House and Home,* pp. 185–9.

48. Benson, *British Coalminers,* p. 95.
49. **A. Russell,** 'The Quest for Security: The Changing Working Conditions of the British Working Class in the Twentieth Century', Ph.D. University of Lancaster, 1982, p. 589.
50. Daunton, *House and Home,* p. 176. Also Englander, *Landlord and Tenant,* p. 298.
51. Englander, 'Birmingham', pp. 124–6.
52. Daunton, *House and Home,* p. 305. Also Englander, *Landlord and Tenant,* p. 250.
53. Daunton, *House and Home,* p. 305. Also pp. 176, 296, 304; Englander, *Landlord and Tenant,* pp. 235, 298, 311.
54. **R. M. Reeve,** *The Industrial Revolution 1750–1850*, University of London Press, 1971, pp. 117–18.
55. **J. Stevenson,** *British Society 1914–45*, Penguin, 1984, p. 227.
56. **G. Orwell,** *The Road to Wigan Pier,* Penguin, 1963, p. 45.
57. Cullingworth, *Housing,* pp. 21–4; Burnett, *Social History,* pp. 240–8.
58. Burnett, *Social History,* p. 141.
59. Cited Daunton, *House and Home,* p. 8. Also p. 7; Burnett, *Social History,* pp. 159–66; **E. Gauldie,** *Cruel Habitations: A History of Working-Class Housing 1780–1918,* Allen & Unwin, 1974, p. 140.
60. **J. F. C. Harrison,** *The Common People: A History from the Norman Conquest to the Present,* Fontana, 1984, p. 375. Also Cullingworth, *Housing,* p. 25; **J. Bullock,** *Bowers Row: Recollections of a Mining Village,* EP Publishing, 1976, pp. 10–11.
61. Daunton, *House and Home,* p. 246. Also pp. 31, 228, 238–47; White, *Worst Street,* p. 48.
62. **J. Halliday,** *Just Ordinary, But . . . An Autobiography,* The Author, 1959, pp. 15–16. Also McKibbin, 'Work and Hobbies', p. 132.
63. Cullingworth, *Housing,* pp. 21–4.
64. Merrett, *State Housing,* p. 12.
65. Daunton, *House and Home,* p. 305; **M. Loane,** *From Their Point of View,* Arnold, 1908, pp. 261–4.
66. **Department of the Environment,** *Housing Policy. Technical Volume Part 1,* HMSO, 1977, p. 38; Burnett, *Social History,* p. 244.
67. **Norfolk Federation of Women's Institutes,** *Within Living Memory: A Collection of Norfolk Reminiscences,* Norfolk Federation of Women's Institutes, 1972, p. 25.
68. *Twentieth Annual Report of the Ministry of Health 1938–39,* p. 94.
69. White, *Worst Street,* p. 48.
70. **W. G. Hoskins,** *The Making of the English Landscape,* Penguin, 1970, p. 228.

Part Two

FAMILY AND COMMUNITY

Chapter 4

FAMILY

No student of nineteenth- and twentieth-century Britain can fail to appreciate the crucial role that the family played in the lives of working people. Moreover, most historians seem agreed upon the significance of two of the developments that occurred during the period covered by this book: an improvement in the material conditions of the working-class family, and a reduction in the number of children that were to be found within it.[1]

But there the agreement ends. Deprived of the apparent precision provided by the census and similar statistical data, historians disagree profoundly about most other aspects of working-class family life. They argue over whether the family was strengthened or weakened by the material and demographic changes that were taking place; they quarrel bitterly over the functions that the family performed in an industrialising, capitalist society. According to orthodox Marxist theory, the family served, both economically and ideologically, to maintain the existing social order.[2] According to revisionist Marxist theory, 'the resilience of the family' derived, in part at least, 'from workers' defence of an institution which affects their standard of living, class cohesion and ability to wage the class struggle'.[3] Other scholars stress the 'instrumentality' of family relationships. In mid-nineteenth-century Preston, suggests Michael Anderson, it was 'advisable, or even well-nigh essential, for kinsman to make every effort to keep in contact with and to enter into reciprocal assistance with kinsman, if life chances were not to be seriously imperilled.'[4] Edward Shorter disagrees:

> . . . the modern nuclear family was born in the shelter of domesticity. Thus sentiment flowed into a number of familial relationships. Affection and inclination, love and sympathy, came to take the place of 'instrumental' considerations in regulating the dealings of family members with one another.[5]

It is not easy to determine the truth of the matter. Nonetheless it will be argued, and with some confidence, that the years between 1850 and 1939 saw fundamental changes in family life, and that these changes led eventually to the emergence of what, paradoxically, is often thought of today as the 'traditional' working-class family. As families grew smaller, healthier, more prosperous and more inward-looking, there emerged the generation that has been described so sympathetically by Richard Hoggart:

> . . . they were of the newer world. That world had many advantages to offer: cheaper and more varied clothes, cheaper and more varied food; frozen meat at a few pence the pound, tinned pineapples for next to nothing, cheap tinned savouries, fish-and-chips round the corner. It had cheap and easy travel on the new trams, and ready-packeted proprietary drugs from the corner-shops. This . . . generation had fewer children, and on their account, in particular, felt the pressure of the greater organization of urban life: they were glad that 'the lad's chances in life' had improved, but they began to worry about whether he would get his scholarship.[6]

This new generation emerged first in the industrial sectors of the economy. Nor is this surprising. For although it is impossible to measure precisely the correlation between material conditions on the one hand and health, family size and personal relationships on the other, it is perfectly clear that improvements in the former exercised a profound, and beneficial, effect upon the latter. Consequently the same families that gained most from the changes taking place in working conditions, incomes and housing were also those most likely to benefit from advances in health, from reductions in family size, and from improvements in the quality of personal relationships.[7]

It was seen in Chapter 1 that the working conditions of many of those employed in the industrial sectors of the economy changed, and changed for the better, during the period covered by this book. In cotton, coal, engineering and motor manufacturing the working day began to shorten, the work itself became less exhausting, and the risk of accident and disease began to diminish. It was seen in Chapter 2 that the beneficiaries of these improvements were also likely to be the recipients of the highest incomes. It was seen in the last chapter that the high, and rising, wage earnings of these workers enabled them to monopolise the best of the available accommodation: they were the most likely either to buy a home of their own or to obtain the tenancy of a council house. Working-class owner-occupation was most common, it will be recalled, in the cotton towns of Lancashire, the mining region of South Wales, the engineering and shipbuilding centres of London and the North-East, and the 'new' manufacturing towns of the Midlands.

Housing improvements contributed not just to the comfort of family life, but also of course to its health. 'The years between 1880 and 1914', points out F. B. Smith, 'are the crucial ones in the great transition from the age-old pattern of mass morbidity and mortality occasioned by infectious diseases, poor nutrition and heavy labour' . . . 'The putative causes of this transition are complicated. . .' but 'One leading cause is improvement in the environment' and especially 'the removal of damp and delapidated (*sic*) housing'.[8]

More important still was the ability of well-paid workers to afford a nutritious and appetising diet. Dietary historians confirm the common-sense observations of contemporary commentators that the better-off ate best: they ate more, they ate a more varied diet, and they ate more regularly. 'Not until income exceeded 30s. per week', explains D. J. Oddy of the late nineteenth-century working class, 'was there a marked improvement in standards'; families earning 30s. or more ate twice as much meat and drank twice as much milk as those earning less than 18s.[9] But even those earning between 21s. and 30s. a week could expect to eat reasonably well.

> Meals are more regular. For dinner, meat and vegetables are demanded every day. Bacon, eggs and fish find their place at other times. Puddings and tarts are not uncommon, and bread ceases to be the staff of life. Skill in cookery becomes very important, and though capable of much improvement, it is on the whole not amiss. In this class no one goes short of food.[10]

In the mid 1930s the better-off were still consuming by far the most meat and milk – together now with eggs, fruit, vegetables and fish: 'in the poorest group the average consumption of milk, including tinned milk, is equivalent to 1.8 pints per head per week; in the wealthiest group 5.5 pints. The poorest group consume 1.5 eggs per head per week; the wealthiest 4.5'.[11]

It is clear then that there was a close correlation between material conditions and standards of health; and that in the industrial sectors of the economy changes at the workplace combined with rising incomes, better housing and improved nutrition to strengthen the population's resistance to ill-health. Reviewing the state of the nation's health in 1936, John Boyd Orr concluded that 'as income increases, disease and death-rate decrease, children grow more quickly, adult stature is greater and general health and physique improve'.[12]

Nonetheless two qualifications need to be made. The first is that the combination of (somewhat) easier work and a richer and more varied diet (that included growing amounts of salt, sugar and tobacco) increased the risk of obesity, diabetes, renal complaints, cancer, heart disease and high blood pressure.[13] The second is that income alone was not sufficient to guarantee adequate medical treatment. Indeed, in the early years of the period the ability to purchase professional care was by no means an unmixed blessing.[14] Moreover, improvements in the quality of a family's accommodation sometimes aggravated the difficulties of securing proper medical attention. It was noticed that the health of mothers living on new council estates 'does not always improve as much as that of children. Sometimes the health of women even declines.' There were several explanations: the isolation of the estates, their higher cost of living, the burden of looking after a larger house, and the shortage of resident doctors – a problem compounded by the lack of public telephones and the inadequacies of public transport.[15]

Nonetheless there was generally a positive correlation between material conditions and standards of health care. In the industrial sectors of the economy working-class purchasing power improved at much the same time, and at much the same rate, as the capacity of the medical profession to help its patients.[16] By the turn of the century a good number of men from cotton and coalmining families were able to afford certain of the medical attention that they needed. In the cotton industry workers normally dealt with their doctors on an individual basis.[17] In coalmining they tended to make their arrangements collectively, many of the miners' pit clubs, friendly societies and trade unions contracting with local doctors or contributing towards the support of voluntary hospitals and provident dispensaries. By the end of the nineteenth century, for instance, nearly two-thirds of the 80,000 miners in Lancashire and Cheshire were members of the coalfield's miners' permanent relief society and eligible for the medical care to which this entitled them.[18]

Improvements in material conditions and standards of health had a demonstrable effect upon family life. It was in the 1870s that the death rate generally began to fall: from 21 to 22 per 1,000 of the population (in England and Wales) between 1850 and 1875; to 18.7 in the early 1890s; 14.3 in 1911–15; and a fraction over 12 per 1,000 at the end of the period. It was not until the early years of the new century that the infant death rate began to decline. But when it did, it fell very rapidly: from 163 per 1,000 live births (in England and Wales) in 1899; to 110 in 1910; 80 in 1920; and 53 per 1,000 in 1938. The result was that whereas in 1850 the average expectation of life had stood at 40 for men (and 42 for women), by 1890 it had risen to 44 (and 47); by 1901 to 45 (and 49); and by 1910–12 to 52 (and 55). By the end of the period the average man could expect to live to the age of 61 and the average woman to 66 – a rise of more than 50 per cent in less than a century.[19]

The close correlation between material conditions and standards of health meant of course that working people benefited less from these advances than those belonging to other classes in society. But it meant too that within the working class death rates tended to fall most sharply, and life expectancy to increase most rapidly, among those employed in the expanding sectors of the economy. Such an assertion will come perhaps as something of a surprise for it is commonly supposed that the cotton towns and coalmining villages included some of the most unhealthy places in which it was possible to live and work.[20] It is difficult to know. It seems possible that the infant mortality rate began to decline in the cotton towns well before the end of the nineteenth century.[21] It seems certain that by the end of the century coalminers had a level of occupational mortality nearly one-fifth below that of the rest of the male working population. The explanation, Professor Church concludes, is to be found in coalmining's 'higher-than-average wages and earnings. . . . There does seem to be a demonstrable connection between the untypically sharp fall in mortality of miners after the 1870s on the one hand, with the untypically sharp rise in wages which they encountered over the period from the 1880s to 1913, on the other.'[22]

Statistics alone cannot reveal the full extent – let alone the many ramifications – of the improvements that were taking place in working-class health. F. B. Smith is one of the few historians to explore the impact of these improvements on family size and family relationships: 'the steadily growing numbers of people retired or widowed, liable to the physical and social disabilities attendant upon ageing; and the belated social and official condonation of birth control . . . the probable increase in attention and income which parents and grandparents in all classes devote to children of smaller families'.[23]

The improving material conditions enjoyed by the better-off sections of the working class were accompanied by, and helped to produce, a number of demographic changes – most notably the decline in the size of the family. It is well known that from the 1880s onwards the age of first marriage began to creep upwards, the birth rate began to fall, and the size of the family began to decline.[24] Whereas couples marrying in the 1860s had more than six children, those marrying in 1915 had fewer than two-and-a-half, and those marrying in the late 1920s barely two. 'The family size of those married 1925–9 is 60 per cent lower than the mid-Victorian average; and by 1930, 81 per cent of all families consisted of three or less children.'[25]

It was among skilled workers and those employed in textiles that the size of the working-class family first began to fall. By 1911 the typical textile worker had 3.19 children – compared to the 'unskilled' worker's 3.92, the agricultural labourer's 3.99, and the miner's 4.33.[26] It seems doubtful whether it will ever be possible to identify for certain the process whereby this – or any other – group of workers discovered that it was both desirable and possible to limit the size of its families. The process has been linked with any number of factors: from work patterns and standards of living, to ethnic composition and religious character, to the economic, social and psychological cost-benefits of child-rearing.[27]

Among cotton workers at least the key factor seems to have

been the employment opportunities that were available to married women. It was claimed as early as 1832 that: 'Where individuals are congregated in factories I conceive that means preventive of impregnation are more likely to be generally known and practised by young persons.' The explanation was repeated three-quarters of a century later: 'The most striking thing . . . seems to be the association between the presence of textile factories with consequent industrial employment of women and a rapid fall in the birth rate. . . . It is probable that the woman who works in the factory meets more people and the knowledge gained by one woman reaches a far wider area than when her acquaintance is limited to people in the same street or village and thus in the textile districts knowledge as to the possibility of a limitation of family is more widespread.'[28]

Whatever its roots, the decline in fertility had, as might be expected, the most profound consequences for working-class family life. Falling fertility meant smaller families; and smaller families tended to raise expectations, to foster fresh attitudes, and to facilitate the development of new and more satisfying personal relationships.

The difficulties of studying the material foundations and size of the working-class family are formidable indeed. But they are as nothing compared to the complexities of trying to examine the relationships that existed within the family. The sources are elusive and there is a tendency to assume that 'relationships within the working class were intrinsically . . . more lacking in feeling than relationships amongst other classes, just because they took different forms'.[29] Nonetheless, a certain generalisation is possible. It will be argued here that in the high-wage sectors of the economy the improvement in material conditions and the decline in family size were associated with – and helped to cause – significant changes in the nature of family relationships.

There are signs by the late nineteenth century of certain changes in the patterns of working-class courtship.[30] But there are few indications of these changes resulting in the enjoyment of more intense or satisfying sexual relationships. Nor is this paucity of evidence very surprising for the sexual relationship is one of the most elusive and sensitive issues with which the historian ever has to deal: sexual fulfilment is difficult to define and virtually impossible to measure. Edward Shorter has tried to use rates of illegitimacy and pre-nuptial pregnancy as a measure of sexual liberation. Between 1750 and 1850, he maintains, the increase in the number of illegitimate children born in Europe can be traced to a change in the attitudes of lower-class women, a change so profound as to amount to a sexual revolution.[31] Shorter's arguments have been subjected to the most withering criticism. The link that he makes between illegitimacy, pre-marital pregnancy and sexual liberation is assumed rather than proved; and in Britain at least the rise in illegitimacy and pre-marital pregnancy was halted, and then reversed, at the end of the nineteenth century.[32]

Tempting though it is to ridicule the empirical bases of Shorter's arguments, it is difficult to find more convincing indicators of sexual attitudes and behaviour. Oral evidence provides the least unsatisfactory alternative. It is doubtful, concludes Elizabeth Roberts from her oral investigation of working-class women in Barrow, Lancaster and Preston, 'if sexual relationships in marriage were as important to couples earlier in the century as they are to our contemporaries. Sexual intercourse was regarded as necessary for the procreation of children or as an activity indulged in by men for their own pleasure, but it was never discussed in the evidence as something which could give mutual happiness. No hint was ever made that women might have enjoyed sex.'[33]

There is a good deal of evidence to support the view that working-class marriages were based less upon sexual satisfaction than upon a growing sense of companionship. Of course companionable marriages had always existed. But it does appear that the combination of improving material conditions and declining family size tended to foster closer family relationships; it encouraged family members to spend more time at home, to spend more time together and, it seems, to enjoy one another's company.[34]

Change came slowly. Families continued to quarrel; husbands, wives and children continued to go their separate ways (the late nineteenth-century commercialisation of sport providing men with a new excuse to escape from their families). It is not easy, for instance, to tell which of the following childhood memories of family life in Preston dates from the mid-nineteenth century, and which from the early twentieth. The son of a moulder recalls that his father used to call

> at the alehouse on Saturday night, and spent half his money before
> he came home; my mother would sit crying, not knowing how the shop
> bill would be paid. About twelve o'clock my father would come home
> drunk as a pig.[35]

The daughter of a weaver recalls that after she was born, her father 'wouldn't work at all.'

> . . . my mother used to give him so much money a week to look
> after me. I can remember going to those country pubs. He'd walk,
> and walk me there and I can always remember him sitting me once
> on a windowsill outside a pub and it was high up and I couldn't get
> off and I was outside waiting for him coming out.[36]

Yet change there was. Although male activities such as drinking and gambling retained much of their popularity, both gradually became more family-based. It became less unusual for wives to join their husbands in the pub and more common for husbands to stay at home to drink.[37] It became increasingly common to bet at home: whereas the nineteenth-century miner had gambled on street games, his twentieth-century counterpart was likely to enter newspaper competitions and have a weekly flutter on the football pools.[38]

Nor were these the only changes. It seems that as families grew smaller, better off and more comfortably housed, husbands and wives spent more of their time together in domestic activities: reading, talking, gardening, doing odd jobs, playing with the children, listening to the radio, and going out as a family.[39] It is easy to prove that families from the high-wage sectors of the economy were the first to go away on holiday together. John Walton has shown how 'the seaside holiday habit had become . . . deeply rooted in the Lancashire textile district by the turn of the century. By the 1890s, whole towns had a deserted appearance at the Wakes, with shops closed and churches having to join forces to raise even the semblance of a choir for Sunday service.'[40]

It is less easy to prove that families from the high-wage sectors were the first to spend time together on a day-to-day basis. But the oral and autobiographical evidence really is too insistent to be ignored; it shows that by the end of the nineteenth century workers in cotton, engineering and coal were beginning to have the time, the money and the energy that they needed to enable them to enjoy being with their families. The daughter of a Lancashire weaver recalls how her father used to prepare home-made treats – toffee or ice cream according to the weather. A boy brought up in the Durham coalfield remembers that families had sing-songs together and that 'Parents would spend time to listen to hear their children repeating their multiplication tables, counting on a bead counter, etc.'[41] Patchy and impressionistic though it is, such evidence helps to confirm the validity of David Vincent's observation that it was 'the prosperity of the labouring poor' in the second half of the nineteenth century that facilitated the emergence of 'a more "humane" form of family life'.[42]

This more 'humane' form of family life developed first among the better off and became epitomised by that shrine to working-class domesticity, the front parlour. 'The women are proud when they can exhibit a parlour to Sunday visitors,' sneered one observer of Bolton life in 1899: 'It is shut up six days of the week, and is only kept for brag.'[43] Other commentators were less condescending. When James Haslam visited the home of a Lancashire weaver a few years later, he explained that 'The "front place" was usually occupied among them as "t'best room". It was usually occupied at week-ends, when the family had thrown off their factory clothes till Monday morning, or it would be used when they were having "company" – that is, a special visit of neighbours or friends.'[44] It was this apparently irrational use of space that constituted the parlour's very justification: it demonstrated the existence, for all to see, of resources surplus to immediate requirements; it reflected, as Martin Daunton has pointed out, a transitory stage in the growth of working-class achievements and aspirations, a stage that 'permitted the purchase of furniture and fittings but which did not sanction their frequent use'.[45]

Material improvement and demographic change stimulated the emergence of more humane and companionable family relationships. But these new relationships did little to alter the fundamental balance of power within working-class marriages. Male and female spheres remained clear and separate: the husband's responsibility was to provide his family with as steady an income as possible and to treat his wife and children with proper care and consideration; the wife's responsibility was to look after the house, bring up the children and make the family's income stretch as far as possible.[46] Elizabeth Roberts reaches an appropriately cautious conclusion: 'Although the increased sharing of leisure, and the pattern of husbands and wives sharing domestic work in families where the wife had full-time employment, presaged the more usual companionate marriages evident after the second world war, it must be emphasised that separate roles were the norm throughout the period' from 1890 to 1940.[47]

The close correlation between work, income, accommodation, health, family form and family relationships meant that material and domestic disadvantage tended to be mutually reinforcing. The same families that gained least from improvements in material conditions were also likely to benefit least from reductions in family size or from changes in the nature of family relationships.

The association between traditional work patterns and poverty was made clear in the first two chapters of the book. It was seen in Chapter 1 that the working conditions of most of the population changed remarkably little between 1850 and 1939: in most jobs the hours of work remained long and/or irregular, while the work itself continued to be physically demanding and sometimes highly dangerous. It was seen in Chapter 2 that, although most working people did eventually become much better off, a small minority remained stranded below the poverty line, and a much larger minority hovered uncomfortably close to it.

The association between poverty and poor housing was established in Chapter 3. It is true that as the period progressed a growing number of the less well off managed to secure the tenancy of a council house: it has been estimated that by 1937, for example, as many as one-third of all council tenants were unskilled workers such as dockers and builders' labourers. But they often found the cost of moving onto a council estate surprisingly expensive. The rents were high of course; but so was the cost of getting to work or visiting the shops; and so too was the expense of taking over a larger house. In fact, so expensive did ex-slum-dwellers find it to furnish their new homes that local authorities in Leeds, Glasgow, Birmingham, Bolton, Rotherham and some of the London boroughs found it necessary to organise their own subsidised furniture schemes.[48] But as was seen in the previous chapter, the great majority of the working population did not live in council property (or in their own homes) but in accommodation which they rented privately and which rarely provided them with anything but the most rudimentary standards of convenience, comfort and health. In 1942, to take but one example, 16 per cent of families with incomes of less than £300 a year still washed their clothes, and 30 per cent still took their baths, in water that had to be heated on a stove or over an open fire.[49]

Well known too is the association between poverty and poor nutrition. It was shown earlier in this chapter that the poor rarely ate an adequate diet. In the late nineteenth century, it will be recalled, families earning less than 18s. a week ate half as much meat and drank half as much milk as those earning 30s. or more; in the mid-1930s the poor ate only a third of the eggs and drank less than a third of the milk that was consumed by the rich. But even statistics such as these do not reveal the full impact of inadequate nutrition upon family life. In poor families the available food was rarely divided out equally: 'me and the children goes without dinner', explained a York housewife, '– or mebbe only 'as a cup o'tea and a bit o'bread, But Jim ollers takes 'is dinner to work, and I give it him as usual; 'e never knows we go without, and I never tells 'im.'[50] The nation as a whole might have become 'nutrition-conscious' by the end of the period, but the link between poverty and malnutrition remained: 'It has been shown by the best authorities', concluded Margery Spring Rice in 1939, 'that a large part of the population is too poor to buy enough of the kind of food necessary for the maintenance of sound health. No unemployed married man with a family under the Assistance Board, nor any married man in such poorly paid trades as agriculture, receives enough money to buy adequate food for himself, wife and children.'[51]

The fact that the poor generally did the hardest work, received the lowest incomes, lived in the worst accommodation and ate the most inadequate diet meant that they also suffered from the poorest health.[52] It is true that the inability of the poor to purchase professional medical care did not disadvantage them very greatly during the early part of the period; indeed, insofar as their poverty kept them away from insanitary hospitals and incompetent doctors it almost certainly worked to their advantage.[53] But their poverty meant that they were unable to benefit from the improving standards of medical care that were becoming available towards the end of the nineteenth century: 'Unless you were really dying you never sent for a doctor because . . . [you] hadn't the money to pay.'[54]

Some families relied upon familiar, if unqualified, sources of medical assistance. The son of a Bolton railway porter remembers going to a local woman for advice: she was cheaper than the doctor; there was no queuing; and her treatment seemed to work.[55] Other families continued to treat themselves with traditional remedies. Dockers' families in Bristol retained their faith in a wide range of do-it-yourself cures: toothache was treated by chewing salt, tobacco or horseradish; sore throats were dealt with by sticking a hot, linseed meal poultice onto the neck; and bad chests by eating raw fat bacon, by rubbing in camphorated oil, or by wearing a brown paper shirt smothered in goose grease.[56] In Poplar, recalls John Blake,

> Any household illness had to be cured by old fashioned remedies, as a doctor's fee could not always be afforded. Epsom Salts, Brimstone and Treacle, Carbonate of Soda, Camphorated Oil and Amber, Russian Tallow and Brown Paper, Vinegar and Brown Paper for a headache, Bread Poultice applied to any septic condition. . . . Another remedy used in those early days was hot fomentations of lint and iodine, applied to the skin for rheumatic or similar complaints.[57]

Many families treated themselves with patent medicines, the consumption of which began to increase in the 1870s. The most noticeable change between the late nineteenth century and the end of the period was that, as the population grew more prosperous and more long-lived, so advertisements for Morrison's, Holloways and Beecham Pills gave way to those extolling the virtues of Yeast-Vite and Phyllosan. 'Even in 1873, researchers reported finding that 16 per cent of sufferers with symptoms of illness in Britain took no action and 63 per cent made some attempt at self-care. Only 20 per cent of sufferers actually visited a doctor.'[58]

The relationship between poverty and ill-health may be demonstrated in a number of ways. Mortality statistics provide one convenient index. They show that even when the death rate did begin to fall, it fell least quickly among the families of the unskilled, the poorly paid and the unemployed. It was found that in the early 1930s unskilled workers had a death rate 15 per cent higher than the skilled, and that towards the end of the decade areas of high unemployment like Wigan and the Rhondda had rates two-thirds higher than centres of 'new' industry such as Oxford.[59] Moreover, there were found to be similar, if smaller, variations within areas of high unemployment: when the Medical Officer of Health for Stockton-on-Tees compared the families of unemployed and employed workers, he discovered that the former had a death rate more than one-third higher than the latter.[60]

Statistics of infant mortality reveal more grimly still the relationship between disadvantage and ill-health.[61] A parliamentary report prepared in 1913 showed that whereas the infant mortality rate in wage-earning families generally was 133 per thousand live births (and 77 per thousand in the middle and upper classes), the rate among unskilled labourers stood at 152 per thousand. Maud Pember Reeves revealed the correlation between material conditions and infant mortality in the most striking way. In Lambeth, she discovered, the infant death rate in families paying 6s. 6d. or more a week in rent was 12 per cent (120 per thousand); in families paying less than 6s. in rent the death rate was 40 per cent (400 per thousand).[62] There were also pronounced regional disparities. In 1935 the south-east of England had an infant mortality rate of 47 per thousand live births; Wales a rate of 63 per thousand; the north of England a rate of 68 per thousand; and Scotland a rate of 77 per thousand.[63]

Even the statistics of infant mortality do not reveal completely the relationship between poverty and ill-health. But there is other statistical evidence to which the historian can turn. Late nineteenth- and twentieth-century social investigators showed time and time again that children from poor families were shorter, lighter and altogether less healthy than their better-off contemporaries. Seebohm Rowntree found that in turn-of-the-century York, for example, boys from the poorest class of homes were three-and-a-half inches shorter and eleven pounds lighter than those from the best homes.[64] A few years later the Reverend W. E. Rees reported the results of a survey of 42,000 Salford children which showed that 13-year-old boys from the 'poor working class quarter' were some 7 per cent shorter and 17 per cent lighter than those from the 'better quarter'.[65] Later surveys confirmed the link between deprivation and ill-health: it was found in 1933, for instance, that at least one-third of the children living in the poorer districts of Newcastle-upon-Tyne needed to be classified either as unhealthy or as physically unfit.[66]

Unhealthy children grew into unhealthy adults and so the cycle of deprivation continued.[67] The poor continued to work the hardest, to eat the least nutritious diet, to die the youngest and (when they did survive, marry and have children) to lack the health and energy needed to participate fully in a humane and companionable family life.

The poor did not lack the health and energy needed to have children. Indeed it is a well-known paradox that it was those least able to afford large families who were most likely to have them. Throughout the period covered by this book it was the unskilled, the casually employed and the poorly paid who tended both to marry young and to have more children than other workers.[68] In 1911, it will be remembered, the typical agricultural labourer had 3.99 children and the unskilled worker 3.92, compared to the textile worker's 3.19. It has been found that well into the 1920s the 'average number of live births credited to the wives of labourers, the most fertile of the manual working group, . . . [was] not far short of double the number credited to the wives of professional men and of salaried employees' and was between 11 and 24 per cent greater than the number credited to the wives of wage earners generally.[69]

It is no easier to explain the failure of the poor to control their fertility than it was to account for the success of the better off in controlling theirs. It cannot be assumed that because the employment opportunities available to married women provided the key to explaining the declining fertility of cotton families, it must be the absence of such opportunities that accounted for the higher fertility of families in the traditional sectors of the economy. The explanation is more complex, revolving as it does around the survival of a whole 'culture of poverty'. The poor, it seems, were often ignorant about the workings of their own bodies and poorly informed about mechanical methods of birth control, so that when they did practise contraception they tended to rely upon simple, but unreliable, techniques such as the safe period and coitus interruptus.[70] The poor, it seems, were also less likely than other groups to want to control their fertility. Some couples were opposed to contraception on moral and/or religious grounds; others wished to prove their virility and/or feminity; while others hoped that a large family would protect them against the poverty of old age. A large family, it seemed to many of the poor, could be both economically rational and emotionally satisfying.[71]

It is clear then that any study of working-class fertility remains beset by major difficulties of evidence and interpretation. But so too does the broader study of family relationships among the poor. Nonetheless there are certain signs of change in patterns of courtship between 1850 and 1939: illegitimacy rates were always high but it does appear that it was becoming increasingly common for couples to have some sexual experience before marriage.[72]

But this was no erotic revolution. Young men and women continued to choose their partners from a narrow geographical and social circle, and on the basis, it has even been suggested, of their *lack* of sexual attractiveness.[73] Whatever the couple's inclinations, the opportunities for sexual intimacy were often rather restricted in the growing towns and cities. One London servant explained, and was able to prove, that her lovemaking was regulated by the timetable of the metropolitan railway: the crucial moments were the few minutes on each trip that the train was stationary in a dark siding. It cannot be assumed that such ingenuity was indicative of widespread sexual promiscuity. It is true that domestic servants generally were notorious for their large numbers of illegitimate children. But the explanation lay not in the servants' sexual behaviour, 'which appears indistinguishable from that of others of similar background'. The explanation was more mundane; it lay in the large numbers of women in domestic service, and 'in the contradictions between the marked immobility of women in service and the contrasting rapidity of movement of the men to which such women most frequently found themselves attached.'[74]

Given the unromantic beginnings of some marriages, and the difficult material circumstances of most, it is scarcely surprising that few couples ever enjoyed sexual passion on the grand scale. Ill-health, money worries, a lack of privacy and the fear of pregnancy all militated against the development of truly satisfying sexual relationships. Mr and Mrs 'L' lived in London with her parents: 'His in-laws are quite nice and well-meaning, but . . . he doesn't feel at home. They have only their bedroom to retire to, and everyone knows what is going on. "I'm self-conscious." '

> Alec Y . . . a lorry-driver of thirty-six, five and a half years married, hints there are difficulties at times in the sex side of his marriage and says it is his wife's fear of pregnancy which is responsible. Mrs. Y, whose three children are all under five, confirms his statement and says she didn't want to start her family so soon or have them so quickly. She is now afraid she may have been 'caught' yet again and will be 'very annoyed' if this is so. Unenthusiastic about intercourse, she explains that this worry 'was always in the back of me mind. I was afraid'.[75]

The social survey evidence suggests, and the autobiographical evidence confirms, that for most men sex became a habit, for most women a duty. 'Husbands are valued in an inverse relation to sexuality,' explained two mid-twentieth-century investigators: ' "he's very good, he doesn't bother me much", "he's not lustful", "he wouldn't trouble you at all", "he's pretty good that way; if I say no, he doesn't go on".'[76] Well known is Robert Roberts's graphic description of sexual attitudes and behaviour in the Salford slum in which he was brought up at the beginning of this century.

> I remember the savage dissatisfaction with his spouse of a young brass moulder. 'Last night,' he said (during what was made plain had been the 'very lists of love'), 'she goes an' asks me not to forget to leave twopence for the gas!' The wife of a fettler in the same group was prone, it turned out, to reach her *crise d'extase* whilst eating an apple. A third, swathed in clothes, permitted her husband only the act *per se* and, on her mother's advice, allowed no 'dirty' manual contact whatever. 'It's about as exciting', he said, 'as posting a letter!'[77]

It was difficult for couples in the traditional sectors of the economy to compensate for any lack of sexual fulfilment in their marriages. Everything conspired against them. The survival of heavy work, low and uncertain incomes, large families, poor health, and inadequate and overcrowded accommodation all inhibited the emergence of companionable and enjoyable family relationships. So great was the burden that it tended to drive the members of the family apart and, when it did bring them together, to generate all kinds of domestic tension.

The combination of material and demographic disadvantage meant that while wives struggled to keep the home together, their husbands and children often sought their pleasures elsewhere.[78] The poorer the family, the more likely were the children to take a part-time job, or play outside and congregate on street corners.[79] The poorer the family, the more likely were the husband and wife to grow apart. Lady Bell saw this happen in Middlesbrough: 'Many a workman . . . finds the hours when the housewife is busy and the house upside down a comfortless time enough to live through if he has nowhere else to go. And not only in the morning, but all day and every day, this is the permanent condition of many a house where the woman is not skilled in the domestic arts, and comfort is unknown.'[80] Maud Pember Reeves saw it happen in Lambeth:

> The young couple . . . marry and live contentedly on 20s. a week . . . and they do not for the first year or two realise that even two or three children will develop into a burden which is too great for their strength. . . . Moreover, the separation of interests soon begins to show itself. The husband goes to the same work – hard, long and monotonous – but at least a change from the growing discomfort of the home. He gets accustomed to seeing his wife slave, and she gets accustomed to seeing him appear and disappear on his daily round of work, which gradually appeals less and less to her imagination, till, at thirty, she hardly knows what his duties are – so overwhelmed is she in the flood of her own most absorbing duties and economies. Her economies interfere with his comfort, and are irksome to him; so he gets out of touch with her point of view.[81]

Poor families did spend a good deal of time together – often in fact considerably more than those with higher incomes and more regular employment. There is some evidence that, as in other sectors of the economy, families began to derive increased enjoyment from the time that they spent together. Some small amounts of drinking and gambling were redirected towards the home: a growing number of men joined their families in domestic activities such as reading, gardening, listening to the radio and going to the cinema.[82] During the 1930s the cinema was easily the most popular form of mass entertainment in working-class districts, a popularity that reached its height in areas of high unemployment.[83] A growing number of men also began to help around the home: cooking, doing some of the household chores and playing with the children. The daughter of a factory worker-turned-navvy remembers her childhood during the 1920s: 'When you came in of a night . . . the parents . . . used to sit down and play cards with you or ludo, snakes and ladders, draughts, games like that.'[84]

There is much more evidence that when poor families spent time together, it led not to companionship and enjoyment, but to the generation of all kinds of domestic tension. Sometimes these tensions erupted into violence. How often this happened, it is impossible to discover: women with black eyes would say to their neighbours, 'Oh I was chopping some stick and the stick flew up and hit me in the eye.'[85] But it does seem that although domestic violence generally was in decline from about the 1890s, it remained most common in poor families where the idea of male domination lingered longest. It was reported from London in 1900 that 'wife-beating was so common among a certain class that plenty of wives take it as a perfect matter of course, and did not appear to mind very much unless they were seriously damaged'.[86] A St Helens woman, who was not born until after the First World War, remembers that

> Men were tyrants. . . . There was an awful lot of wifebeating and women were the underdogs. . . . My mother slept in the outside lavatory at times. The men that didn't drink and behaved like that were the worst of all. . . . The wifebeating came from the Victorian era. When it happened, women went to neighbours' houses. Then the husband would come and kick the door down to get the wife out. . . . It was just a way of life.[87]

The 'absolute rule for all sub-affluent marriages', claims Geoffrey Best, 'was like it or lump it.'[88]

But this is to exaggerate. Even in the worst of the nineteenth-century slums, domestic tensions rarely resulted in constant physical violence.[89] But domestic tensions could lead to a virtually endless round of sulking, complaining and bickering. Living with in-laws was never easy: 'Mr. and Mrs. J. live with her parents. He says, "they are very kind, and I get on well enough with them, but you feel tied". She says, "there's no privacy; there's always an audience. You have to restrain yourselves, and the only time you can talk is in bed, and then you're tired." '[90] Taking in a lodger was also stressful. Margaret Loane reported in 1908 how 'A childless married woman whom I have known for many years took a lad of nineteen as a lodger. . . . A few months later my old friend referred to her lodger as the worst bargain she had ever made.' He was 'good-natured enough, and he don't drink nothing naming, nor yet smoke, and he's pretty careful with the furniture'. The trouble was that

> It was agreed that he was to set in the kitchen when he chose, but of course we never thought as he wouldn't have the manners to keep away when we was at meals. But no; sure as ever we've got a bit of anything nice and hot, there he'll stick, and he'll sniff and he'll sniff, and stare, and pass remarks, and sigh, till one or the other of us – and I must own it's oftenest me – will say, 'Like a bit?' and then, without no more asking than you'd give a dog, he pegs into it until what I meant for next day's dinner looks pretty foolish.[91]

Even when families lived alone, they were never short of things to argue about. Husbands and wives quarrelled over money; over the husband's drinking and gambling; over the wife's performance of her household duties; and increasingly, perhaps, over the family's inability to attain the domestic ideal against which even the most disadvantaged were beginning to measure their lives.[92] Parents and children could argue over virtually anything; and adolescence invariably brought with it many new sources of dispute: what clothes to wear; how late to stay out; what proportion of the child's wages to pay into the household budget.[93]

Generalisation is difficult. The evidence is fragmentary and often contradictory: two mid-twentieth-century commentators cite the example of a London road-sweeper who 'said that his father and mother "thought the world of one another", and then went on to tell how his father drank, was jealous and violent, used to beat his mother and that she "retaliated" '.[94] Nonetheless, it does seem indisputable that in the traditional sectors of the economy it was the persistence of material and demographic disadvantage that impeded the development of caring and companionable family relationships. (The son of a building worker explains that his mother – a part-time cleaner – 'was kind but she was hard, if you understand, but she had to be hard because of so many children'.[95]) It is difficult to dissent from Eliot Slater and Moya Woodside's view of working-class marriage in London between the wars.

> Seen through the eyes of children, it is open discord between the parents which is impressive and remembered in after-years – 'fights over everything', 'always at logger-heads', 'life was a lot of squabbles', 'not too good if Father was in beer', 'I wouldn't like to get on like them in my later life' . . . Only the most perceptive and intelligent recognized an incompatibility expressed at a less flagrant level, and sensed discord even if concealed. 'A brittle atmosphere', 'undercurrents', 'there was no open discord; it was just an awful atmosphere' epitomize the child's sense of insecurity. But periodical conflicts and disagreements, and a relation between the parents of very attenuated affection seem to be almost standard.[96]

The years between 1850 and 1939 saw fundamental changes in working-class family life. The close correlation between material, demographic and personal factors led, in the industrial sectors of the economy, to the emergence of a smaller, healthier, more prosperous and more inward-looking family – its achievements and aspirations encapsulated in that shrine to working-class domesticity, the front parlour. However, the intimacy of the relationship between material, demographic and personal factors had another, less welcome consequence: it meant that families in the traditional sectors of the economy shared only slowly and uncertainly in the improvements that were taking place elsewhere. It was a dichotomy that was to have significant repercussions in many aspects of working-class life.

NOTES AND REFERENCES

1. **M. Anderson,** *Approaches to the History of the Western Family 1500–1914,* Macmillan, 1980; **E. Roberts,** 'Working Wives and their Families', in **T. Barker** and **M. Drake** (eds), *Population and Society in Britain 1850–1980,* Batsford, 1982.
2. **J. Weeks,** *Sex, Politics and Society: The Regulation of Sexuality since 1800,* Longman, 1981, p. 25.
3. **J. Humphries,** 'Class Struggle and the Persistence of the Working-Class Family', *Cambridge Journal of Economics,* 1, 1977, p. 241.
4. **M. Anderson,** *Family Structure in Nineteenth Century Lancashire,* Cambridge U.P., 1971, p. 137.
5. **E. Shorter,** *The Making of the Modern Family,* Fontana, 1977, p. 15.
6. **R. Hoggart,** *The Uses of Literacy: Aspects of Working-Class Life with Special Reference to Publications and Entertainments,* Penguin, 1958, p. 26.
7. **J. Stevenson,** *British Society 1914–45,* Penguin, 1984, p. 205; **D. J. Oddy,** 'The Health of the People', in Barker and Drake, *Population and Society,* p. 125.
8. **F. B. Smith,** 'Health', in **J. Benson** (ed.), *The Working Class in England 1875–1914,* Croom Helm, 1984, pp. 38–9. Also **F. B. Smith,** *The People's Health 1830–1910,* Croom Helm, 1979, pp. 230–1.
9. **D. J. Oddy,** 'Working-Class Diets in Late Nineteenth-Century Britain', *Economic History Review,* xxiii, 1970, pp. 318, 320.
10. Cited *ibid.,* p. 321.
11. **J. B. Orr,** *Food Health and Income: Report on a Survey of Adequacy of Diet in Relation to Income,* Macmillan, 1936, p. 49.
12. *Ibid.,* p. 49.
13. Smith, 'Health', pp. 52–4; *Twentieth Annual Report of the Ministry of Health 1938–39,* pp. 43–4.
14. Smith, *Health,* pp. 56, 250–53. Also Manchester Polytechnic, Manchester Studies, Transcript 630, p. 8; Transcript 664, p. 11.
15. **R. Jeavons** and **J. Madge,** *Housing Estates: A Study of Bristol Corporation Policy and Practice between the Wars,* University of Bristol, 1946, pp. 77–8.
16. Smith, *Health,* pp. 250–3; **J. M. Winter,** 'The Decline of Mortality in Britain 1870–1950', in Barker and Drake, *Population and Society,* p. 110.
17. Manchester Studies, Transcript 664, p. 10; Transcript 708, p. 4.
18. **J. Benson,** 'The Compensation of English Coal-miners and their Dependants for Industrial Accidents, 1860–1897', Ph.D. University of Leeds, 1974, p. 440; **J. Benson,** *British Coalminers in the Nineteenth Century: A Social History,* Gill & Macmillan, 1980, pp. 184–5.
19. Smith, *Health,* pp. 65, 113–14; **E. H. Hunt,** *British Labour History 1815–1914,* Weidenfeld & Nicolson, 1981, p. 35; Stevenson, *British Society,* pp. 148, 203; Winter, 'Decline of Mortality', p. 102; *Twentieth Annual Report of the Ministry of Health 1938–39,* p. 35.
20. E.g. Benson, *British Coalminers,* p. 132.
21. **R. Burr-Litchfield,** 'The Family and the Mill: Cotton Mill Work,

Family Work Patterns and Fertility in Mid-Victorian Stockport', in **A. S. Wohl** (ed.), *The Victorian Family: Structure and Stresses,* Croom Helm, 1978, p. 193. But cf. Hunt, *Labour History,* p. 48; **E. Roberts,** *A Woman's Place: An Oral History of Working-Class Women 1890–1940,* Blackwell, 1984, pp. 167–8.

22. **R. Church,** *The History of the British Coal Industry, Volume 3: Victorian Pre-eminence,* Clarendon Press, 1986, p. 596.

23. Smith, 'Health', p. 57.

24. **R. B. Outhwaite,** 'Age of Marriage in England from the late Seventeenth to the Nineteenth Century', *Transactions of the Royal Historical Society,* xxiii, 1973; Harrison, *Common People,* p. 386; Anderson, *Approaches,* p. 20.

25. Weeks, *Sex,* p. 202. Also Hunt, *Labour History,* p. 38.

26. Hunt, *Labour History,* p. 38. Also Weeks, *Sex,* pp. 46, 69–73.

27. **N. L. Tranter,** *Population and Society 1750–1940: Contrasts in Population Growth,* Longman, 1985, pp. 107–23.

28. Cited Roberts, 'Working wives', p. 153. See also **D. Gittins,** 'Married Life and Birth Control between the Wars', *Oral History,* 3, 1975, p. 55; **D. Gittins,** 'Women's Work and Family Size between the Wars', *Oral History,* 5, 1977, p. 87.

29. Weeks, *Sex,* p. 59.

30. *Ibid.,* p. 74.

31. Shorter, *Modern Family,* esp. pp. 87–103.

32. **J. W. Scott** and **L. A. Tilly,** 'Women's Work and the Family in Nineteenth-Century Europe', *Comparative Studies in History and Society,* 17, 1975, pp. 55–56; **L. Stone,** 'The Domestic Revolution', *Times Literary Supplement,* 28 May 1976; Anderson, *Approaches,* p.21.

33. Roberts, *Woman's Place,* pp. 83–4.

34. **J. M. Mogey,** *Family and Neighbourhood: Two Studies in Oxford,* Oxford U. P., 1956, pp. 62, 71–2; **M. Young** and **P. Willmott,** *Family and Kinship in East London,* Penguin, 1957; **J. R. Gillis,** *For Better, For Worse: British Marriages 1600 to the Present,* Oxford U.P., 1986.

35. Anderson, *Family Structure,* p. 70.

36. Roberts, *Woman's Place,* p. 121.

37. *Ibid.,* pp. 122–3.

38. *News of the World,* 12 January 1930; Benson, *British Coalminers,* p. 161; **N. Dennis, F. Henriques** and **C. Slaughter,** *Coal is Our Life: An Analysis of a Yorkshire Mining Community,* Tavistock, 1974, pp. 159–60.

39. **S. Constantine,** 'Amateur Gardening and Popular Recreation in the 19th and 20th Centuries', *Journal of Social History,* xiv, 1981; **R. McKibbin,** 'Work and Hobbies in Britain, 1880–1950', in **J. M. Winter** (ed.), *The Working Class in Modern British History: Essays in Honour of Henry Pelling,* Cambridge U.P. 1983.

40. **J. K. Walton,** 'The Demand for Working-Class Seaside Holidays in Victorian England', *Economic History Review,* xxxiv, 1981, p. 257. Also Manchester Studies, Transcript 664, p. 3; **J. Stevenson** and **C. Cook,** *The Slump,* Quartet Books, 1979, pp. 25–6; **J. A. R. Pimlott,** *The Englishman's Holiday: A Social History,* Harvester, 1977.

41. Benson, *British Coalminers*, p. 136. Also Manchester Studies, Transcript 664, p. 4.
42. **D. Vincent,** 'Love and Death and the Nineteenth-Century Working Class', *Social History*, 5, 1980, p. 247
43. **J. Burnett,** *A Social History of Housing 1815–1985*, Methuen, 1986, p. 172. Also **M. J. Daunton,** *House and Home in the Victorian City: Working-Class Housing 1850–1914*, Arnold, p. 279.
44. Daunton, *House and Home*, p. 283. Also Manchester Studies, Transcript 628, p. 6.
45. Daunton, *House and Home*, p. 280. Also Burnett, *Housing*, p. 172.
46. **S. Meacham,** *A Life Apart: The English Working Class 1890–1914*, Thames & Hudson, 1977, pp. 64, 73, 116, 208–9; **W. Seccombe,** 'Patriarchy Stabilized: The Construction of the Male Breadwinner Wage Norm in Nineteenth-Century Britain', *Social History*, 11, 1986, pp. 59, 62; Roberts, *Woman's Place*, pp. 110–14.
47. Roberts, *Woman's Place*, p. 124.
48. Jevons and Madge, *Housing Estates*, pp. 23–4, 35, 45.
49. Daunton, *House and Home*, p. 243.
50. Cited Hunt, *Labour History*, p. 123. Also Bristol, RO56, p. 23.
51. **M. S. Rice,** *Working-Class Wives: Their Health and Conditions*, Penguin, 1939, p. 155. These, and similar, views came in for a good deal of contemporary criticism: see Stevenson, *British Society*, p. 215. The fact that a large number of children in a family was one major cause of poverty meant that there was always a disproportionate number of children living below the poverty line.
52. **C. Webster,** 'Healthy or Hungry Thirties?', *History Workshop*, 13, 1982.
53. Smith, *Health*, pp. 28, 254–5, 368.
54. Manchester Studies, Transcript 664, p. 10.
55. Manchester Studies, Transcript 652, pp. 12–13. Also 869, NP; **W. M. Williams,** *The Sociology of an English Village: Gosforth*, Routledge & Kegan Paul, 1956, p. 59.
56. Bristol, R007, p. 22; R008, p. 20; R011, p. 37; R030, p. 13. For the nineteenth century, see Smith, *Health*, pp. 109–11, 303, 418–19.
57. **J. Blake,** *Memories of Old Poplar*, Stepney Books Publications, 1977, p. 14.
58. Smith, *Health*, pp. 343–5. Also Hoggart, *Uses of Literacy*, p. 47; **E. Slater** and **M. Woodside,** *Patterns of Marriage: A Study of Marriage Relationships in the Urban Working Classes*, Cassell, 1951, pp.246–7.
59. Stevenson, *British Society*, p. 216. Also **G. M. Howe,** *Man, Environment and Disease in Britain: A Medical Geography of Britain Through the Ages*, David & Charles, 1972, p. 205.
60. **S. Constantine,** *Unemployment in Britain between the Wars*, Longman, 1980, pp. 33–4. The link between unemployment and ill-health was never accepted by the Ministry of Health.
61. For the debate about the relationship between unemployment and infant mortality, see Constantine, *Unemployment*, p. 32; Winter, 'Mortality', p. 233.
62. **M. P. Reeves,** *Round About A Pound A Week*, Bell, 1913, p. 26. Also Smith, *Health*, pp. 124–8; Meacham, *Life Apart*, p. 156.

63. Stevenson, *British Society*, p. 217.
64. Meacham, *Life Apart*, p. 157.
65. Smith, *Health*, p. 176.
66. Stevenson, *British Society*, p. 215.
67. White, *Worst Street*, p. 49; Slater and Woodside, *Patterns of Marriage*, p. 277.
68. But see Outhwaite, 'Age of Marriage', p. 69.
69. **A. M. Carr-Saunders, D. C. Jones** and **C. A. Moser,** *A Survey of Social Conditions in England and Wales: As Illustrated by Statistics,* Clarendon Press, 1958, p. 25.
70. Slater and Woodside, *Patterns of Marriage,* pp. 194, 207, 276; Weeks, *Sex,* pp. 187–8.
71. Slater and Woodside, *Patterns of Marriage,* pp. 140–2, 206–10; Weeks, *Sex,* p. 69.
72. Weeks, *Sex,* p. 208; Slater and Woodside, *Patterns of Marriage,* pp. 113–14; **J. R. Gillis,** 'Servants, Sexual Relations, and the Risks of Illegitimacy in London, 1801–1900', *Feminist Studies,* 5, 1979, p. 143.
73. Slater and Woodside, *Patterns of Marriage,* pp. 94–5, 107; White, *Worst Street,* pp. 198–9.
74. Gillis, 'Servants', p. 158.
75. Slater and Woodside, *Patterns of Marriage,* pp. 170, 197.
76. *Ibid.*, p. 168. Also Weeks, *Sex,* p. 209.
77. **R. Roberts,** *The Classic Slum: Salford Life in the First Quarter of the Century,* Penguin, 1973, pp. 55–6.
78. **P. N. Stearns,** 'Working-Class Women in Britain, 1890–1914', in **M. Vicinus** (ed.), *Suffer and be Still: Women in the Victorian Age,* Methuen, 1980, p. 104; Seccombe, 'Patriarchy', p. 62.
79. Howkins, *Poor Labouring Men,* pp. 32–3; Bristol, RO11, p. 71; RO58, p. 24.
80. **Lady Bell,** *At The Works: A Study of a Manufacturing Town,* Arnold, 1907, p. 130.
81. Reeves, *Pound A Week,* pp. 154–5.
82. Stevenson, *British Society,* p. 398; Slater and Woodside, *Patterns of Marriage,* p. 86; Constantine, 'Amateur Gardening'; Bristol, Transcript RO59, p. 4. Also **E. J. Hobsbawm,** *Industry and Empire,* Penguin, 1969, p. 22.
83. **J. F. C. Harrison,** *The Common People: A History from the Norman Conquest to the Present,* Fontana, 1984, p. 376; Hobsbawm, *Industry and Empire,* p. 221; **J. Richards,** 'The Cinema and Cinema-Going in Birmingham in the 1930s', in **J. K. Walton** and **J. Walvin** (eds), *Leisure in Britain 1780–1939,* Manchester U.P., 1983, p. 33.
84. Bristol, Transcript RO56, p. 17.
85. Bristol, Transcript RO11, p. 43. Also White, *Worst Street,* p. 191; **D. Woods,** 'Community Violence', in Benson (ed.), *Working Class,* pp. 169–72, 185–6, 191.
86. Cited Woods, 'Community Violence', p. 190. Also White, *Worst Street,* pp. 140, 149–51, 153, 160.
87. **C. Forman,** *Industrial Town: Self Portrait of St Helens in the 1920s,* Granada, 1979, p. 128.

88. Cited Woods, 'Community Violence', p. 188.
89. *Ibid.*, p. 194; White, *Worst Street*, p. 141.
90. Slater and Woodside, *Patterns of Marriage*, p. 152.
91. **M. Loane,** *From their Point of View*, Arnold, 1908, pp. 57–8.
92. White, *Worst Street*, p. 143.
93. Bristol, Transcript RO11, pp. 21, 48; RO56, p. 41; RO58, p. 12; Roberts, 'The Family', pp. 26–9; White, *Worst Street*, pp. 192–3, 199, 202; Weeks, *Sex*, p. 73.
94. Slater and Woodside, *Patterns of Marriage*, p. 40. Also pp. 52–64.
95. Bristol, Transcript RO59, p. 9. Also Smith, *Health*, p. 399; **P. Taylor,** 'Daughters and Mothers – Maids and Mistresses: Domestic Service between the Wars', in **J. Clarke, C. Critcher** and **R. Johnson,** *Working-Class Culture: Studies in History and Theory*. Hutchinson, 1979, pp. 126–9; Meacham, *Life Apart*, pp. 160–61.
96. Slater and Woodside, *Patterns of Marriage*, p. 43.

Chapter 5

KINSHIP, NEIGHBOURHOOD AND COMMUNITY

Kinship, neighbourhood and community have long been central, not just to the academic concerns of social scientists, but to the everyday attempts of ordinary people to understand and interpret their lives. The years following the Second World War saw the establishment of the Institute of Community Studies and the publication of a number of well-known, and generally well received, studies of English and Welsh community life.[1] Moreover, there remains to this day a deep-seated nostalgia for a time (and a place) when families kept in touch with one another, knew their neighbours and lived together in stable, tightly knit local communities.[2]

It is striking, therefore, that neither kinship, nor neighbourhood nor community has received the historical attention that it deserves. The explanation seems to be that in their pursuit of the male, institutional solidarities of the workplace and the labour movement, historians have sometimes tended to overlook the less obvious, more personal and predominantly female solidarities of kinship, neighbourhood and community. But this neglect is not due simply to the failings of male labour historians. It springs too from the very elusiveness of the subject: from the theoretical complexities of defining, and distinguishing, the terms kinship, neighbourhood and community; and from the empirical difficulties of finding the evidence that is required to examine them historically.

'It is almost impossible', admits Elizabeth Roberts, 'to define precisely who were or who were not regarded as family by working-class people.' Certainly the kin relationship manifested itself in various forms and may be measured in a number of different ways: by census-based indicators such as co-residence; or, as Roberts herself suggests, by non-statistical indicators such as the group of people 'from whom, and to whom, support and help would either be received or offered'.[3] But of course neither type of indicator necessarily reveals anything at all about the quality of the kin relationship. Neither reveals what the members of a co-resident

117

or mutually supportive family felt about the relatives with whom their lives were so intimately entwined – nor indeed what relationships were like in families whose members lived apart and either could not or would not help one another.

The working-class neighbourhood is harder still to define. It is easy enough to identify a family's immediate next-door neighbours, but much more difficult to decide how far beyond these the neighbourhood itself extended. In urban areas, suggests Standish Meacham, the neighbourhood normally comprised the street in which a family lived, together with those immediately surrounding it. But, as Meacham himself points out, the neighbourhood needs to be defined socially as well as spatially: 'Neighbourhood meant more than houses and streets. It meant the mutually beneficial relationships one formed with others; a sort of social symbiosis.'[4] Used in this sense, neighbourhood meant neighbourliness; a neighbourliness that 'did not imply the intimacy of friendship' but 'implied reciprocity – looking out for one another'.[5] But this neighbourliness – the very stuff of popular nostalgia – did not develop automatically just because people lived together in the same neighbourhood. The neighbourliness of the working-class neighbourhood cannot be assumed; its existence has always to be demonstrated.[6]

The discussion of working-class community is fraught with even more complications than that of kinship or of neighbourhood. However, it is not acceptable to use the term simply 'as a convenient hold-all for those aspects of working-class life which in part at least transcend the workplace'.[7] Community, like neighbourhood, needs to be defined both spatially and socially: as a geographical area and as a group of people to which its members feel that they belong.[8] Used in this sense, a community is defined not just 'by who its members are, but by what they do'. It arises from 'people from the same area sharing the same attitudes, beliefs and interests, and expressing their communality of interest through social interaction'.[9] The difficulty is how to identify and measure this 'communality of interest'. Scholars have tackled the problem in various ways, studying everything from marriage patterns and residential mobility to church attendance and voting behaviour. But none of these measures is entirely satisfactory; it is difficult, after all, to imbue political affiliation or the choice of a marriage partner with an unambiguous message about the nature and strength of community consciousness.[10]

Despite all these difficulties, a certain broad generalisation is possible. It seems, for instance, that in the industrial sectors of the economy the solidarities of kinship, neighbourhood and community were well established by the beginning of the period, but that they proved somewhat vulnerable to the economic and social changes that took place towards the end of the century.

The extended family played an important part in the life of the better-off mid-nineteenth-century worker. Yet despite the attention that has been lavished upon the history of the coal industry and its workforce, surprisingly little is known about kinship ties among the nineteenth-century coalmining population. However it seems probable that by the middle of the century mining families were already displaying some of the solidarities for which they were to become so well known. Fathers helped their sons to find a job in the pit; parents gave their children a home until (and even after) they were married; and both parents and children tried hard to keep in touch and did their best to help one another. As the Houghton-le-Spring Board of Guardians explained in 1838, 'the Working Class in this Mining District being so inter-married and related to each other, those who may need parochial relief can be and have been kept considerably cheaper and better by giving them Weekly relief and allowing them to remain with their friends, than could possibly be done by keeping them in the Workhouse'.[11]

A good deal more is known about kinship ties in the cotton districts. The pioneering investigations of Michael Anderson show that in mid-nineteenth-century Preston, for example, more than 95 per cent of the population lived in the same household as one of their relatives. But, as Anderson points out, 'Kinship does not stop at the front door' for 'many, perhaps even a majority of people did deliberately live near one or more kinsmen and many others probably tried to'.[12] Relatives helped each other to find work and looked to one another for other forms of support. The diary of the Clitheroe weaver, John Ward, shows that although he was in contact with his brother on only nine occasions between 1861 and 1864, he felt sure that he could rely upon him for friendship and sympathy and even, it seems, for material assistance.[13]

These kinship ties were threatened both by economic prosperity and by geographical mobility. It is not hard to imagine the disruptive effects of economic prosperity; how a new job, higher pay or a more comfortable home might encourage the better-off members of a family to regard themselves as superior to – or at least as different from – their less successful relatives.[14] Nor is it difficult to envisage the deleterious consequences of geographical mobility; how hard it would be for working people to maintain contact with family members who moved away from the immediate neighbourhood. It is true that the migration of the extended family as a group might strengthen kinship ties but if, as normally happened, it was the nuclear family – or some part of it – that moved, the result was likely to be a weakening of ties with the relatives who were left behind.[15]

Working people were much more mobile than is generally realised. Between 1855 and 1938 almost 12 million people emigrated from England and Wales to countries outside Europe. It was a movement in which miners and skilled workers played a prominent part:

it is known, for example, that skilled workers comprised the largest single group of late nineteenth-century emigrants to the United States of America. During the 1920s 'A Newcastle upon Tyne Migration Committee was formed for the purpose of bringing an agricultural life in the Dominions within the reach of boys from the Tyneside and neighbouring district'. One result, it appears, was that 'Many heartbreaking scenes were recorded on the Newcastle quayside as parents bade goodbye to their children, many of whom they knew they would never see again.'[16]

There was a much larger movement of population within the country as families travelled about in search of work.[17] The mobility of the colliery population is particularly well documented. It is true that, as time went by, it became increasingly uncommon for mining families to move long distances in the search for work. As large pits came to have longer lives, as rail (and then road) communications improved, and as home ownership became more common, so fewer and fewer families cared to face the upheaval of moving home. Yet long-distance migration persisted. Economic depression, the opening of a new coalfield, or the expansion of an old one all continued to uproot large numbers of men. In the early years of the twentieth century, for instance, the Doncaster coalfield drew miners from Durham and South Wales, while South Wales itself attracted nearly 100,000 new workers between 1901 and 1910.[18] Later in the century families left these (now declining) areas for Kent and the East Midlands. The result was that between 1925 and 1938 employment in the tiny Kent coalfield increased three-fold: from 2,044 to 6,641.[19] Such long-distance migration could have the most devastating consequences. The wife of a Kent miner remembers their move from Monmouthshire in 1930: 'I hated Deal. Was I homesick. I started to cry didn't I Ted? I said "Ooh I think I'll go back I don't like it here." I would've gone back within the hour if they'd been a train coming. . . . We were such a big family, such a close family.'[20]

Short-distance migration was always a great deal more common. Michael Sill has found that in mid-nineteenth-century Durham most migration was 'short range with many of the coalminer heads of households having been born in the contiguous mid-Wear valley section of the Durham coalfield'.[21] Coalowner Joseph Pease told the 1873 Select Committee on the Dearness and Scarcity of Coal that although migration out of the district was rare, internal migration was common with, so he claimed, a quarter of the colliery population constantly on the move.[22] Half a century later short-distance migration provided the bulk of the labour needed for the expansion of the east Nottinghamshire coalfield. Robert Waller has shown, for instance, that most of the men hired at Harworth colliery between 1925 and 1931 had 'last worked in the pits nearest to it'. But as Waller is at pains to point out, the fact that 'the migration was primarily short-distance' does not mean that we should 'underestimate the break involved in moving to Harworth. In a time before many miners possessed motor cars, Harworth was remote enough to be beyond reasonable walking distance of even the nearest pit community.'[23] This emphasis upon the disruptive effects of short-distance migration is well founded: even short-distance migration made co-residence impossible, and reduced sharply the level of emotional and material support that members of the extended family were able to offer to one another.[24]

The mobility of better-off workers was occasioned not just by their need to find work, but by their desire to secure better accommodation.[25] It has been seen that during the inter-war years both council estates and private developments tended to be built on the fringes of urban areas, often at some distance from established centres of working-class population. This made it difficult for members of the extended family to keep in regular contact and maintain their day-to-day pattern of lending, borrowing and visiting.

> For many families visiting the relatives in the former neighbourhood becomes an affair for the week-end or for special occasions. Dressing up is required, everyone is on their best behaviour, stiffness and formality creep in, enjoyment escapes away, and the social contacts are subsequently broken.[26]

Yet the extended family displayed a considerable resilience. Even council tenants managed to maintain surprisingly close ties with their relatives – and not just at weddings, christenings, funerals and other rites of passage. An investigation carried out on an Oxford council estate during the early 1950s revealed that nearly a third of all householders continued to meet regularly with their relatives from other parts of the city.[27] In fact the historian of the Dagenham estate goes so far as to claim that 'Local extended families, which had such a central place in the older districts, have grown up in almost identical form' in the new neighbourhood.[28]

Nor did the decline of the coal and cotton industries do much, it seems, to weaken existing ties of kinship. It is true that family employment began to disappear from the textile districts. But kinship ties continued to manifest themselves in many other ways. Orphaned children were cared for by members of the extended family – indeed, some children lived with relatives even when both their parents were alive.[29] But even when relatives did not live together under the same roof, they continued to play a major part in one another's lives: in the 1920s, recalls the daughter of a Lancashire weaver, 'grandmothers were very important . . . more so than what they are now'.[30]

The solidarities of mining families proved similarly – and at times notoriously – resilient. In 'traditional' mining settlements like those in west Yorkshire, most early twentieth-century families 'were related by marriage', claims Jim Bullock; 'and often cousin married cousin. This happened twice in my own family, for my eldest brother married a cousin, and so did my sister next but one to me.'[31] Even after the Second World War miners' wives in Featherstone were said to be living mostly 'within easy reach of kinsfolk and old childhood friends of their own generation'.

> This gives at least greater scope for social contacts from day to day than . . . the working-class wife on a new estate in the larger towns. These contacts with neighbours and relatives form the foremost part of the . . . . mother's extra-familial life. . . . Besides her neighbours the typical housewife . . . sees a good deal of her kinsfolk. Among the older-established families the visiting of relatives is a well-developed institution. At week-ends, visits will be exchanged and many wives see one or another of their kinsfolk every day.[32]

It remains difficult to know whether or not to agree with Michael Anderson about the calculative basis of the kin relationship. But it is easy enough to agree with him about the resilience of the relationship among the better off. For whatever the basis of the kin relationship, and however powerful the barriers to its survival, the solidarities of the extended family did prove remarkably powerful. 'Whatever may or may not have happened to the extended family since the second world war . . . it remained of the greatest importance as a provider of social services, social contacts, and to a lesser degree financial assistance in working-class life in the period 1890–1940.'[33]

The working-class neighbourhood was, like the extended family, well established among better-off workers by the beginning of the period. Indeed, kinship and neighbourliness tended to be mutually reinforcing. In mid-nineteenth-century Lancashire, explains Patrick Joyce, 'it was kin relationships that supplied the kernel of neighbourhood community identification'.[34] But once again it is the work of Michael Anderson that proves especially illuminating. He provides several examples of neighbours ('some of whom were also undoubtedly kin') proffering generous assistance at times of domestic crisis. He cites the case of weaver's wife Nancy Beswick who, together with her husband, brought home a sick neighbour, fed him, took his wife to the Poor Law overseers, and helped the stricken family in many other ways. He cites an 1849 report in the *Morning Chronicle*:

> In most cases the doors of the houses stand hospitably open, and younger children cluster over the thresholds and swarm out upon the pavement. . . . Every evening after mill hours these streets . . . present a scene of considerable quiet enjoyment. The people all appear to be on the best of terms with each other, and laugh and gossip from window to window, and door to door. The women, in particular, are fond of sitting in groups upon their thresholds, sewing and knitting; the children sprawl about beside them, and there is the amount of sweethearting going forward which is naturally to be looked for under such circumstances.[35]

Such neighbourliness needed to be of considerable resilience if it was to withstand the strains to which it was subjected: the persistence of population mobility; the growth of prosperity; the emergence of the privatised family; and the expansion, followed by the contraction, of the great nineteenth-century staple industries. It is not surprising then that working-class neighbourliness proved more vulnerable than kinship to the economic and social changes that took place towards the end of the century.

The solidarities of the neighbourhood tended, still more than the ties of kinship, to break down whenever there was a significant level of population mobility. Neighbours, after all, were less likely than relatives to keep in touch with a family that moved away from the immediate area.[36] The solidarities of the neighbourhood tended to break down too whenever its members began to attain higher and/or more regular incomes. Indeed, it was only the relatively well off who could afford – and only those aspiring to respectability who would wish – to distance themselves from the support systems of the neighbourhoods in which they lived. 'There can be little doubt', concludes Elizabeth Roberts, 'that increasing affluence . . . helped to weaken old neighbourhood ties.'[37]

The solidarities of the neighbourhood broke down most visibly on the council estates that were built in the years following the First World War. Living on an estate tended to impede the development of any form of neighbourhood consciousness. The estates were new and incoming families had few relatives to ease their integration into the neighbourhood and its ways. Often, indeed, the newcomers did not remain for very long: 5 per cent of Bristol tenants, 10 per cent of those at Watling, and as many as 17 per cent of those in Dagenham moved on every year.[38]

Nor did the design of the estates do much to encourage feelings of neighbourliness. The low density of the housing and the inadequate provision of public amenities made it difficult for tenants to get to know one another. It was the policy of the Bristol council to discourage the opening of licensed premises – in fact for several years the city's estates were also short of shops, libraries, churches, cinemas and community centres. 'One Anglican Church, one cinema and one public-house for more than 12,000 residents', it was pointed out, 'represents less than a bare minimum of amenity.'[39] Dagenham was little better served. In 1932 the huge estate had just five pubs and there remained 'a complete absence . . . of the "front parlour" shop and the "general shop just round the corner" '.[40] The consequences were predictable: 'One reason people have so little to do with neighbours is the absence of places to meet them.'[41]

Yet working-class neighbourliness did not break down in any simple or unambiguous fashion. Council tenants sometimes became very friendly with their immediate, next-door neighbours – but only, it seems, as a means of compensating for the lack of contact with those living further afield. In Oxford, it was explained 'the greater degree of acceptance of next-door neighbours in the housing estate should be looked at in conjunction with the frequent expressions of distaste for "the people at the end of the road" . . . ':

> For most families the surrounding neighbourhood, apart from the two or three families met face to face, was considered an unfriendly place, even a place where people hostile to some of the things you cherished might be living. In face of such an attitude a strengthening of relations within the family and a cautious exchange of gossip between immediate neighbours might be expected to take place.[42]

Textile and mining families managed still more successfully to maintain the ties of neighbourhood throughout the difficult inter-war years. Nor perhaps is this so surprising for, as has been seen already, it was prosperity rather than poverty that posed the most serious challenge to the survival of working-class neighbourliness. 'I worked with cotton' until 'eventually all the mills closed down', recalls Rochdale spinner Jimmy Buckley. But 'All our neighbours were very good. Everybody knew each other and everybody was friendly'.[43] Coalminer W. H. Davies recalls 'the neighbourliness and togetherness that prevailed in the mining valleys' of South Wales. When Davies was born in 1903, his mother was 'so ill that she was not expected to survive the confinement. . . . Nothing helped her more in her fight for survival than the kindness of neighbours, behaviour so typical of mining communities in those days.'[44] Such coalfield neighbourliness was not destroyed by the mounting pressures of the inter-war period. The authors of *Coal is our Life* lay great emphasis upon the part that neighbourhood ties continued to play in the lives of miners' wives in Featherstone. 'Every day a woman will receive a visit from one or other of the neighbours, or she will make such a visit herself. The usual practice, in fact, is for a group of three or four to gather over cups of tea and "have five" (i.e. five minutes, which can be stretched indefinitely).'[45]

Nonetheless, it seems clear that neighbourliness did prove more susceptible than kinship to the economic and social changes of the late nineteenth and twentieth centuries. Neighbours, it seemed, were always likely to prove less reliable than relatives. 'In point of services,' conclude Young and Willmott, 'neighbours do not make up for kin.'[46]

The working-class community was, like neighbourliness and the extended family, already well established among better-off workers by the middle of the nineteenth century. But like neighbourliness, the ties of community proved vulnerable to the economic and social improvements that took place towards the end of the century.

The emergence of clearly defined communities of relatively well-paid workers has been explained in a number of ways:

by the strength of their kinship and neighbourhood ties; by their geographical isolation; and by the stability and/or the homogeneity of their underlying economic and social structures.[47] Each explanation has its adherents and each, no doubt, has its merits. But any monocausal interpretation needs to be approached with considerable scepticism. Communities come into being, it seems, where a number of factors reinforce one another: where the economic and social structure is relatively homogeneous, 'where families have lived and worked in the same area for a long time, and where neighbours are also kin'.[48]

Whatever the precise balance of forces conducive to the emergence of community consciousness, there is no doubt that by the middle of the nineteenth century certain groups of workers and their families were displaying an identifiable 'communality of interest'. For the most part, these communities were occupationally based: the silk weavers of Spitalfields; the watchmakers of Clerkenwell; the textile workers of Lancashire and Yorkshire; and the miners of the Yorkshire, Scotland, Durham and Northumberland coalfields. The strength of the miners' community feeling is well known: 'During the first half of the century', explains Professor Church 'the objective differences between the patterns and hazards of miners' working lives and their modes of living compared with other occupational groups were sufficient to have produced an environment, varying in the degree of uniqueness, which virtually imposed shared experiences of a kind which produced the phenomenon sometimes described as "community".'[49] The cotton workers' sense of community emerged somewhat later. Patrick Joyce argues that it was only with 'the advent of a measure of prosperity after mid-century, and of population stability and residential continuity . . . that the full extension of community beyond kin . . . developed very rapidly'.[50]

The solidarities of these communities did not survive intact for very long. They were undermined both by a growth in the instability and heterogeneity of their social and economic structures and by a decline in the kinship and neighbourhood ties to which these changes gave rise. The solidarities of textile communities seem to have been particularly short-lived. Even Patrick Joyce admits that 'Population movement beyond mid-century continued to disrupt the stability within which the sense of community could cohere.'[51] Nor were mining settlements the stable, homogeneous communities of popular imagination. There was a constant, and in some coalfields an increasing, movement of men in and out of the industry. It is true that by the end of the century a growing number of miners were reluctant to keep moving house and chose instead to commute to and from work. But this, too, could undermine community solidarity – indeed it was said that some South Wales coalowners preferred to employ commuter-miners because their eagerness to catch their bus or train at the end of the shift made them a particularly difficult group for the unions to organise. And of course even the most stable settlement contained its own internal tensions: there was a sharp division between the hewer and the oncost worker, a wide gap between the young man at the height of his earning power and the old man seeing out his days on the surface. Snobbery, recalls one South Wales miner, was 'exactly as we find it today. . . . The woman who lived in the main road would not admit even a nodding acquaintance with an equally respectable person living in a side street.'[52]

If mining settlements sometimes lacked the stability and homogeneity within which community solidarities could flourish, it is scarcely surprising that such ties were slow to develop on council estates or among those employed in the so-called 'new' industries. It was hard to maintain unity at Cowley during the Pressed Steel strike of 1934, and Arthur Exell found it difficult to organise a tenants' group on the private Florence Park estate: 'The problem was how to form a committee as we did not know each other very well.'[53] But it was on the new council estates that the weakness of community consciousness – like the decline of kinship and neighbourliness – was to prove most noticeable. It could be seen on the Knowle and Bedminster estates outside Bristol: during the late 1930s the majority of new houses were let to ex-slum-dwellers with the result that it became 'very difficult to secure co-operation between the different classes of tenants and to achieve a sense of unity'.[54] This absence of community feeling was common, it seems, to almost all council developments. The Watling estate, concluded Ruth Durant in 1939, 'is not much more than a huge hotel without a roof; the constant turnover of its population is the greatest single handicap to its developing into a community'.[55]

Certain limited generalisation is now possible. It is clear that the ties of the better off to the community were somewhat weaker than those to the neighbourhood, and much less strong than those to the extended family. It is clear in fact that in the high-wage sectors of the economy the solidarities of both community and neighbourhood were markedly less secure than has commonly been supposed.

However, it would be misleading to generalise about kinship, neighbourhood and community on the basis of our knowledge of developments in the high-wage sectors of the economy. For the fact is that the family ties, neighbourliness and community feeling that remain so cherished in the popular memory did survive relatively unscathed. But they did so not in the high-wage but in the low-wage sectors of the economy. Nor is this so surprising; for if it is true that prosperity tended to undermine the ties of kinship, neighbourhood and community, it can come as no great surprise to find that poverty was likely to sustain them.

Poverty facilitated and encouraged the maintenance of kin

relationships because it discouraged family members from moving too far from the parental home. This is not to say that the poor were necessarily immobile; often indeed it was their poverty that forced them to move home. Domestic servants and farm labourers both travelled surprisingly long distances in the search for work. The agricultural depression of the 1880s led to a surge of overseas emigration; it has been found, for example, that in rural counties such as Cornwall and Gloucestershire 'long-term economic distress was responsible for a high degree of occupational and geographical mobility. . . . Eventually, and possibly as a last resort, persons suffering as a result of economic dislocations emigrated.'[56]

But when farm labourers moved home, it was less likely to be to the New World than to the next village. A study of demographic change in north Cardiganshire during the third quarter of the nineteenth century shows that although fewer than half the agricultural labourers remained in their parish of birth, 'the greater part of the migration was restricted to a "local" area of about eight miles radius'.[57] The community studies carried out during the 1950s confirm that even at this late date migration had not dislodged the extended family from its place in rural society. Indeed, these studies reveal how common it still was for relatives to live near one another. Alwyn Rees found that in one mid-Wales village two-thirds of all households had a close relative living elsewhere within the parish[58]; W. M. Williams discovered that in the Cumberland village of Gosforth, 'Just over half the occupiers and their wives . . . have "family relationships" with at least one other household in the parish, and many "families" extend over six or more households.'[59]

The urban poor were much more mobile than agricultural labourers – and more mobile too than most other sections of the working class.[60] But they too tended to move only short distances: '. . . in the main,' concludes David Englander, 'the migrations of the casual poor were circular and confined to a narrow radius.'[61] Michael Anderson shows that in one area of Preston only 14 per cent of men (and 19 per cent of women) were living in the same house in 1861 as they had been in 1851. But he shows too that 'almost 40% were found in the same house or within 200 yards of the house that they had occupied ten years earlier' and that probably 'another 10–20% were living within less than half a mile'.[62] The situation changed remarkably little during the following hundred years. In their celebrated study of mid-twentieth-century Bethnal Green, Michael Young and Peter Willmott revealed that 53 per cent of their sample had been born in the borough; and that of the remainder, more than half had been residents for at least 15 years. They discovered in fact that two-thirds of the borough's population still lived within two or three miles of their parents.[63] Richard Hoggart underlines the point.

> Unless he gets a council-house, a working-class man is likely to live in his local area, perhaps even in the house he 'got the keys for' the night before his wedding, all his life. He has little cause to move if he is a general labourer. . . . He may have a cousin who teaches, married a girl in Nottingham and settled there; he may have a brother who met a girl in Scotland during the war and brought her down here. But by and large the family live near and have 'always' lived near: each Christmas Day they all go to tea at Grandma's.[64]

The immobility of the poor, and the survival of the extended family, were occasioned by the same combination of factors in both countryside and town. Of crucial, and continuing, importance was the dependence of the poor upon the facilities and services provided by their immediate locality; they relied heavily upon local labour markets, upon the extended family and, as will be seen later, upon neighbourhood-based systems of support. Their dependence upon local labour markets was inimical to even relatively short-distance mobility; any attempt to move away from the family and neighbourhood was constrained not just by the nature of seasonal and casual work but by ignorance about employment opportunities elsewhere. Gareth Stedman Jones explains the dilemma:

> . . . the casual labourer, if married, found himself trapped in a vicious circle. For casual labour virtually necessitated family work in order to attain a bearable level of subsistence. But on the other hand family work, which was normally of an unskilled kind, redoubled the immobility of the casual labourer. For the uncertain gamble of obtaining more regular work elsewhere entailed not only risking his own livelihood but also that of his wife.[65]

The immobility of the poor, and the importance that they attached to their kinship ties, were reinforced (in what becomes almost a circular argument) by the very resilience of the extended family. The poor worked hard – and successfully – to maintain the solidarities of kinship. Relatives saw each other as often as they could, with mothers and daughters in particular keeping in regular and close touch. In mid-twentieth-century Bethnal Green, discovered Young and Willmott, wives saw their mothers an average of three times a week. The mother, they concluded, was still 'the head and centre of the extended family'.[66]

Relatives helped out whenever they could. They would 'speak for' one another: a father would approach the foreman about getting his son a job; a mother would talk to the landlord about obtaining a relative the tenancy of a nearby house.[67] Relatives would offer each other all sorts of other assistance. 'Blood ties', concluded Williams of rural Gosforth, remained 'stronger than considerations inspired by social class. . . . Co-operation between relatives in major and minor matters of everyday life is continuous . . . and is emphasised in such crisis situations as serious illness.'[68] It was the same in urban areas.

In the vast majority of cases, concludes Elizabeth Roberts from her study of Barrow, Preston and Lancaster, 'kin living within easy (and cheap) travelling distance invariably offered a wide range of help in a wide variety of situations'.[69] Willmott and Young wax almost lyrical about the role played by the extended family in a poor area such as Bethnal Green: 'Money apart, Bethnal Green could almost have been designed expressly for aged parents, so well is it suited to their needs, providing them with company, care, and, at least if they are mothers, a place of eminence in the family.'[70]

It is perfectly clear then that in both countryside and town the poor continued to rely heavily upon the emotional and material support provided by their relatives. Nor was this all; for alongside the extended family, and intimately connected to it, there survived a powerful sense of working-class neighbourliness.

Of course poverty did not foster neighbourliness in any inevitable or straightforward fashion.[71] Poverty could exacerbate, as well as diminish, the tensions of neighbourhood life. When Robert Roberts recalled the Salford slum in which he was brought up in the early years of the twentieth century, he remarked that

> some sociologists have been apt to write fondly about the cosy
> gregariousness of the old slum dwellers. Their picture, I think, has
> been overdrawn. Close propinquity, together with cultural poverty, led
> as much to enmity as it did to friendship. There could be much personal
> unhappiness and fear of one neighbour by another, especially if a bullying
> woman was a member of a large family group in the district.[72]

Roberts is right. Sometimes poverty (or the fear of poverty) made it difficult even to contemplate helping the neighbours. Sometimes poverty (and the fear of poverty) encouraged neighbours to prey upon one another. Certainly poverty was one of the fundamental causes of the quarrelling and violence that remained endemic in so many poor neighbourhoods. In all events, it would be a mistake to believe that 'the poor did not steal from the poor' and to derive from this appealing adage unrealistic notions about the neighbourliness of working-class life.[73]

Nonetheless there seems little doubt that poor neighbourhoods, with their overcrowded housing, their immobile inhabitants and their close ties of kinship, did tend to promote, rather than retard, a spirit of neighbourliness. In fact the greater the poverty, the stronger the neighbourliness that was likely to develop.[74] In poor districts neighbours, like relatives, provided one another with a wide range of emotional and material support. The neighbourliness of late nineteenth- and early twentieth-century rural life is celebrated in a number of well-known agricultural autobiographies.[75] Indeed, even after the Second World War neighbours in Gosforth saw no need to lock their back doors at night, went into one other's houses without knocking, and fed each other's children several times a week.[76]

Neighbourhood-based systems of support were most fully developed, it seems, among the urban poor. It has been claimed that in Victorian and Edwardian London, for example, 'Neighbourhood proximity created intimate ties of working-class mutual dependence and complex forms of social life and group morality organised largely through women.'[77] These ties of mutual dependence never really disappeared. Women continued to provide one another with advice on everything from how to cook a cheap meal to where to go for a safe abortion. A Burnley woman remembers that between the wars 'everybody' knew how to get rid of an unwanted pregnancy: 'Neighbours, neighbours, yes, neighbours. . . . You would never have to mention her name or tell or anything but – of course everybody knew.'[78] Neighbours called upon each other's specialist skills. There was 'a hierarchy of specialisation in any group of streets', recalls Richard Hoggart. 'This man is known to be something of a "scholar" and has a bound set of encyclopedias which he will always gladly refer to when asked; another is a good "penman" and very helpful at filling in forms; another is particularly "good with his hands", in wood or metal or as a general repairer; this woman is expert at fine needlework and will be called in on special occasions.'[79]

Neighbours, like relatives, helped each other to cope with every type of domestic crisis. It was seen in Chapter 2 that it was common to organise a whip-round for an injured neighbour, to buy a drink for the man without work, or to cook a meal for the family whose mother was incapacitated. It was common too for women to help each other with the day-to-day burden of child care. In nineteenth- and early twentieth-century London, claims Ellen Ross, 'Neighbours and indeed neighbourhoods functioned as auxiliary parents.' Ross cites the experience of George Sims who visited a very poor south London neighbourhood during the 1880s. He met a woman living in a 'wretched room' with six children, two of whom were 'only staying' until their own mother was released from prison for assaulting a policeman. The woman was looking after the two extra children, she explained, because it was 'only neighbourly-like'. Ross is also ab ɔ to provide a certain amount of much-needed statistical evidence: a survey carried out in the early years of the new century revealed that as many as 30 per cent of working mothers left their young children in the care of neighbours.[80] Even such limited statistical precision is difficult to obtain for later in the century. But this does not mean that there is any reason to doubt the continuing importance of the material and emotional security provided by neighbours in poor working-class districts. 'Home may be private,' explains Richard Hoggart,

> but the front door opens out of the living-room on to the street,
> and when you go down the one step or use it as a seat on a warm
> evening you become part of the life of the neighbourhood . . . to the
> insider, these are small worlds, each as homogeneous and well-defined

as a village. . . . They know it, as do all its inhabitants, in intimate detail – automatically slipping up a snicket here or through a shared lavatory block there; they know it as a group of tribal areas.[81]

The density and resilience of these neighbourhood ties did much to ensure the survival of community solidarities. For just as kinship helped to link the nuclear family to its neighbourhood, so very often did neighbourliness lay the foundations of community life.[82] The attachment of rural workers to their communities has become well nigh legendary. E. H. Hunt cites the case of the Suffolk farm worker John Edmunds who left his parish of birth just once, to take some corn to Wickham Market six miles away. Safely back at home, he lit up his pipe and was heard to say, 'Thank God I'm back in good owd England.'[83] There is other, less anecdotal evidence. P. J. Perry concludes from his pioneering investigation of working-class marriage in 27 west Dorset parishes between 1837 and 1936 that the lives of the rural poor long remained community orientated. He concedes that 'the percentage of intra-parochial marriages fell from more than 50 per cent to just over 30 per cent during this period, most markedly in the last 30 years as the financial situation of the countryman sharply improved and rural bus services became established and extensive'. But as he is at pains to point out, 'it must equally be remembered that, as late as 1927–36, three-quarters of all working-class marriages were to a distance of less than 12 miles; the impact of the motor car, and of general and considerable working-class affluence, are apparently post-war developments'.[84]

It is not always appreciated that in urban areas, too, the poor continued to display a considerable degree of community consciousness. It is true that unemployment, poverty, mobility and kinship could all be destructive of community life. 'Don't let them fool you with all this stuff about what a great community it was. You'd have eight or ten families in a street, and they'd all be related somehow, but there might be another family, just as big. There'd be a lot of feuding going on. You'd have friendly neighbours so long as you were in with the family; otherwise things could be pretty rough.'[85] But even those factors seemingly most destructive of community life sometimes proved surprisingly supportive of it. So although population mobility normally disrupted community consciousness, Scottish, Welsh and Irish immigrants to England all developed their own particular forms of community coherence[86]; and although community coherence usually (and most obviously) centred around friendship and co-operation, it could also feed upon gossip, rumour, dissension and violence. As Jerry White points out, it would be wrong to assume that the violence of a street such as Campbell Bunk was necessarily destructive of community consciousness. Indeed: 'At one level it actively reinforced the feeling of proud exclusivity, that Campbell Road set higher standards of toughness than elsewhere. . . . Violence helped bolster the image of an identifiable community for the benefit of outsiders.'[87]

Nonetheless the survival of identifiable communities depended essentially upon the resilience of kinship and neighbourhood ties. In mid-nineteenth-century Preston, explains Michael Anderson, 'The sense of community . . . was probably reinforced by the fact that neighbours, workmates, co-villagers, friends and even fellow church members, would usually have been the same people, so that the attractions and solidarity which developed in one relationship would reinforce the others and make it that much more difficult to break community norms, since so many different kinds of satisfactions might all have been foregone at the same time.'[88] In mid-twentieth-century Bethnal Green, confirm Young and Willmott, relatives remained 'a vital means of connecting people with their community'. Indeed: 'Far from the family excluding ties to outsiders, it acts as an important means of promoting them. . . . The kindred are, if we understand their function aright, a bridge between the individual and the community.'[89]

If the community consciousness of the poor derived essentially from the twin pillars of kinship and neighbourhood, it manifested itself in any number of different forms: in sporting activities, in special interest groups and, most strikingly of all, in street life and in community-based systems of mutual support.[90] The streets provided the largest and most accessible forum for the communal life of the poor. It was in the streets that members of the community came together to talk and play, to work and shop, and to observe (and sometimes resist) the incursions of intruders such as school board visitors, rent collectors and police officers.[91] Historians have tried to use the hostility shown towards these outsiders as a measure of community identity. Clearly this is a somewhat hazardous procedure: responses were complex and/or ambivalent, and could be influenced as much by personal, family or class concerns as by considerations of a community nature. Yet the attempt is well worth making. It shows that for most of the nineteenth century the poor were intensely hostile to the police, and suggests that this hostility resulted in large measure from resentment at what was regarded as unwarranted, extraneous interference in the life of the community. Unfortunately the procedure takes us little further; for although it shows that the hostility of the poor abated very considerably towards the end of the century, it does not reveal whether this was due to declining community solidarity, to more sensitive policing methods or, perhaps, to broader economic and social changes.[92]

Fortunately there are other guides to levels of community solidarity, and of these the most useful are the community-based systems of mutual support. According to Jerry White, 'one factor binding together the community of Campbell Bunk in the 1920s and 1930s was poverty and the collective servicing of needs which poverty inspired'.[93] This collective servicing depended not just upon the informal help of relatives and neighbours, but upon the more formal assistance provided by the publicans, landlords, pawnbrokers, moneylenders and corner-shopkeepers who were active in the community. 'With some poor folk,' explains Robert Roberts, 'to be "taken on at a tick shop" indicated a solid foot at last in the door of establishment. A tick book, honoured each week, became an emblem of integrity and a bulwark against hard times.'[94] The credit relationships built up within the community were of immense value and could be re-established elsewhere only with considerable difficulty, and only over a long, and hazardous, period of time.

The resilience of community consciousness can no longer be in doubt. The social investigators of the 1950s were astonished at the vitality of the community life they uncovered among the poor. 'Since family life is so embracing in Bethnal Green,' remarked Young and Willmott, 'one might perhaps expect it would be all-embracing. The attachment to relatives would then be at the expense of attachment to others. But in practice this is not what seems to happen.' What they discovered was a powerful community consciousness, 'a village in the middle of London, an orderly community based on family and neighbourhood groupings'.[95]

The lack of interest shown by some historians in working-class kinship, neighbourhood and community has been both unnecessary and unfortunate. It has been unnecessary because, as must be clear by now, a good deal of reasonably confident generalisation can certainly be made. It can be shown that in the high-wage sectors of the economy the ties of kinship, neighbourhood and community were well established by the middle of the nineteenth century, but that all three (and particularly neighbourhood and community) proved somewhat vulnerable to the social and economic changes that took place towards the end of the century. It can also be shown that in the low-wage sectors of the economy the ties of community, neighbourhood and kinship, far from disintegrating, survived remarkably unscathed until well beyond the end of the period. The lack of interest in these issues has been unfortunate because, as will be seen in the two subsequent chapters, they are of considerable, and far-reaching, significance. It will be shown that an understanding of kinship, neighbourhood and community is central to the analysis of working-class values and attitudes, and crucial to any examination of working-class participation (and non-participation) in the various branches of the labour movement.

NOTES AND REFERENCES

1. **J. M. Mogey,** *Family and Neighbourhood: Two Studies in Oxford,* Oxford U.P., 1956; **W. M. Williams,** *The Sociology of an English Village: Gosforth,* Routledge & Kegan Paul, 1956; **P. Willmott,** *The Evolution of a Community: A Study of Dagenham after Forty Years,* Routledge & Kegan Paul, 1963; **M. Young** and **P. Willmott,** *Family and Kinship in East London,* Penguin, 1957.

2. **A. Macfarlane,** 'History, Anthropology and the Study of Communities', *Social History,* 5, 1977, p. 631; **M. Stacey,** 'The Myth of Community Studies', *British Journal of Sociology,* 20, 1969, p. 134; **R. E. Pahl,** *Patterns of Urban Life,* Longman, 1970, p. 100; **R. Dennis,** *English Industrial Cities of the Nineteenth Century: A Social Geography,* Cambridge U.P., 1984, p. 285.

3. **E. Roberts,** *A Woman's Place: An Oral History of Working-Class Women 1890–1940,* Blackwell, 1984, p. 169.

4. **S. Meacham,** *A Life Apart: The English Working Class 1890–1914,* Thames & Hudson, 1977, p. 45. Also pp. 52–3, 55, 59.

5. *Ibid.,* p. 55. Also Williams, *Gosforth,* p. 141; **E. J. Hobsbawm,** 'The Nineteenth-Century London Labour Market', in **E. J. Hobsbawm** (ed.), *Worlds of Labour: Further Studies in the History of Labour,* Weidenfeld & Nicolson, 1984, p. 138.

6. Pahl, *Urban Life,* pp. 115, 119.

7. **J. Rule,** *The Labouring Classes in Early Industrial England 1750–1850,* Longman, 1986, p. 155.

8. **R. Durant,** *Watling: A Survey of Social Life on a New Housing Estate,* King, 1939; **T. Young,** *Becontree and Dagenham: A Report made for the Pilgrim Trust by Terence Young,* Becontree Social Survey Committee, 1934, p. 88; **R. Frankenberg,** *Communities in Britain: Social Life in Town and Country,* Penguin, 1966, p. 15; **C. G. Pooley,** 'The Residential Segregation of Migrant Communities in Mid-Victorian Liverpool', *Transactions of the Institute of British Geographers,* 2, 1977, p. 367.

9. Dennis, *Industrial Cities,* pp. 270, 285. Also Durant, *Watling,* pp. ix, 15.

10. *Ibid.,* pp. 10, 248, 250, 264, 268, 284, 286.

11. **R. Colls,** *The Pitmen of the Northern Coalfield: Work, Culture, and Protest, 1790–1850,* Manchester U.P., 1987, p. 259. Also **J. Benson,** *British Coalminers in the Nineteenth Century: A Social History,* Gill & Macmillan, 1980, p. 141; **R. Church,** *The History of the British Coal Industry, Volume 3 1830–1913: Victorian Pre-eminence,* Clarendon Press, 1986, pp. 230–1.

12. **M. Anderson,** *Family Structure in Nineteenth Century Lancashire,* Cambridge U.P., 1971, pp. 56, 61.

13. **J. Ward,** 'The Diary of John Ward of Clitheroe, Weaver, 1860–1864', *Transactions of the Historic Society of Lancashire and Cheshire,* 105, 1953; Anderson, *Family structure,* pp. 63, 119; Rule, *Labouring Classes,* p. 175; **P. Joyce,** *Work, Society and Politics: The Culture of the Factory in Later Victorian England,* Methuen, 1982, p. 55.

14. Roberts, *Woman's Place,* p. 182.

15. *Ibid.*, p. 169; Young and Willmott, *Family and Kinship*, pp. 170–85.

16. **J. Davison,** *Northumberland Miners 1919–1939,* NUM (Northumberland Area), 1973, p. 97. Also **N. L. Tranter,** *Population and Society 1750–1850: Contrasts in Population Growth,* Longman, 1985, p. 38; **C. J. Erickson,** 'Who were the English and Scots Immigrants to the United States in the Late Nineteenth Century', in **D. V. Glass** and **R. Revelle** (eds), *Population and Social Change,* Arnold, 1972, p. 352; **D. Baines,** *Migration in a Mature Economy: Emigration and Internal Migration in England and Wales, 1861–1901,* Cambridge U.P., 1985.

17. Tranter, *Population and Society,* pp. 37, 144; Roberts, *Woman's Place,* pp. 181–3; **R. Lawton,** 'Peopling the Past', *Transactions of the Institute of British Geographers,* 12, 1987, p. 266.

18. Benson, *British Coalminers,* pp. 126–7.

19. **R. E. Goffee,** 'The Butty System and the Kent Coalfield', *Bulletin of the Society for the Study of Labour History,* 34, 1977, p. 42; **P. J. Waller,** *The Dukeries Transformed: The Social and Political Development of a Twentieth-Century Coalfield,* Clarendon Press, 1983, pp. 34–5.

20. **G. Harkell,** 'The Migration of Mining Families to the Kent Coalfield between the Wars', *Oral History,* 6, 1978, p. 106.

21. **M. Sill,** 'Mid-Nineteenth Century Labour Mobility: The Case of the Coal-Miners of Hetton-le-Hole, Co. Durham', *Local Population Studies,* 22, 1979, p. 50.

22. Church, *Coal Industry,* p. 219.

23. Waller, *Dukeries,* p. 34.

24. Roberts, *Woman's Place,* p. 181.

25. For the nineteenth century, see **D. Englander,** *Landlord and Tenant in Urban Britain 1838–1918,* Clarendon Press, 1983, pp. 8–9.

26. Mogey, *Family,* p. 83. Also Young and Willmott, *Family and Kinship,* p. 131; Willmott, *Evolution of a Community,* p. 109.

27. Mogey, *Family,* p. 81.

28. Willmott, *Evolution of a Community,* p. 109.

29. Roberts, *Woman's Place,* pp. 172–4; Anderson, *Family Structure,* p. 115. Cf. Manchester Polytechnic, Manchester Studies, Transcript 247, Tape 1, p. 8.

30. Manchester Studies, Transcript 628, p. 3. Also Roberts, *Woman's Place,* pp. 177–8, 180.

31. **J. Bullock,** *Bowers Row: Recollections of a Mining Village,* E P Publishing, 1976, p. 57.

32. **N. Dennis, F. Henriques** and **C. Slaughter,** *Coal is Our Life: An Analysis of a Yorkshire Mining Community,* Tavistock, 1956, pp. 203–4.

33. Roberts, *Woman's Place,* pp. 182–3.

34. Joyce, *Work,* p. 105.

35. Anderson, *Family Structure,* p. 104. Also p. 147.

36. Harkell, 'Migration', p. 108.

37. Roberts, *Woman's Place,* p. 198. Also p. 197; **E. Ross,** ' "Not the Sort that Would Sit on the Doorstep": Respectability in Pre-World War I London Neighbourhoods', *International Labor and Working Class History,* 27, 1985, p. 52; Avon County Reference Library, Bristol People's Oral History Project, Transcript R007, p. 26.

38. Mogey, *Family,* p. 85; Durant, *Watling,* p. 16; Willmott, *Evolution of a Community,* p. 20; **R. Jevons** and **J. Madge,** *Housing Estates:*

A Study of Bristol Corporation Policy and Practice between the Wars, University of Bristol, 1946, p. 64.

39. Jevons and Madge, *Housing Estates*, p. 83. Also p. 91; **M.D. Summerbell,** 'Bristol's Housing Policy 1919–1930', M.Sc. (Econ), University of Bristol, 1980, pp. 192, 206.

40. Young, *Becontree and Dagenham*, p. 100. Also p. 190.

41. Young and Willmott, *Family and Kinship*, p. 142. Also Meacham, *Life Apart*, pp. 52–3.

42. Mogey, *Family*, p. 153. Also Durant, *Watling*, pp. 21–2, 32–49, 50–1.

43. **M. Gray,** *The Worst of Times: An Oral History of the Great Depression in Britain*, Wildwood House, 1985, pp. 147, 153.

44. **W. H. Davies,** *The Right Place, The Right Time: Memories of Boyhood Days in a Welsh Mining Community*, Christopher Davies, 1972, p. 62. Also p. 66.

45. Dennis, Henriques and Slaughter, *Coal is Our Life*, p. 203.

46. Young and Willmott, *Family and Kinship*, p. 147.

47. For a valuable discussion see Dennis, *Industrial Cities*, pp. 25, 250–1, 264–5, 270.

48. *Ibid.*, p. 250.

49. Church, *Coal Industry*, p. 612. Also pp. 611–15; Colls, *Pitmen*, pp. 11–12, 305–6; Benson, *British Coalminers*, pp. 82–3.

50. Joyce, *Work*, p. 117. Also Dennis, *Industrial Cities*, p. 278.

51. Joyce, *Work*, p. 103. Also **D. Martin,** 'Women Without Work: Textile Weavers in North-East Lancashire 1919–1939', M.A. University of Lancaster, 1985, p. 4.

52. **J. Benson,** 'Coalmining', in **C. Wrigley** (ed.), *A History of British Industrial Relations 1875–1914*, Harvester, 1982, p. 193. Also Benson, *British Coalminers*, pp. 189–91; Bristol, Transcript RO14, p. 10.

53. **A. Exell,** 'Morris Motors in the 1930s. Part II: Politics and Trade Unionism', *History Workshop*, 7, 1979, p. 52. Also **R. C. Whiting,** *The View from Cowley: The Impact of Industrialization upon Oxford*, Clarendon Press, 1983, pp. 92–3.

54. Jevons and Madge, *Housing Estates*, p. 25. Also pp. 68, 78.

55. Durant, *Watling*, p. 119. Also pp. 45–8.

56. **R. Duncan,** 'Case Studies in Emigration: Cornwall, Gloucestershire and New South Wales, 1877–1886', *Economic History Review*, 16, 1963–4, p. 288.

57. **G. J. Lewis,** 'Mobility, Locality and Demographic Change: The Case of North Cardiganshire, 1851–71', *Welsh History Review*, 9, 1979, p. 353.

58. Frankenberg, *Communities*, p. 49.

59. Williams, *Gosforth*, p. 72.

60. **C. G. Pooley,** 'Residential Mobility in the Victorian City', *Transactions of the Institute of British Geographers*, 4, 1979, p. 261.

61. Englander, *Landlord and Tenant*, p. 8. Also Pooley, 'Residential Mobility', p. 272.

62. Anderson, *Family Structure*, pp. 41–2. Also Pooley, 'Residential Mobility', p. 271; **E. Hopkins,** 'The Decline of the Family Work Unit in Black Country Nailing', *International Review of Social History*, 22, 1977, p. 188.

63. Young and Willmott, *Family and Kinship*, pp. 36, 104. Also Mogey, *Family*, p. 81.
64. **R. Hoggart**, *The Uses of Literacy: Aspects of Working-Class Life with Special Reference to Publications and Entertainments*, Penguin, 1958, p. 62.
65. **G. S. Jones**, *Outcast London: A Study in the Relationship between Classes in Victorian Society*, Clarendon Press, 1971, p. 87. Also pp. 81–6; Lewis, 'Mobility', pp. 353–4.
66. Young and Willmott, *Family and Kinship*, pp. 49–61. Also Meacham, *Life Apart*, p. 60; Roberts, *Woman's Place*, pp. 172, 177–8; Mogey, *Family*, p. 81.
67. Young and Willmott, *Family and Kinship*, pp. 41, 94–7, 103; Meacham, *Life Apart*, p. 177.
68. Williams, *Gosforth*, p. 84.
69. Roberts, *Woman's Place*, p. 170.
70. **P. Willmott** and **M. Young**, *Family and Class in a London Suburb*, Routledge & Kegan Paul, 1960, p. 123.
71. Roberts, *Woman's Place*, pp. 188–9; **D. Gittins**, 'Women's Work and Family Size between the Wars', *Oral History*, 5, 1977, p. 97.
72. **R. Roberts**, *The Classic Slum: Salford Life in the First Quarter of the Century*, Penguin, 1971, p. 47.
73. **J. White**, *The Worst Street in North London: Campbell Bunk, Islington, Between the Wars*, Routledge & Kegan Paul, 1986, pp. 97, 100–1; Meacham, *Life Apart*, pp. 50, 52; Pahl, *Urban Life*, p. 119.
74. Meacham, *Life Apart*, pp. 47–8, 51; White, *Worst Street*, p. 72; Roberts, *Woman's Place*, pp. 195, 200; Ross, 'Doorstep', pp. 53–4.
75. E.g. **F. Thompson**, *Lark Rise to Candleford*, Penguin, 1973; **M. Penn**, *Manchester Fourteen Miles*, Caliban Books, 1979.
76. Williams, *Gosforth*, p. 143.
77. Ross, 'Doorstep', p. 54.
78. Gittins, 'Women's Work', p. 89. Also White, *Worst Street*, p. 74.
79. Hoggart, *Literacy*, p. 22.
80. Ross, 'Doorstep', p. 12. Also **C. Forman**, *Industrial Town: Self Portrait of St Helens in the 1920s*, Granada, 1979, p. 142.
81. Hoggart, *Literacy*, pp. 58–60.
82. Anderson, *Family Structure*, p. 103; Meacham, *Life Apart*, p. 47; Young and Willmott, *Family and Kinship*, p. 116; Willmott and Young, *Family and Class*, p. 131.
83. **E. H. Hunt**, *British Labour History 1815–1914*, Weidenfeld & Nicolson, 1981, p. 144.
84. **P. J. Perry**, 'Working-Class Isolation and Mobility in Rural Dorset, 1837–1936: a Study of Marriage Distances', *Transactions of the Institute of British Geographers*, 46, 1969, pp. 138–9.
85. Forman, *Industrial Town*, p. 142. Also Meacham, *Life Apart*, p. 52; Dennis, *Industrial Cities*, p. 265.
86. Pooley, 'Residential Segregation', esp. pp. 375–80.
87. White, *Worst Street*, p. 100. Also Dennis, *Industrial Cities*, p. 286.
88. Anderson, *Family Structure*, p. 103. Also Joyce, *Work*, p. 118.
89. Young and Willmott, *Family and Kinship*, pp. 104, 116.
90. E.g. **T. Mason**, *Association Football and English Society 1863–1915*, Harvester, 1980, p. 235; Dennis, *Industrial Cities*, p. 278.

91. Ross, 'Survival Networks', pp. 17–18; White, *Worst Street,* p. 79; Bristol, Transcript RO56, p. 33; RO58, p. 15.
92. **D. Woods,** 'Community Violence', in **J. Benson** (ed.), *The Working Class in England 1875–1914,* Croom Helm, 1984, pp. 181–2, 184; White, *Worst Street,* pp. 4, 114–15, 121, 161.
93. White, *Worst Street,* p. 4.
94. Roberts, *Classic Slum,* p. 82. Also **M. Tebbutt,** *Making Ends Meet: Pawnbroking and Working-Class Credit*, Leicester U.P. 1983; Stedman Jones, *Outcast London,* pp. 87–8; Hoggart, *Literacy,* pp. 60–1; Englander, *Landlord and Tenant,* p. 259.
95. Willmott and Young, *Family and Class,* p. vii.

Part Three

RESPONSES

Chapter 6

INDIVIDUAL, NATION
AND CLASS

The assessment of ideas and attitudes (or ideology) is probably the most complex task that can be undertaken in this, or any other, investigation of working-class life. Certainly it is a subject that arouses intense – and often acrimonious – differences of opinion. Indeed, Marxists and non-Marxists cannot even agree upon what constitutes ideology: to the non-Marxist, ideology means almost any cluster of ideas and attitudes; to the Marxist, it means only those ideas and attitudes that justify (or conceal) inequality, and so legitimate the existing distribution of wealth and power.[1] Yet neither these conceptual problems, nor the more obvious empirical difficulties, have dissuaded historians from generalising about working-class ideology in the years between 1850 and 1939. Right-wing historians applaud the good sense of working people in accepting the secure position that they enjoyed within a stable, prosperous and increasingly democratic society.[2] Left-wing historians bemoan the failure of working people to recognise, and challenge, the disabilities under which they laboured; they lament the continuing readiness of the British working class to acquiesce in its own subordination.[3]

The current surge of interest in popular culture has produced a number of valuable, and often fascinating, historical studies of working-class ideology. Historians and others interested in popular culture have begun to investigate a bewilderingly wide range of issues: from the jokes that made working people laugh, to the views that they held about sex, morality and the law; from the aspirations that they had for their children, to the part which they believed that luck would play in the realisation of their dreams.[4] There is a space here to consider only a few of these many issues – issues that have been chosen, not just for their intrinsic interest, but because they are inter-related and because they contribute to the wider concerns of the book as a whole. Accordingly attention will be focused upon working people's attitudes towards just three aspects of their lives:

the possibility of individual advance; the country in which they lived; and the class in which they found themselves.

It would be absurd to claim that changes in working-class economic (and social) life led directly and inevitably to changes in working people's attitudes and values. Indeed, both academic inquiry and common-sense observation attest to the crudity of such economic determinism and confirm the complexity of the relationship between material conditions and ideology.[5]

Yet relationship there was. Indeed, it is striking that it was in the high-wage sectors of the economy that attitudes towards individual advance and nationality underwent the most profound changes during the period under review. It will be shown that in these sectors the growth of individualistic and patriotic ideals combined with one another to impede the development of a coherent sense of working-class consciousness.

Attitudes towards the possibility of individual advance changed most radically of all. As time went by, the better off began to find fewer satisfactions either in their work or in their religion, and they turned instead to the material comforts that were becoming more widely available.

There is a great deal of evidence to suggest that well-paid workers were becoming less interested in their work. Women, of course, had rarely derived much satisfaction from paid employment. Even when they worked in high-wage industries, they – along with almost everybody else – tended to regard their employment as temporary and/or as supplementary to a man's.[6] So although it is said that female munition workers blossomed during the First World War, they soon found themselves laid off when peace was restored.[7] The women who remained in factory employment often regarded it with considerable distaste. Recalls a Preston weaver who started work in 1933: 'I hated it. I used to tell my mother and she would tell me there was no other work and I would have to stick it. I said, "I will only stick it because you have asked me to, Mother. I would rather stop at home with you."'[8]

There is evidence that male workers too began to derive less satisfaction from their work.[9] It is true that boys were usually proud to leave school and that miners continued to display a love/hate relationship with their work – it was said that 'more coal was filled by miners in the pubs than they ever fill while they are at the pit.'[10] But there can be little doubt that most other men employed in the industrial sectors of the economy found their work becoming increasingly, and unambiguously, unattractive. It was seen in Chapter 1 that it was in cotton, engineering and the so-called 'new' industries that employers adopted the strategies most characteristic of modern manufacturing; they increased their supervision, extended mechanisation, and imposed more systematic systems of wage payment. It was in these industries, not surprisingly, that employees grew most alienated from their work.[11] The motor industry assembly line became, and has remained, synonymous with such workplace alienation.

> The moment you clocked on in the morning until you finished work in the evening you were not a human being but part of a process, and you were numbered. Company spies invested with a little authority were constantly on the move ready to pounce on you for the slightest misdemeanour. The toilet arrangements were those of the stable; none of the w.c.'s had doors, so that those who were forced to use them did so under possible supervision of a company spy. The whole process was one of, in my opinion, human degradation.[12]

The motor industry assembly line was not typical even of manufacturing industry. But there is no doubt that work was becoming depersonalised throughout much of manufacturing; and there is no doubt that this depersonalisation had far-reaching consequences: it hastened the decline of male, work-centred culture, and it discouraged workers (both male and female) from regarding their work as the means by which they were most likely to fulfil their dreams of individual advance.[13]

Those employed in the high-wage sectors of the economy grew equally disinclined to await the rewards and satisfactions of the afterlife. Indeed, it has been suggested that there was an inverse relationship between industrialisation and organised religion, that the 'degree of involvement in the work processes of modern industrial society correlates negatively with the degree of involvement in church-oriented religion'.[14] But these are difficult issues with which to deal. There were, after all, several forms of religious belief; several ways in which those with a religious belief could 'belong' to a religious organisation; and several functions that a religious organisation could perform for its members other than providing them with access to the supernatural.[15]

It is these non-spiritual factors that form the basis of most of the following discussion. The adoption of this behavioural perspective derives not from any profound theoretical position, but from the simple recognition that religious activity is a great deal easier to study than religious belief. It is clear that in the years before the First World War organised religion played a considerable role in the lives of the skilled and the better off. It is not a role that can be measured simply by examining the statistics of church membership and attendance (it was found that in the 1880s, for instance, attendance in working-class areas did not average more than 20 per cent of the population). Yet as Hugh McLeod points out: 'Christianity and the Christian churches had a pervasive influence in nineteenth-century Britain. . . . Children whose parents seldom attended church still learnt prayers on their mother's knee, heard grace said at meals, sang hymns with their parents, went to Sunday School, and very often to a denominational day school.'[16] It was the local church and chapel that celebrated rites of passage, marked the passing of the seasons, and provided the community with a range both of social services and of leisure facilities. The Church of England played its part; it was said that in the Colne district of Lancashire, for example, 'people would go anywhere where they could get a bit of a do like a lantern lecture or something like that . . . Band of Hope an that sort of thing, an it was somewhere to go, an it was cheap.'[17] But it was the non-conformists who were particularly active in the social, cultural and political life of their communities. In late nineteenth- and early twentieth-century cotton towns and mining villages the methodist chapel provided the centre of many people's social and communal life. 'There was something for almost everyone', recalls a west Yorkshire miner:

> penny readings, love feasts, temperance classes, Pleasant Sunday
> Afternoons, choir practices, 'tonic sola-fa' classes, Sunday school
> classes, concerts, Band of Hope sessions and a whole range of
> fund-raising activities. You could spend every night of the week
> at the chapel and most of the weekend too.[18]

Yet even the chapels did not manage to sustain their role in the years following the First World War. Their decline can be seen most obviously in the figures of membership and attendance. For although the membership of the various methodist denominations increased by just over 8 per cent between 1901 and 1931, the proportion of the adult population that this represented declined by very nearly 26 per cent.[19] The decline of the churches' influence can be seen more vividly in the oral, autobiographical and social survey evidence. When Charles Booth's investigators visited Deptford at the turn of the century, they met artisans and skilled engineers who thanked 'Cobden and Bright and everybody but God for their prosperity'.[20] When Mass Observation investigators visited the semi-suburban London borough of 'Metrop' in 1947, they discovered that no more than 10 per cent of the population attended church on a regular basis – in fact when one man was asked whether he went to church, he replied that he did, 'but when asked for the approximate date of his last attendance could recall no visit since church parade in the 1914–18 War'.[21]

The decline of the churches' social role is clear, the reasons for it less so. But thanks to the efforts of Robert Moore we now understand a good deal about the process whereby the methodist chapels lost their hold over the (Durham coalmining) communities that they served. Before the First World War, explains Moore, 'the chapels provided a wide range of activities which engaged the time and attention of members to the virtual exclusion of all other activities'. But after the war the village communities became 'much more socially differentiated than before. By this we mean that specialised agencies were beginning to form for particular social functions rather than a few institutions (like the chapels) performing many.' It was difficult for the chapels to adapt: 'It seems that once the crucial coincidence of chapel, [trade-union] lodge and Liberal Party was broken, the chapels were isolated from an important network of power and influence. From then the entertainment and educational activities of the chapels ceased to service and sustain the network of institutions but rather operated only to sustain the chapels themselves.'[22]

It is difficult to use membership lists and attendance figures to evaluate (or explain) the changing social role of the churches; but it is more hazardous still to use the evaluation (or explanation) of the churches' social role as the basis on which to assess the extent of religious belief. Nonetheless it does appear that the decline in the social impact of religion was accompanied by a decline in religious belief: 'the advance in material comforts', observes A.J.P. Taylor, 'made men less concerned with pie in the sky'.[23] Yet there remained a pervasive strand of residual belief.

> Metrop people were asked: 'Do you believe there is a God, or there isn't, or haven't you made up your mind?' About two-thirds of men and four-fifths of women said they did believe, or believed more or less. . . . Irrespective of their own religious beliefs, the majority of people in Metrop consider that religion should be taught in schools. Even among those who openly doubt the existence of God, the majority hold this view. Throughout the survey an attitude of 'goodwill' towards the *idea* of religion and religious faith is apparent, frequently in conjunction with a hostile attitude towards the Church, and a personal religious faith of an exceedingly vague and unorthodox kind.[24]

However, the survival of such residual religious belief is not sufficient to invalidate the conclusion that the churches were losing their hold over the spiritual, as well as the social, life of the communities that they served. The evidence, patchy and ambiguous though it may be, makes it clear beyond reasonable doubt that as time went by, fewer and fewer of the better off were prepared to look to, and wait for, the rewards that they were promised in the afterlife.

The better off looked elsewhere for the consolation. They found it, some of them, in the educational aspirations that they had for their children. Believing education to be a possible avenue of long-term economic and social advance, they encouraged their children to attend school regularly, to work hard and to stay on beyond the compulsory school-leaving age (which was ten in 1876, 11 in 1893 and 14 in 1899). John Hurt believes that already in 1870 'parents in working-class industrialised areas valued the greater emphasis that was now placed on preparing the children for the ascertainable needs of a tangible world'.[25] But it is easy to exaggerate. Brian Jackson and Dennis Marsden discovered that even in the late 1940s and early 1950s 'A visit round the homes' of the 'minority of working-class parents whose children successfully complete the grammar school course' shows 'that by and large they come from the most prosperous, house-owning reaches of the working class'.[26]

The majority of the better off found their consolation, not in the education of their children, but in the material benefits of the new consumerism. It can be imagined that many of the economic and social developments discussed in earlier chapters of the book combined together to increase working-class demand for goods and services. It has been seen, for example, that workers in manufacturing (and to a lesser extent in mining) started to enjoy a growing margin of income above that required for mere subsistence, and began to benefit from a more emotionally satisfying family life that tended to foster new needs and expectations. These changes in demand were matched by changes in the capacity of the economy to meet them: food supplies improved, and entrepreneurs in both manufacturing and marketing began to cater seriously for the new working-class consumer.[27]

It is not surprising that attitudes began to change. When real incomes rose, the first priority was to obtain enough food to eat and adequate accommodation in which to live. But once these basic needs had been met, priorities began to alter. The better off wished to enjoy some of the trappings of their new-found, if often insecure, prosperity. They wanted to eat a more varied diet and wear more fashionable clothes; they planned to live in a more comfortable and better furnished home; and they expected to enjoy some at least of the new forms of leisure that were becoming available to those with the money to pay for them.[28]

Fashion assumed a new significance. The extension of factory methods of production to clothing and footwear enabled the new multiple stores (like Hepworths and Freeman Hardy Willis) that were opening in the 1870s and 1880s to sell to the new mass market. 'By the first decade of the twentieth century', concludes W.H. Fraser, 'a proportion of the working class not only had the opportunity of being well clad, but could clothe themselves from an increasing variety and range of items. There was now enough choice for the working-class girl to be able to concern herself with fashion and style and not solely with price.'[29] Indeed, according to J.B. Priestley, one of the most striking features of the 'new post-war England' was to see 'factory girls looking like actresses'.[30]

When they settled down to married life factory girls, like other well-paid workers, began to furnish their homes with visible signs of their affluence: they bought clocks, mirrors and pianos – and then furniture, electrical goods and other products of the new consumer industries.[31] 'We have got more pianos and perambulators,' claimed a south Yorkshire miners' leader in 1873; but, as he went on to explain, the piano was 'a cut above the perambulator'.[32] Once again it was the combination of new methods of production and new forms of retailing that enabled the better off to enjoy their prosperity. But it was the reorganisation of credit facilities that proved of particular importance; for whereas the poor continued to rely upon traditional forms of credit for the purchase of basic necessities, the better off were encouraged to use new forms of credit for the purchase of consumer goods. During the First World War South Wales miner B.L. Coombes and his wife moved into two rented rooms: 'I remember how proud I felt when I saw them furnished for the first time, and realised that all that shining new furniture was ours – even if most of it still had to be paid for.'[33] In fact the use of hire purchase multiplied 20 times between 1918 and 1938, and brought 'a wide range of household goods such as furniture within the reach of sections of the community who could not previously have afforded them'.[34]

The better off also began to turn to new, and often more expensive, forms of leisure.[35] It was seen in Chapter 4 that families in the high-wage sectors of the economy were the first to enjoy the benefits of an annual holiday: the 'seaside holiday habit', it will be recalled, 'had become . . . deeply rooted in the Lancashire textile district by the turn of the century'. Chapter 4 showed too that families in the high-wage sectors were the first to enjoy time together on a day-to-day basis. But this too could be expensive, for it might involve the purchase of a whole range of leisure goods: from pianos and bicycles to newspapers and magazines, and all the other items required for the serious pursuit of a home-based hobby such as gardening or stamp collecting.[36] Moreover, the new pattern of leisure probably involved the husband in a weekly or fortnightly visit to watch a game of professional soccer: Tony Mason is in no doubt that 'as the popularity of the game increased, notably in the north and midlands in the 1880s . . . most watchers were . . . working people and the majority of *them* were . . . skilled workers . . . with relatively high wages and relative security of employment'.[37] In fact Mason's conclusion may be extended far beyond the soccer terraces; for it was the better off who were the first to participate in most of the new forms of leisure that were becoming available to the working class during the final quarter of the nineteenth century.

Gradually, it seems, workers in the high-wage sectors of the economy came to regard themselves as consumers rather than as producers; in fact they came to regard the new consumerism, rather than job satisfaction, religious certainty, or educational achievement, as the most accessible avenue of individual (and family) advance. This new consumerism had something of an anaesthetising effect: wearing their more fashionable clothes, living in their more comfortably furnished homes, and spending their free time in more varied and interesting ways, the new working-class consumer was unlikely perhaps to dwell upon the inequalities that remained at the heart of British society.[38]

Indeed there is a considerable, albeit easily exaggerated, body of evidence to suggest that during this period the better off came to feel a considerable loyalty towards the country in which they lived. It was a loyalty that could take various forms and express itself in various ways: in the dislike or hatred of foreigners; in the veneration of the monarchy; in celebrations like those after the relief of Mafeking; in the membership of uniformed and quasi-military organisations; or, most strikingly of all, in volunteering for military service at times of national emergency.[39]

Wherever they turned, the better off were subjected to a barrage of patriotic (as well as nationalistic and imperialist) propaganda. They heard it at school, Sunday school and church; they read it in their newspapers and library books; and they were likely to meet it again when they visited the music hall or the cinema.[40] A recent study of imperialist propaganda in the cotton districts of Lancashire shows that although Empire Day was not recognised officially until 1916, it was observed eight or nine years earlier by schools in Burnley, Blackburn and Wigan. It was celebrated with particular enthusiasm in Blackburn where, it is said, 'headmasters tended to write more about Empire Day than about any other topic except the school inspector's report or the curriculum'.[41] It is on the basis of this type of evidence that historians such as J.M. MacKenzie conclude that popular imperialism was securely established by the end of the nineteenth century – 'being for the Empire', he claims, 'was surely rather like being against sin'.[42]

It is a plausible argument, but one that is not easy to substantiate. For although it is simple enough to show that both children and adults were subjected to a stream of patriotic propaganda, it is remarkably difficult to find convincing evidence as to its impact.[43] In their attempts to uncover such evidence, historians have turned to three major sources of information: the membership of voluntary, uniformed organisations; the popularity of royal celebrations; and the extent of voluntary enlistment into the armed forces.

The membership of voluntary, uniformed organisations appears to offer one promising indicator. Indeed Hugh Cunningham undertook his study of the Volunteer Movement precisely in order to examine working-class attitudes towards the country in which they lived.[44] At first sight, his analysis appears to provide convincing evidence of 'upper' working-class patriotism. For despite the commitment in time, effort and money that volunteer membership demanded, the movement attracted one-third of late nineteenth- and early twentieth-century men at some time in their lives. Over half the volunteers were working-class, and of these more than half 'seem to have been predominantly from the upper working class'.[45] Yet Cunningham is not convinced that those who joined necessarily did so for patriotic reasons. He cites the colonel of the 3rd Volunteer Battalion of the

Lancashire Fusiliers, whose members were mechanics in the Salford cotton trade: 'The bulk of my men join because they like the show, the dress, and they like the camp. I do not think they join from very high patriotic motives.'[46] The conclusion, believes Cunningham, is inescapable. 'From the point of view of the individual . . . volunteering was primarily a recreation.'[47]

Other scholars have turned to the study of youth organisations such as the Boys' Brigade (which was founded in 1883), the Church Lads' Brigade (1891) and the Boy Scouts (1907). The Scouts (with a membership of 32,000 in 1920, and 422,000 in 1930) was by far the largest and most important[48]; the Scouts, like other uniformed groups, appealed primarily to the sons of skilled workers – 'it was often too expensive a game for the sons of unemployed or unskilled workers to play'.[49] Yet, as with the Volunteer Movement, it is difficult to know what tempted recruits to join and what patriotic (or other) lessons they learned once they were members. Stephen Humphries believes that 'Larking about . . . acted as the major obstacle that frustrated the endeavours of uniformed youth movements . . . to instil order, regularity and patriotic duty into the working-class younger generation.' Indeed 'interviews suggest that sport, the band and the annual camp were the activities that most attracted members and that drilling and military manoeuvres were usually regarded as tiresome concessions to authority, to be avoided wherever possible'.[50]

One or two other scholars have turned to royal occasions and celebrations as a means of measuring working-class patriotism. They have examined popular attitudes towards events such as Queen Victoria's Golden Jubilee (of 1887) and Diamond Jubilee (1897), the coronation (1902) and funeral (1911) of King Edward VII, and the coronation (1911) and Silver Jubilee (1935) of King George V.[51] Yet once again the evidence is difficult to interpret. There is little doubt that working-class participation in such national celebrations derived from a mixture of motives: from patriotic fervour, from local pride and civic duty, and from the simple desire to have a good time.[52] The socialist pioneer Keir Hardie claimed, for example, that the crowds celebrating the Diamond Jubilee of 1897 were enjoying a day's holiday more than they were demonstrating their loyalty to crown and country. 'The cheering millions would be there and cheer just as lustily if the occasion were for the installation of the first president of the British Republic.'[53]

But this is to exaggerate. Elizabeth Hammerton and David Cannadine have shown from their meticulous examination of the Diamond Jubilee in Cambridge that 'there was no hostility to the celebration of the Jubilee per se. . . . To the extent to which there was conflict, it was over *how* to celebrate, not whether to celebrate. In so far as there was disagreement, it took place within the shared assumption that there should, indeed, be a celebration.'[54] Certainly the study of royal celebrations does seem to suggest that there occurred a significant change in popular attitudes some time during the 1870s. It was from this time onwards that the monarchy began to act as a symbol of national unity, and that royal celebrations began to serve as a focus of genuine and widespread patriotic commitment.[55]

However, for many historians the most convincing evidence of working-class patriotism derives neither from these royal celebrations nor from the membership of voluntary organisations, but from the levels of voluntary recruitment to the armed forces that were reached at times of national crisis. These historians assume, not unreasonably, that offering to fight, and perhaps die, for one's country constituted the ultimate test of patriotic loyalty.

It is not surprising, therefore, that working-class volunteering to fight in the Boer War (of 1899–1902) has been seen traditionally as proof of the popularity of patriotism and imperialism in late Victorian and Edwardian Britain. But once again the evidence is far from unambiguous. The American historian Richard Price has been merciless in exposing the inadequacies of arguments based upon such evidence: starting from the paradox that voluntary recruitment grew more popular as the war itself grew more unpopular, he concludes that working-class volunteering was a function, not of popular patriotism, but of poverty and of conditions in the labour market.[56]

The best evidence of working-class patriotism is to be found a few years later, at the outbreak of the First World War. The war, claims A.J.P. Taylor,

> produced a great surge of patriotic enthusiasm; all lesser passions were laid aside. . . . Soon Kitchener's finger pointed balefully from every hoarding: 'Your Country needs YOU.' . . . Kitchener asked for an initial one hundred thousand – 175,000 men volunteered in the single week ending 5 September; 750,000 had enlisted by the end of September. Thereafter the average ran at 125,000 men a month until June 1915 when it slackened off. In all over two and a half million men enlisted before voluntary recruitment came to an end in March 1916.[57]

Workers from the high-wage sectors were well to the fore. A *Times* correspondent reported on the mood of the industrial areas at the end of August 1914:

> The truth of the matter is that the working class through and through is as intensely national as any other class. There is no greater miscalculation of the agitator than that which credits miners and factory workers with a sort of first principle objection to war in any form. In a crisis the economic plea is swept aside by the appeal of patriotism. One would have said that if the doctrine of 'the international brotherhood of the workers' was to make headway anywhere it would be in South Wales. It is abundantly clear to-day that even the miners who hold the doctrine will not allow it to run counter to the ideal of national unity. The miners, in fact, have

silently joined with the organized workers in all other parts of Britain in presenting a united front to the common enemy.[58]

The *Times* correspondent was right. A quarter of a million miners (more than 20 per cent of the workforce) volunteered for military service in the first year of the war; in fact, so serious did the loss of manpower become that in 1916 the government prohibited the enlistment of any more workers from the coal industry.[59] Indeed, it has been argued recently that even wartime disputes, such as the South Wales strike of 1915, can be seen as evidence of the miners' patriotism: 'Though the strike had been called to achieve higher wages, it also entailed the question of patriotic status. In demanding higher wages, the miners, as a group, were also demanding official acknowledgement and reward for their patriotic sacrifices and their unsurpassed contribution to the war effort.'[60]

There is here a good deal of special pleading. Yet it is important not to react too strongly against such exaggerated claims. For although the debate about working-class patriotism is by no means settled, it does seem that by the end of the nineteenth century miners and others in the leading sectors of the economy did feel a considerable, and growing, loyalty towards the country in which they lived.[61] It was a loyalty that had important repercussions: for the fact that loyalty to the nation as a whole was inimical to loyalty towards any particular part of it, meant that the emergence of patriotism (like the growth of individualism) tended to impede the development of working-class consciousness.[62]

Working-class consciousness itself is probably the most complex, and is certainly the most contentious, of all the issues with which the historian of labour has to deal. There are two major difficulties. It is hard to know which evidence will reveal most clearly what working people thought about their own, and other people's, position within society. As E.P. Thompson has pointed out (of an earlier period): 'The same man who touches his forelock to the squire by day – and who goes down to history as an example of deference – may kill his sheep, snare his pheasants or poison his dogs at night.'[63]

It is more difficult still to know which definition of class consciousness the historian of labour is best advised to adopt. For class consciousness could (and can) take so many forms. It was possible for different workers (and indeed for the same worker at different times) to assume a number of contradictory stances: to deny the existence of class; to recognise, and welcome, its existence; to recognise, and accept, its existence; to recognise, and resent, its existence; or to so resent the class system as to seek to overthrow it.[64] One way out of this labyrinth has been provided by the sociologist Michael Mann. Mann distinguishes most helpfully between four tiers of class consciousness: what he calls class identity – 'the definition of oneself as working-class'; class opposition – 'the perception that the capitalist and his agents constitute an enduring opponent to oneself'; class totality – 'the acceptance of the two previous elements as the defining characteristics of *(a)* one's total social situation and *(b)* the whole society in which one lives'; and finally class alternative – 'the conception of an *alternative* society, a goal toward which one moves through the struggle with the opponent'.[65] It is Mann's four-tier model which forms the basis of the discussion that follows.

There is no doubt that during the period covered by this book a growing number of workers in manufacturing and mining came to define themselves as working class. Nor is this surprising for it is agreed by historians of both left and right that there existed (and still exists) an intimate – albeit complex and elusive – relationship between material conditions and class consciousness.[66] It seems almost certain, therefore, that economic and social changes of the sort discussed in this and earlier chapters proved crucial in bringing working people to think of themselves as working class.[67] It was the workers in the high-wage sectors of the economy who had to deal first with the emergence of powerful employers, the growth of the factory system, the establishment of single-industry communities, and the imposition of new and more severe forms of work discipline. These developments tended to be mutually reinforcing; by widening the gap between employers and employed, narrowing the gap between skilled and unskilled, and reducing the opportunities for social mobility, they all served to strengthen the workers' identification of themselves as working class.[68] Standish Meacham cites the case of the turn-of-the century 'Salford factory operative'

> living in a two-up, two-down brick house, one of twelve in a drearily 'respectable' terrace; handing his wife the weekly pay packet and hoping she could make do with it; sending his children to a Board school until they came of age and took their place inside the mill; voting Lib-Lab or Labour, or not bothering to vote at all: that man was conscious of himself as working class. His friends, similarly circumstanced, thought of him, as they thought of themselves, as working class.[69]

Eric Hobsbawm cites the case of the miners' leader Herbert Smith.

> He was probably as close to the average pitman as any leader, even among miners, even in South Yorkshire, has ever been: a slow, hard, reliable man, keener on cricket and Barnsley Football Club whose matches he attended religiously, than on ideas; a man more inclined to ask opponents to step outside than to argue. Herbert Smith advanced steadily from checkweighman to the presidency of the Yorkshire miners and eventually, in the 1920s, the Miners' Federation. In 1897, at the age of thirty-five, he decided to support the ILP. . .
>
> . . . his choice . . . expressed a visceral, a militant and profound class consciousness which found visible expression in his dress. Herbert Smith was famous for his cap. A biography of his has been written under the title

The Man in the Cap. He wore it like a flag. . . .Among the millions of men in caps he was certainly exceptional; but he was exceptional only as a particularly majestic tree in a large forest. There were innumerable others, less prominent, less political, less active, who recognised themselves in his image, and we should recognise them also.'[70]

But the very greatest caution is necessary. For while it is certainly true that more and more workers in the high-wage sectors did begin to identify themselves as working-class, it is also true that a very large number remained slow to display even the most rudimentary sense of class identity. Yet on reflection this is not so surprising; for it has been seen time and again in this book how sharp were the differences (of skill, income, accommodation, fertility, religion, gender, age and so on) that continued to divide working people one from another.

There were divisions between workers within the same high-wage industry – the cotton spinner looked down upon the piecer, the coal hewer upon the surface worker, and the homeowner upon the private tenant. There were divisions between workers from different high-wage industries. The institutional manifestations of these divisions will be discussed in the following chapter; all that need be said for the moment is that an examination of working-class political and trade-union activity offers little comfort to those seeking evidence of inter-industry collaboration, and so of broad working-class identification.

There were divisions between workers from the high-wage and low-wage sectors of the economy. It has been seen that the former tended to be more prosperous, to maintain greater control over their work, to live in more comfortable accommodation, to enjoy better health, to have smaller families and to be less dependent upon the ties of kinship and community. Indeed, it is to such divisions, and the emergence of a 'labour aristocracy' of high-wage earners drawn largely (though not exclusively) from textiles, mining and iron and steel, that Marxist historians have turned in their attempts to explain the lack of 'true' (that is, revolutionary) class consciousness among the workers of Victorian and Edwardian Britain.[71] Certainly it is possible to find examples of the better off, not only distancing themselves from other working-class groups, but identifying themselves specifically as members of the middle class – a classic case of what Marxists call 'false' consciousness. The best evidence comes, it is true, from after the end of the period. But the evidence is startling; it shows that in the 1950s the proportion of manual workers who considered themselves to be middle class ranged from 13 per cent in Dagenham, 23 per cent in Greenwich, and 31 per cent in Hertford, to 48 per cent in Woodford. It was found that in Woodford, for example, many manual workers judged class not by occupation or education but by income and consumption. Of the 170 manual workers (out of a sample of 355) who considered themselves middle-class, 10 per cent believed that they belonged to the lower-middle class, 35 per cent to the middle-middle class, and 3 per cent to the upper-middle class.[72]

With workers in the high-wage sectors failing so often to identify themselves as working-class, it is not surprising that they failed still more conspicuously to attain the higher reaches of Mann's four-tier model of class consciousness. Search as one may, it is difficult to find convincing evidence of the better off perceiving capitalists and their agents as permanent class opponents, let alone defining themselves and their society in class terms, or conceiving of an alternative, non-class-based form of social organisation. For every activist dreaming of the overthrow of capitalism and the establishment of the socialist commonwealth, there must have been hundreds – if not thousands – of the better off saving for a new piano and looking forward to a holiday at the seaside.

Nonetheless, the failure of workers in the high-wage sectors to perceive employers and their agents as permanent class opponents does seem rather puzzling. Certainly it has been argued with some force that working people came to regard the middle class with considerable, and growing, hostility. Proponents of this view point to strike activity, the growth of trade unionism, the emergence of the Labour Party, the formation of the Triple Alliance in 1914, and the calling (though not the calling-off) of the General Strike of 1926.[73] Proponents of this view can also point to the less tangible evidence of individual experience. 'Opposition was a consequence of economic fact', claims Standish Meacham, . . .'as long as even a skilled workman with a large family remained condemned to a graceless life of semi-poverty, there would be consciousness of "them" and "us".'[74]

Like a number of other labour historians, Standish Meacham is somewhat prone to exaggerate the extent to which the better off became locked into class opposition. The fact is that even when working people did regard capitalists and their agents as permanent class opponents, they were as likely to ignore, or joke about, them as they were to engage them in any kind of struggle. 'Rather than chafe at their supposed "betters",' admits Meacham, 'they turned their backs on them.'[75] The 'new' factory worker of the twentieth century was no more threatening: he was 'neither deeply involved with his work-mates nor deeply antagonistic to his employer; on the whole his attitude to both more nearly approximates one of indifference'.[76]

Often, of course, such acquiescence in the inequalities of the class structure was brought about by fear and/or by the demands of earning a living. Work, as F.M.L. Thompson has pointed out, was perhaps 'the supreme instrument of social control'.[77] 'Wage advances', Stephen Marglin has argued, 'were to the capitalist what free samples of heroin are to the pusher: a means of creating dependence'.[78] Yet very often – and more often than is usually admitted by labour historians – such acquiescence was brought about by an adherence to the principles of individualism and a fondness for the security that a hierarchical class structure seemed to provide.[79] The new-found availability of oral evidence makes it possible to recreate more fully than ever before the extent to which employers (though not their agents) were admired rather than envied, and respected rather than reviled. It shows the resilience of such attitudes even in an environment as apparently inhospitable as that provided by the cotton industry in early twentieth-century Lancashire. A worker from Nelson recalls that even in a large 640-loom mill he was able to call the boss by his first name: 'Practically every manufacturer in town was a man that 'ad risen up from the bottom by his own endeavours.'[80] It was the same, we are told, in nearby Accrington: weaver Charles Rogers remembers that 'The boss only lived a few doors away from where we lived you see. In those days the bosses did not live far and wide. The bosses were people who were men who had come from the rank and file of the industry.'[81]

So although it is tempting to stress the class consciousness of workers in the high-wage sectors of the economy, it is a temptation that needs to be resisted. The better off did not always identify themselves as working class; indeed, by the end of the period (or soon after) they were more likely to regard themselves as members of the middle class than as fighters for a new social order. Nonetheless it remains difficult to know precisely why workers in the high-wage sectors did not become more class conscious. But part, at least, of the explanation seems to lie in the changing attitudes that were discussed at the beginning of this chapter; for it appears clear that the growth of individualistic and patriotic values combined together most effectively to impede the development of a fully fledged class consciousness among the better off.

If it is accepted that there existed a relationship between material conditions and ideology, then it is only to be expected that those in the low-wage sectors of the economy should take a different view of the world from those in the high-wage sectors. And indeed they did – though not, perhaps, in quite the way that might be expected. For although individualistic aspirations were slower to emerge in the traditional sectors, and although patriotic loyalties advanced no more quickly, they coalesced still more effectively to impede the development of any real sense of class consciousness.

Attitudes towards the possibility of individual advance changed more quickly than is sometimes supposed. It is true that workers in the traditional sectors neither derived much satisfaction from their work, nor anticipated many rewards in the afterlife, nor set much store by the value of education. But they did change their attitude towards the possession of material goods: if the poor remained unable to attain many of the benefits of the new consumerism, this did not prevent them from aspiring towards them – and resenting their inability to obtain them.

Workers in the traditional sectors rarely demonstrated a great deal of commitment to their work. Elizabeth Roberts has found that throughout the period from 1890 to 1940 women in Barrow, Lancaster and Preston 'shared a common attitude to wage-earning work; it was not in itself a good thing, but was undertaken because the family income was perceived to be inadequate without their contribution'.[82] J.M. Mogey found a similar lack of interest when he undertook his study of Oxford in the early 1950s. A labourer in a gas works spoke for many: 'I'm one of those that's so interested in my work that I never notice what's going on around me.'[83] Most workers, both male and female, took this same instrumental view of their work: work had only one purpose, to provide them with the money that they needed in order to live.

But even in the traditional sectors of the economy, some jobs demanded a good deal of initiative, and this encouraged, or at least did nothing to discourage, the maintenance of individualistic attitudes. Industries such as building and dock labouring compelled workers to apply for work each day, to ingratiate themselves with the foreman and, very often, to dovetail together a number of different ways of earning a living.[84] Occupations such as begging, petty crime and penny capitalism did still more to encourage individualistic attitudes. Jerry White explains how such individualism took hold in what was called 'the worst street in North London': the inhabitants' rejection of wage labour 'encouraged a feeling of "looking out for number one". The economic competition between the street earners, competing for pitches and customers; the violent intra-communal conflicts; the strong sense of having to "hold your own" in Campbell Bunk – all contributed to a feeling that one's own interests were, in the last ditch, paramount.'[85]

White's analysis is most convincing; and it is certainly true that the survival of self-employment, and its impact upon popular ideology, needs to be examined more carefully than it has been up to now. But it is also the case that the great majority of workers in the low-wage sectors of the economy were always employed in wage labour, and continued to regard their work as a means less of possible advance than of immediate day-to-day survival.

Nor is there much evidence that those dependent upon the low-wage sectors looked to the rewards and satisfactions of an afterlife. But the complexity of this issue will be recalled from earlier in the chapter; it will be remembered too that there was said to be a negative correlation between 'involvement in the work processes of modern industrial society' and 'involvement in church-oriented religion', and that this appeared to be consistent with the declining religious enthusiasm of those in the high-wage sectors of the economy. But this does not mean that those least involved in modern industry – those, that is, from the low-wage sectors – were therefore more likely to partake in the life of the Church. What appears to have happened is that those furthest removed from the work processes of modern industrial society were least likely to involve themselves in organised religion, yet also most likely to retain some vestiges of spiritual belief.

It does seem that those employed in the traditional sectors of the economy were unlikely to attend either church or chapel.[86] It is true that nineteenth-century agricultural communities often sustained reasonable levels of religious attendance. But those who remained on the land in the twentieth century became as reluctant as other workers to worship on a Sunday. 'If the Lark Rise people had been asked their religion,' explains Flora Thompson, 'the answer of nine out of ten would have been "Church of England", for practically all of them were christened, married, and buried as such.' But as she goes on to emphasise, 'in adult life, few went to church between the baptisms of their offspring'.[87]

Even fewer of the poor went to church in urban areas. 'It was not that the Church of God had lost the great towns,' explained Bishop Winnington-Ingram in 1896, 'it never had them.'[88] The religious census of 1851 revealed, and later newspaper censuses confirmed, that the poor rarely attended church. The census carried out by the *Daily News* in 1902–3 showed that whereas in the upper-working-class areas of London just over 16 per cent of the adult population attended divine service, in the poor districts of the capital the figure sunk to well below 12 per cent.[89] Hugh McLeod has taken 'as representative of three sections of [London] society at the beginning of the twentieth century a Hampstead barrister, a Lewisham clerk and a Bethnal Green costermonger'. His conclusion is that 'the first would be likely to spend some part of an average week attending church services, probably Anglican; in the case of the second, it would be harder to predict, but if he did attend church it would probably be Nonconformist; in the case of the third it would be most unlikely that he would attend any sort of church'.[90]

That there was a decline in the attendance of the poor there can be no doubt. But whether this decline was caused by, or even associated with, a decline in religious belief is (once again) very difficult to determine. For even when the poor did attend church, they often did so for non-spiritual reasons. Gareth Stedman Jones reports that in some parts of late nineteenth-century London 'poor parishioners were accustomed to attend three or four different churches in order to receive charitable assistance from each'.[91] Hugh McLeod confirms that in Bethnal Green 'the hand to mouth economy of large parts of the local population' meant that 'the church was chiefly seen as a source of material help. "Why, Mrs Jones, you're out early", the caretaker of a . . . school had said on meeting the mother of one of the children on Sunday morning. "Yes, sir. I'm going to church." "Going to church?" "Yes, sir, I've lost my mangle."'[92] By the turn of the century, concluded Charles Booth, 'the quiet poor, if they attend any religious service, are more or less bribed'.[93] The cynicism of the poor seems to be confirmed by much of the available oral evidence. The son of a south Devon agricultural labourer recalls that he used to attend chapel regularly during the 1920s:

> Actually we went 'cos 'twas somewhere to go, a bit of a laugh, like. Prayers used to be automatic, they did, babble, babble, babble, and that was the end of that, like. . . .We was thinking more of whether we was going to get any tea when we got home, that's what we were thinking about.[94]

In fact the spiritual hold of the churches weakened rather less than the decline of church attendance, and the cynicism of many attenders, would lead one to suspect. Often, it seems, the poor retained both a respect for, and some residual belief in, the teachings of the Church. Jeffrey Cox concludes from his study of the south London borough of Lambeth between 1870 and 1930 that although 'the working classes . . . were in a sense "indifferent to the claims of organised religion", they were not irreligious as a class'.[95] Richard Hoggart points to the fact that working people continued to believe in the purposiveness of life, in a life after death, and in Christianity as a system of ethics: '"Ah like fair dealings" may seem an inadequate guide to the cosmos and can be self-righteous, but – said sincerely by a middle-aged man after a hard life – it can represent a considerable triumph over difficult circumstances.'[96]

It is difficult to know to what extent this residual belief remained more important than among other working-class groups. But it is possible to be sure that the survival of such belief does not seriously undermine the view that the Churches were losing even the limited influence that they had once exercised over the lives of the poor.

The poor were less interested than other groups in the opportunities offered by the educational system. Indeed it has been said, and with good reason, that parental indifference tended to increase along with parental poverty.[97] Very often the poor could not afford, and did not wish, to take advantage of the educational facilities that were becoming available. It was not cheap to equip a child properly for school, and it could entail a considerable financial sacrifice to forego the income that a working child could bring into the family. Moreover, many parents did not believe that there was much to be gained from a formal education. 'Don't worry about your education', a bricklayer's wife used to tell her children during the 1930s: '. . .as long as you can read and as long as you can write and as long as you know what's in your wage packet, that's all you need to know, the rest will come to you as you live your life.'[98] Whatever the cause of the poor's lack of involvement in education, the result was the same. Between the 1900s and the 1930s the proportion of children of professional and managerial parents attending grammar schools grew from 37 to 62 per cent – while the proportion of children of semi-skilled and unskilled parents enjoying the benefits of a grammar school education increased from 1 per cent to 10 per cent.[99]

The poor, like the better off, turned to material possessions for the satisfactions that they were unable to obtain elsewhere. But the poor, unlike the better off, were almost bound to be frustrated in their ambitions. The poor were trapped. On the one hand, they lacked the money, the time, the energy and the settled home life that was needed to turn them into true mass-market consumers.[100] On the other hand, they faced great, and growing, pressures to conform to the new consumer ideal. They saw the benefits enjoyed by their better-off neighbours and workmates. They found it hard to resist the blandishments of the door-to-door salesman. In Lark Rise, remembers Flora Thompson, 'a man who kept a small furniture shop in a neighbouring town came round selling his wares on the instalment plan. On his first visit . . . he got no order at all; but on his second one of the women, more daring than the rest, ordered a small wooden washstand and a zinc bath for washing day. Immediately washstands and zinc baths became the rage. None of the women could think how they had managed to exist so long without a washstand in their bedroom.'[101] Moreover, the poor probably found it as difficult as other workers to resist the advertisements carried in the mass media. Richard Hoggart concludes from his examination of what he calls the 'Peg's Paper' type of women's magazine that 'in general, the assumption is that the married women readers are young enough to want to keep up with the unmarried by the use of cosmetics and hair-shampoos'. He goes on to explain how

> Mail-order firms advertise fancy wedge-shoes, nylon underwear for
> – I suppose – the young women, and corsets for the older. For all
> groups, but especially, it appears, the youngish married women with
> little spare money, there are large advertisements (much the biggest
> in these magazines) inviting them to become agents for one of the
> great Clothing or General Credit Clubs which proliferate, chiefly from
> the Manchester area, and usually give their agents two shillings in the
> pound, a fat catalogue, and free notepaper.[102]

The poor made do with modest luxuries. The Carnegie Trust discovered that in the late 1930s, for example, cinema-going was the single most popular activity among the young unemployed, 80 per cent of whom went to the cinema on more than one occasion each week.[103] George Orwell came to a similar conclusion. Following his visit to Wigan and the north of England, he remarked upon the paradox 'that in a decade of unparalleled depression, the consumption of all cheap luxuries has increased'. He elaborated the point in a passage that is worth quoting at some length.

> The two things that have probably made the greatest difference of all are the movies and the mass-production of cheap smart clothes since the war. The youth who leaves school at fourteen and gets a blind-alley job is out of work at twenty, probably for life; but for two pounds ten on the hire-purchase he can buy himself a suit which, for a little while and at a little distance, looks as though it had been tailored in Savile Row. The girl can look like a fashion plate at an even lower price. You may have three halfpence in your pocket and not a prospect in the world, and only the corner of a leaky bedroom to go home to; but in your new clothes you can stand on the street corner, indulging in a private daydream of yourself as Clark Gable or Greta Garbo, which compensates you for a great deal. And even at home there is generally a cup of tea going – a 'nice cup of tea' – and Father, who has been out of work since 1929, is temporarily happy because he has a sure tip for the Cesarewitch .[104]

If the poor were unable to share in all the benefits of the new consumerism, they could participate fully in the pleasures of the new patriotism. Such a claim may come as something of a surprise, for as was seen earlier in the chapter neither the Volunteer Force nor the uniformed youth organisations ever proved very successful in recruiting from the low-wage sectors of the economy. The unskilled never comprised more than a quarter of the recruits to the Volunteer Force[105]; while the Cadets, the Boys' Brigade and the Boy Scouts all found it difficult to attract boys from poorly paid families – it is noticeable in fact that the areas in which scouting most lost its impetus during the 1930s were precisely those parts of the country that had been hit worst by the industrial depression.[106]

The failure of the uniformed organisations to recruit more successfully among the low-paid does not mean that the poor were less patriotic than other sections of the working class. For although the poverty that afflicted so many in the low-wage sectors of the economy discouraged membership of patriotic (and quasi-patriotic) organisations, it also did much to encourage commitment to a locally based form of patriotic loyalty.

It seems that the patriotism of the poor derived, to some extent at least, from social and cultural pressures. The poor, like the better off, were subjected to a growing barrage of nationalistic and imperialistic propaganda. 'Oh ah, you had that drummed into you' at school, recalls the son of a Bristol docker. 'The British Empire and all this that and the other, you know. Britons never shall be slaves . . . and all this that and the other.'[107] But insofar as the poor attended school (as well as Sunday school and music hall) less regularly than other groups, it may be that they were less susceptible than other workers to pressures of this sort.

In all events, the patriotism of the poor seems to have derived chiefly from structural factors: from the parochialism of neighbourhood and community life, and the competitiveness of local labour markets. The former meant that any newcomer tended to be regarded with suspicion; the latter that he or she tended to be regarded as a rival for scarce employment opportunities. 'It was chauvinism,' claims Jerry White, 'an essentially negative response rather than a positive espousal of an idealised English "nation", which under-pinned the . . . patriotism' of the poor.[108] Stephen Humphries explains the process whereby poverty produced chauvinist and racist expressions of patriotic feeling.

> Working-class racism was most deeply felt in inner-city communities and tended to be concentrated in dockland areas in, for example, south-east London, Liverpool and Cardiff, where prolonged periods of socio-economic decline coincided with the arrival and growth of immigrant groups. In such a situation racist views developed to provide an immediate explanation for the deterioration of the local neighbourhood, and there was an increasing tendency, especially among the unskilled and unemployed, to associate the experience of poverty with the severe competition from immigrants for scarce resources such as jobs and housing and with the formation of a reserve army of immigrant labour that was frequently mobilized by employers to undercut wages paid to the white working class.[109]

Whatever the precise balance of cultural and economic forces, there is ample evidence of the poor's patriotism; indeed despite the complexities of interpretation, there remains a good deal of evidence of what Geoffrey Best has termed the 'flag-saluting, foreigner-hating, peer-respecting side of the plebeian mind'.[110] The oral evidence is particularly insistent: the son of a west country labourer remembers his attitude at the beginning of the twentieth century: 'I used to honestly think as a lad that there was no one like the British. If any one asked you if he was a foreigner, that was it, he was a, you thought he was like a load of rubbish.'[111]

It seems clear, for instance, that the poor shared in the growing enjoyment of national and royal occasions, and subscribed enthusiastically to the view that the monarchy constituted a natural, and potent, symbol of national unity. According to the *Times*, the inhabitants of poor areas took particular delight in the celebrations of Mafeking night:

> . . . the news was received with extraordinary enthusiasm in East London and Saturday was generally observed as a holiday. The Whitechapel and Bow Roads were a mass of flags and bunting, while all the tramcars and omnibuses flew flags . . . a large body of working men with flags and banners perambulated the Bow Road, singing patriotic airs, while hundreds of cyclists wearing photographs of

Colonel Baden Powell formed into procession and paraded the principal
thoroughfares of Poplar and Stepney.[112]

According to the *Daily Mirror*, even the residents of Campbell
Bunk turned out in 1935 to celebrate the Silver Jubilee of King
George V. 'Poor But Loyal' proclaimed the makeshift banner that
they draped across the street – an incident so telling that it was used
by the paper to symbolise the patriotic enthusiasm of even the very
poorest neighbourhoods.[113]

It seems clear, too, that the poor were as willing as any other
group of workers to fight in the nation's wars. But whether such
willingness meant they were as patriotic as other groups is a great
deal more difficult to determine. For the evidence suggests that
although the poor volunteered as much as – if not more than – other
working-class groups, they were more likely than other groups to do
so for economic, rather than patriotic, reasons. It was traditional, as
Sir Ian Hamilton pointed out in 1911, that 'each year about three
fifths of the recruits for the Regular Army enlisted between October
and March' when work was short in industries such as agriculture
and building.[114] Indeed it has been seen already that the increasing
willingness of working people to fight in the Boer War was probably
less a measure of their growing patriotism than of their growing poverty. The same relationship between poverty and enlistment may be
discerned during the First World War; for example, Bristol's *Western
Daily Press* observed at the very outbreak of hostilities that 'In this
city, as elsewhere, there are a great many single young fellows who
are not in employment, and who would welcome the chance to be
doing some real service.'[115]

It remains difficult to judge the patriotism of the poor. Historians
as accomplished as Richard Price, Gareth Stedman Jones and Hugh
Cunningham believe that, in the words of the latter, 'in the late
19th century, at any rate, the British working class remained
largely immune from appeals to nationalism. Patriotism proved
incapable of surmounting the barriers of class'.[116] But this is not
a view that can really be sustained. An alternative, and altogether
more persuasive, view has been put forward by Michael Blanch:
he admits that none of the measures of working-class patriotism is,
individually, very satisfactory, but cumulatively, he maintains, 'they
do suggest, in Birmingham at least, that imperialist and nationalist
sentiment obtained real roots in working-class opinion'. He goes on
to explain that: 'The most responsive groups appear to have been
the unskilled. It is reasonable to suggest that a sizable proportion
of working-class boys passed from schools where nationalist values
were taught, to paramilitary youth, to paramilitary adulthood, and
thence into a "peace-time" army, stimulated by just the sorts of
nationalistic appeal we have tried to identify.'[117] It seems then that
in the low-wage sectors of the economy it was less that patriotism

proved incapable of surmounting the barriers of class and more that class proved incapable of surmounting the barriers of patriotism (and individualism).

Certainly it was difficult for any form of working-class consciousness to develop in the low-wage sectors of the economy. And insofar as working-class consciousness did develop, it remained distinctly unthreatening.

Nonetheless it has been argued, and with considerable force, that the consciousness of those in the traditional sectors of the economy did develop during the years between 1850 and 1939. Proponents of this view point to deskilling, the rise of mass unemployment, improvements in communications, the expansion of the mass media, the introduction of compulsory education and the growth of trade unionism. All these changes, they argue, diminished the differences that existed between different groups of workers, and so encouraged workers to regard themselves (and to act together) as members of a single working class. Proponents of this view agree with Richard Johnson that 'It is probable that working-class culture from the 1880s to the 1930s was more homogeneous and distinct than in any period before or after.'[118] They agree with E.H. Hunt that 'the inter-war years, and especially the years from the Armistice to the general strike, probably have a stronger claim to class consciousness of this [less feeble] kind than the pre-war period. By 1920 there were twice the number of unionists there had been in 1914, sectionalism had been further eroded, and class consciousness was being consolidated by economic adversity and exceptionally persistent and widespread industrial unrest.'[119]

It is not difficult to find powerful evidence in support of the view that those in the low-wage sectors of the economy were beginning to identify themselves as working-class. By the turn of the century many children recognised that class differences existed. They knew that their teachers were different: they were educated, they looked respectable, they came to school by tram, and they pronounced their h's.[120] They knew that the rich had money to spare: 'We used to play that we were much better off and some children would have to pretend they were poor and we were rich and we were giving them money.'[121] They realised, when they were a little older, that class differences could intrude even within the family circle: the daughter of a Bristol labourer recalls that her eldest sister 'was the la-de-da 'cos when she got married she stayed in rooms in Clifton'.[122] There is some evidence too that the poor took a growing pride in their working-class identity: when Willmott and Young examined attitudes towards different types of occupation in the Bethnal Green of the 1950s, they discovered that a substantial minority of their sample placed non-manual jobs at the bottom of the scale, and manual jobs at the top.[123]

Nonetheless it is difficult to sustain the argument that those in low-paid employment came generally to think of themselves as members of a single working class. Indeed, if it is accepted that there existed a fundamental, albeit complex, relationship between material conditions and class consciousness, then it is only to be expected that those dependent upon the traditional sectors of the economy should tend to take a particular view of their own, and other people's, place within the class structure. It will be argued here that, on balance, the social and economic circumstances of life in the traditional sectors of the economy conspired all too successfully to impede the development of wider, class-based loyalties.

There were a number of social and cultural barriers. It was seen earlier in this chapter that both individualism and nationalism tended to undermine loyalty to class. It was seen in the previous chapter that although kinship ties underpinned neighbourhood and community groupings, the latter did not form the basis of wider, class-based loyalties; for the same factors that encouraged unity within a particular neighbourhood or community, tended to make for fragmentation and disunity when dispersed over a wider geographical area.[124]

More crucial still were the economic barriers. Poverty, observes Chas Critcher, has 'to be recognised as an impediment to the development of adequate forms of cultural resistance. The daily experience of poverty can be thoroughly debilitating, tending to atomise and intimidate rather than produce collective action.'[125] Certainly low wages and insecurity of employment tended to heighten the worker's sense of dependence upon his (or her) employer. It was a dependence that was found most often in agriculture, retailing and domestic service, in small family enterprises, and in any job 'that brings him [or her] into direct association with his [or her] employer or other middle class influentials and hinders him [or her] from forming strong attachments to workers in a similar market situation to his [or her] own'.[126] In Cambridge, 'the powerful middle-class patronage wielded by residents and visitors meant that "both working men and shopkeepers learned to be obsequious" '.[127] In Norfolk, 'private charity, especially in winter, was the living proof of the "special" nature of rural society. Its giving and receipt created a bond of dependence, its refusal or rejection was a direct threat.'[128]

The result of these economic and social pressures was that many of the unskilled, casually employed and poorly paid failed to think of themselves as members of a single working class. Tensions and ambiguities abounded. There was always somebody to whom to look up, and always somebody on whom to look down. It will be recalled that Hull shop assistant Rita Greendale had a clear view of the status attached to different types of female employment: 'If you were a shop assistant you never wanted to be a factory girl. We used to look down our noses. Although they earned more money, we used to look down our noses at them. But if you had a job in a department store you were really one up and if you worked in an ordinary store and got taken on in a department store you felt as though you'd lifted yourself a little bit.'[129] Some low-paid workers developed their own idiosyncratic views of the class system. A Bristol woman recalls how she used to envisage a tripartite structure: the working-class – those who were dirty; the upper class – those who were nice because they helped the poor; and the middle class – a group that included people like herself, the daughter of a dock labourer.[130]

With a sense of class identity emerging so uncertainly among the low paid, it is scarcely surprising that other forms of consciousness were slower still to develop. There is almost no evidence of the poor attaining any but the lowest tier of Mann's four-tier model of class consciousness. It is hard to find signs either of class totality (the definition of oneself and one's society in class terms) or of class alternative (the conception of an alternative form of social organisation). Nor, more surprisingly, is it easy to find any significant signs of class opposition (the perception of capitalists and their agents as permanent class opponents).

There are some signs it is true. There was, perhaps, some element of class perception in poaching and in certain other forms of petty crime.[131] There was, no doubt, some element of class perception to be found in more routine aspects of day-to-day life. In fact class perception could emanate from the most unlikely quarters. Domestic servants are commonly held to be among the most deferential and compliant of all workers; yet as Pam Taylor has pointed out, there were some who displayed considerable resentment at their subordination. She cites the case of Winifred Foley: sacked from her job as a kitchen maid in a teachers' training college for speaking to one of the students on the stairs, she 'felt a kind of glory' in her rebellion: 'I sang "the Red Flag" as loud as I dared among the clatter of pots and pans and thought of my Dad and all the down-trodden workers of the world and nearly cried.'[132]

But such resentment was unusual, and such rebellion almost unheard of. By the end of the nineteenth century many of those in the low-wage sectors of the economy, like many of those in the high-wage sectors, had come to accept the class-based nature of the society in which they lived. Acquiescence was easier, and seemed more realistic, than struggle. There was, believes David Kynaston, 'a profound fatalism about the intractability of life's condition'.[133] There appeared, concludes Gareth Stedman Jones, 'no political solution to the class system. It was simply a fact of life. . . .As little Tich put it, in his sketch of the gas-meter collector, "My brother's in the gas trade too, you know. In fact he travels on gas. He's a socialist orator."'[134] Robert Roberts recalls how common acquiescence was in the Salford slum in which he grew up.

The class struggle, as manual workers in general knew it, was apolitical and had place entirely within their own society. They looked upon it not in any way as a war against the employers but as a perpetual series of engagements in the battle of life itself. One family might be 'getting on' – two or three children out to work and the dream of early marriage days fulfilled at last. The neighbours noted it as they noted everything, with pleasure or envy. . . .All in all it was a struggle against the fates, and each family fought it out as best it could. Marxist 'ranters' from the Hall who paid fleeting visits to our street insisted that we, the proletariat, stood locked in titanic struggle with some wicked master class. We were battling, they told us (from a vinegar barrel borrowed from our corner shop) to cast off our chains and win a whole world. Most people passed by; a few stood to listen, but not for long: the problems of the 'proletariat', they felt, had little to do with them.[135]

It would be absurd to deny that the study of working-class ideology remains beset by conceptual and empirical difficulties of the most complex kind. Nonetheless certain generalisation does now appear to be possible. It seems clear that throughout the period covered by the book there existed a profound – albeit complex – relationship between material conditions and popular attitudes. The result was that in the high-wage sectors of the economy the growth of individualistic and patriotic ideals combined together to impede the emergence of wider, class-based loyalties. The result was, if anything, more striking still in the low-wage sectors of the economy; for although individualistic aspirations were slower to emerge, and patriotic loyalties advanced no more quickly, they seemed to combine together still more effectively to impede the development of anything approaching a fully fledged sense of class consciousness. It is impossible to escape the conclusion that as the period progressed working people of all kinds came to accept the inevitability of the class-based society in which they lived. It is difficult to escape the conclusion that it was an inevitability which some – if not many – of them came to regard with a certain satisfaction.

NOTES AND REFERENCES

1. **B. Goodwin,** *Using Political Ideas*, Wiley, 1982, pp. 16–28; **D. J. Manning** and **T. J. Robinson,** *The Place of Ideologies in Political Life*, Croom Helm, 1985, pp. 2–3.
2. **G. Best,** *Mid-Victorian Britain 1851–70*, Fontana, 1979, pp. 290–1; **E. H. Hunt,** *British Labour History 1815-1914*, Weidenfeld & Nicolson, 1981, pp. 329–34.

3. **R. J. Morris,** 'Whatever Happened to the British Working Class, 1750–1850', *Bulletin of the Society for the Study of Labour History*, 41, 1980.

4. See, for example, **D. J. V. Jones,** 'The Poacher: A Study in Victorian Crime and Protest', *Historical Journal*, 22, 1979; **R. McKibbin,** 'Working-Class Gambling in Britain 1880–1939', *Past and Present*, 82, 1979; **J. White,** *The Worst Street in North London: Campbell Bunk, Islington, Between the Wars*, Routledge & Kegan Paul, 1986.

5. **E. H. Carr,** *What is History?*, Penguin, 1961, pp. 93–8.

6. **G. Braybon,** *Women Workers in the First World War: The British Experience*, Croom Helm, 1981, pp. 19, 29–31, 87, 103, 109.

7. *Ibid.*, pp. 205–10. Also **A. Marwick,** *Women at War 1914–1918*, Fontana, 1977.

8. **E. Roberts,** *A Woman's Place: An Oral History of Working-Class Women 1890–1940*, Blackwell, 1984, p.62.

9. For London artisans, see **G. S. Jones,** 'Working-Class Culture and Working-Class Politics in London, 1870–1900; Notes on the Remaking of a Working Class', *Journal of Social History*, 7, 1974.

10. **J. Benson,** *British Coalminers in the Nineteenth Century: A Social History*, Gill & Macmillan, 1980, p. 146. Also Manchester Polytechnic, Manchester Studies, Transcript 247, Tape 1, p. 7.

11. **S. Meacham,** *A Life Apart: The English Working Class 1890–1914*, Thames & Hudson, 1977, p. 132; **B. Jackson,** *Working Class Community: Some General Notions Raised by a Series of Studies in Northern England*, Routledge & Kegan Paul, 1968, p. 74.

12. **W. Greenwood,** *How the Other Man Lives*, Labour Book Service, 1937?, pp. 90–1.

13. Jones, 'Working-Class Culture', pp. 486, 492; **J. Stevenson,** *British Society 1914–45*, Penguin, 1984, p. 195.

14. Cited **A. D. Gilbert,** *Religion and Society in Industrial England: Church, Chapel and Social Change, 1740–1914*, Longman, 1976, p. 147.

15. *Ibid.*, pp. 23–4.

16. **H. McLeod,** *Religion and the Working Class in Nineteenth-Century Britain*, Macmillan, 1984, p. 15. Also p. 13.

17. Manchester Studies, Transcript 628, p. 5. Also 679, p. 2; Avon County Reference Library, Bristol People's Oral History Project, Transcript R007, p. 25; Meacham, *Life Apart*, pp. 199–200; McLeod, *Religion*, pp. 61–2.

18. Benson, *British Coalminers*, p. 170. Also **R. Moore,** *Pit-Men, Preachers & Politics: The Effects of Methodism in a Durham Mining Community*, Cambridge U.P., 1974, p. 130; **P. Wild,** 'Recreation in Rochdale, 1900–1940', in **J. Clarke, C. Critcher** and **R. Johnson** (eds), *Working-Class Culture: Studies in History and Theory*, Hutchinson, 1979, p. 143.

19. **R. Currie** and **A. Gilbert,** 'Religion', in **A. H. Hasley** (ed.), *Trends in British Society since 1900: A Guide to the Changing Social Structure of Britain*, Macmillan, 1972, pp. 442–3, 448–9.

20. **G. Crossick,** *An Artisan Elite in Victorian Society: Kentish London 1840–1880*, Croom Helm, 1978, p. 140.

21. **Mass-Observation,** *Puzzled People: A Study in Popular Attitudes to*

Religion, Ethics, Progress and Politics in a London Borough, Gollancz, 1947, p. 50. Also p. 51; **R. C. Whiting,** *The View from Cowley: The Impact of Industrialization upon Oxford, 1918–1939*, Clarendon Press, 1983, p. 90. Cf. **T. Young,** *Becontree and Dagenham: A Report made for the Pilgrim Trust by Terence Young*, Becontree Social Survey Committee, 1934, pp. 182–9

22.   Moore, *Pit-Men*, pp. 215–16.
23.   **A. J. P. Taylor,** *English History 1914–1945*, Penguin, 1975, p. 223.
24.   Mass-Observation, *Puzzled People*, p. 156.
25.   **J. Hurt,** *Education in Evolution: Church, State, Society and Popular Education 1800–1870*, Paladin, 1972, p. 214.
26.   **B. Jackson** and **D. Marsden,** *Education and the Working Class: Some General Themes Raised by a Study of 88 Working-Class Children in a Northern Industrial City*, Penguin, 1966, p. 65. Also **J. E. Floud, A. H. Hasley** and **F. M. Martin,** *Social Class and Educational Opportunity*, Heinemann, 1956, esp. part III.
27.   **W. H. Fraser,** *The Coming of the Mass Market, 1850–1914*, Macmillan, 1981, pp. ix, 5–7.
28.   *Ibid.*
29.   *Ibid.*, p. 61. Also pp. 118–19.
30.   Cited White, *Worst Street*, p. 193.
31.   Fraser, *Mass Market*, pp. 53, 193, 207. Also **D. Gittins,** 'Women's Work and Family Size between the Wars', *Oral History*, 5, 1977, p. 93.
32.   **C. Ehrlich,** *The Piano: A History*, Dent, 1976, p. 97. Also pp. 91, 98.
33.   **B. L. Coombes,** *These Poor Hands: The Autobiography of a Miner Working in South Wales*, Gollancz, 1939, p. 90.
34.   Cited **M. Tebbutt,** *Making Ends Meet: Pawnbroking and Working-Class Credit*, Leicester U.P., 1983, p. 194. Also Fraser, *Mass Market*, pp. 87, 193–207; **P. Johnson,** 'Credit and Thrift and the British Working Class, 1870–1939', in **J. Winter** (ed.), *The Working Class in Modern British History: Essays in Honour of Henry Pelling*, Cambridge U.P., 1983, pp. 152–3.
35.   Stedman Jones, 'Working-Class Culture', pp. 476+; **H. Cunningham,** 'Leisure', in **J. Benson** (ed.), *The Working Class in England 1875–1914*, Croom Helm, 1984, p. 137.
36.   Cunningham, 'Leisure', p. 143; **R. McKibbin,** 'Work and Hobbies in Britain, 1880–1950', in Winter (ed.), *Working Class*.
37.   **T. Mason,** *Association Football and English Society 1863–1915*, Harvester, 1980, p. 157.
38.   **M. J. Daunton,** *House and Home in the Victorian City: Working-Class Housing 1850–1914*, Arnold, 1983, pp. 265–6, 272; **S. G. Jones,** 'State Intervention in Sport and Leisure in Britain between the Wars', *Journal of Contemporary History*, 22, 1987, pp. 169, 176.
39.   **H. Cunningham,** 'The Language of Patriotism, 1750–1914', *History Workshop*, 12, 1981, pp. 23, 28; **P. Bright,** 'Imperialism and Popular Culture in Lancashire, 1875–1920', M.A. University of Lancaster, 1985, p. 5.
40.   See, for example, Cunningham, 'Patriotism', p. 24; **J. Walvin,** *A Child's World: A Social History of English Childhood 1800–1914*, Penguin, 1982, pp. 129–30, 179–80; **P. A. Dunae,** 'Boys' Literature

and the Idea of Empire, 1870–1914', *Victorian Studies*, 24, 1980; **J. M. Goldstrom,** *The Social Content of Education 1808–1870: A Study of the Working Class School Reader in England and Ireland*, Irish U.P., 1972, pp. 26–8.

41. Bright, 'Imperialism', p. 19. Also pp. 14, 17–18, 20–1.
42. **J. M. MacKenzie,** 'Essays in Revision No. 1: Values of Imperialism', *Social History Society Newsletter*, 11, 1986, p. 4.
43. **J. Springhall,** *Youth, Empire and Society: British Youth Movements, 1883–1940*, Croom Helm, 1977, pp. 107–8; Cunningham, 'Patriotism', p. 26.
44. **H. Cunningham,** *The Volunteer Force: A Social and Political History 1859–1908*, Croom Helm, 1975, p. 153.
45. *Ibid.*, p. 25. Also pp. 2–3, 33–5.
46. Cited *ibid.*, pp. 108–9.
47. *Ibid.*, p. 104. Also pp. 122–3.
48. Springhall, *Youth*, p. 63.
49. *Ibid.*, p. 91. Also pp. 25, 39.
50. **S. Humphries,** *Hooligans or Rebels?: An Oral History of Working-Class Childhood 1889–1939*, Blackwell, 1981, p. 134. Also p. 59; **M. Blanch,** 'Imperialism, Nationalism and Organized Youth', in **J. Clarke, C. Critcher** and **R. Johnson** (eds), *Working-Class Culture: Studies in History and Theory*, Hutchinson, 1979, p. 105.
51. **D. Cannadine,** 'The Context, Performance and Meaning of Ritual: The British Monarchy and the "Invention of Tradition", *c.* 1820–1977', in **E. Hobsbawm** and **T. Ranger** (eds), *The Invention of Tradition*, Cambridge U.P., 1983, pp. 134, 142.
52. Bright, 'Imperialism', pp. 41, 43.
53. Cited **E. Hammerton** and **D. Cannadine,** 'Conflict and Consensus on a Ceremonial Occasion: The Diamond Jubilee in Cambridge in 1897', *Historical Journal*, 24, 1981, p. 114.
54. *Ibid.*, p. 143.
55. Cannadine, 'Monarchy', p. 122.
56. **R. Price,** *An Imperial War and the British Working Class: Working-Class Attitudes and Reactions to the Boer War 1899–1902*, Routledge & Kegan Paul, 1972, pp. 207–13, 216.
57. Taylor, *English History*, pp. 46, 48.
58. Cited **J. Stevenson,** *British Society 1914–45*, Penguin, 1984, pp. 54–5. Also **J. M. Osborne,** *The Voluntary Recruiting Movement in Britain, 1914–1916*, Garland, 1982, p. 117.
59. Moore, *Pit-Men*, p. 197; **M. W. Kirby,** *The British Coalmining Industry, 1870–1946: A Political and Economic History*, Macmillan, 1977, p. 30; **N. K. Buxton,** *The Economic Development of the British Coal Industry: From Industrial Revolution to the Present Day*, Batsford, 1978, p. 159.
60. **A. Mór-O'Brien,** 'Patriotism on Trial: The Strike of the South Wales Miners, July 1915', *Welsh History Review*, 12, 1984, p. 95.
61. For the opposite view, see **H. Cunningham,** 'Jingoism and the Working Classes 1877–78', *Bulletin of the Society for the Study of Labour History*, 19, 1969, p. 8.
62. **S. Joshi** and **B. Carter,** 'The Role of Labour in the Creation of

a Racist Britain', *Race & Class*, xxv, 1984, p. 54; Cunningham, 'Jingoism', p. 8.

63. **E. P. Thompson,** 'Patrician Society, Plebeian Culture', *Journal of Social History*, vii, 1974, p. 399.

64. **R. J. Morris,** *Class and Class Consciousness in the Industrial Revolution 1780–1850*, Macmillan, 1979, p. 37; **A. Marwick,** *Class: Image and Reality in Britain, France and the USA since 1930*, Fontana, 1981, p. 19.

65. **M. Mann,** *Consciousness and Action Among the Western Working Class*, Macmillan, 1973, p. 13.

66. **D. Lockwood,** 'Sources of Variation in Working Class Images of Society', *Sociological Review*, 14, 1966.

67. **E. Royle,** *Modern Britain: A Social History 1750–1985*, Arnold, 1987, pp. 97–100; Hunt, *Labour History*, pp. 331–2; Meacham, *Life Apart*, pp. 15–16.

68. Meacham, *Life Apart*, pp. 22–4, 140; Lockwood, 'Sources', pp. 250–2; **D. Kynaston,** *King Labour: The British Working Class, 1850–1914*, Allen & Unwin, 1976, pp. 65–6, 80, 116–7.

69. Meacham, *Life Apart*, p. 14.

70. **E. J. Hobsbawm,** *Worlds of Labour: Further Studies in the History of Labour*, Weidenfeld & Nicolson, 1984, pp. 212–13.

71. For a valuable guide, see **H. F. Moorhouse,** 'The Marxist Theory of the Labour Aristocracy', *Social History*, 3, 1978. For a wider discussion, see **S. Macintyre,** 'British Labour, Marxism and Working Class Apathy in the Nineteen Twenties', *Historical Journal*, 20, 1977.

72. **P. Willmott** and **M. Young,** *Family and Class in a London Suburb*, Routledge & Kegan Paul, 1960, pp. 114–16. Also **A. J. Reid,** 'The Division of Labour and Politics in Britain, 1880–1920', in **W. J. Mommsen** and **H. G. Husung** (eds), *The Development of Trade Unionism in Great Britain and Germany, 1880–1914*, Allen & Unwin, 1985.

73. **M. J. Haynes,** 'Strikes', in Benson (ed.), *Working Class*; Stevenson, *British Society*, p. 195; Hunt, *Labour History*, p. 334.

74. Meacham, *Life Apart*, p. 14.

75. *Ibid.*, p. 20. Also p. 14.

76. Lockwood, 'Sources', p. 257.

77. **F. M. L. Thompson,** 'Social Control in Victorian Britain', *Economic History Review*, xxxiv, 1981, p. 205. Also Marwick, *Class*, p. 37; Meacham, *Life Apart*, p. 132.

78. **S. Marglin,** 'What Do Bosses Do? The Origins and Functions of Capitalist Production', *Review of Radical Political Economy*, 6, 1974, p. 26.

79. Meacham, *Life Apart*, p. 12; Cunningham, 'Patriotism', p. 19; Marwick, *Class*, pp. 37, 204.

80. Manchester Studies, Transcript 708, NP.

81. *Ibid.*, Transcript 630, p. 7. Also Jackson, *Working Class Community*, p. 89; **P. Joyce,** *Work, Society and Politics: The Culture of the Factory in Later Victorian England*, Methuen, 1982.

82. Roberts, *Woman's Place*, p. 136. Also **J. M. Mogey,** *Family and Neighbourhood: Two Studies in Oxford*, Oxford U.P., 1956, p. 131;

E. **Slater** and **M. Woodside,** *Patterns of Marriage: A Study of Marriage Relationships in the Urban Working Classes*, Cassell, 1951, pp. 81–2.

83. Mogey, *Family and Neighbourhood*, p. 130. Also Slater and Woodside, *Patterns of Marriage*, pp. 76–7.
84. **G. S. Jones,** *Outcast London: A Study in the Relationship between Classes in Victorian Society*, Clarendon Press, 1971, pp. 79–81.
85. White, *Worst Street*, p. 103. Also **J. Benson,** *The Penny Capitalists: A Study of Nineteenth-Century Working-Class Entrepreneurs*, Gill & Macmillan, 1983, pp. 138–40.
86. McLeod, *Religion*, pp. 28–9.
87. **F. Thompson,** *Lark Rise to Candleford*, Penguin, 1979, p. 209. Also **R. Currie, A. Gilbert** and **L. Horsley,** *Churches and Churchgoers: Patterns of Church Growth in the British Isles since 1700*, Clarendon Press, 1977, pp. 102–3; **P. Horn,** *Labouring Life in the Victorian Countryside*, Gill & Macmillan, 1976, ch.8; **A. Howkins,** *Poor Labouring Men: Rural Radicalism in Norfolk 1872–1923*, Routledge & Kegan Paul, 1985, pp. 44–5, 62.
88. Cited Kynaston, *King Labour*, p. 81.
89. *Ibid.*, p. 81.
90. **H. McLeod,** *Class and Religion in the Late Victorian City*, Croom Helm, 1974, pp. 28–9.
91. Jones, *Outcast London*, p. 273. Also **R. Samuel,** *East End Underworld: Chapters in the Life of Arthur Harding*, Routledge & Kegan Paul, 1981, pp. 29–30.
92. Cited McLeod, *Class and Religion*, p. 112.
93. Cited **P. Thompson,** *The Edwardians: The Remaking of British Society*, Paladin, 1977, p. 204.
94. Humphries, *Hooligans*, p. 133.
95. **J. Cox,** *The English Churches in a Secular Society: Lambeth, 1870–1930*, Oxford U.P., 1982, p. 104.
96. **R. Hoggart,** *The Uses of Literacy: Aspects of Working-Class Life with Special Reference to Publications and Entertainments*, Penguin, 1957, p. 119.
97. Meacham, *Life Apart*, p. 172.
98. Bristol, Transcript, RO59, p. 4. Also Meacham, *Life Apart*, p. 172; Slater and Woodside, *Patterns of Marriage*, p. 67; Humphries, *Hooligans*, p. 57.
99. Humphries, *Hooligans*, p. 58.
100. E.g. White, *Worst Street*, p. 194.
101. Thompson, *Lark Rise*, p. 125.
102. Hoggart, *Literacy*, pp. 123–4. Also Fraser, *Mass Market*, pp. 111–21, 136–46.
103. Stevenson, *British Society*, p. 397.
104. **G. Orwell,** *The Road to Wigan Pier*, Penguin, 1937, p. 79. Also **J. Blake,** *Memories of Old Poplar*, Stepney Books Publications, 1977, p. 23.
105. Cunningham, *Volunteer Force*, pp. 33, 50.
106. Springhall, *Youth*, p. 63. Also p. 76; Blanch, 'Imperialism', pp. 105–10, 116.

107. Bristol, Transcript R008, p. 7. Also R003, p. 3; Walvin, *Child's World*, pp. 174–9.
108. White, *Worst Street*, p. 105. Also Hoggart, *Literacy*, pp. 110, 203.
109. Humphries, *Hooligans*, pp. 193, 195–6.
110. Cited **E. P. Thompson,** *The Making of the English Working Class*, Penguin, 1968, p. 916.
111. Bristol, Transcript, RO14, p. 2.
112. Stedman Jones, 'Working-Class Culture', pp. 460–1. Cf. Hoggart, *Literacy*, pp. 110+.
113. White, *Worst Street*, caption to plate 2. See also Hoggart, *Literacy*, pp. 108+; Hammerton and Cannadine, 'Diamond Jubilee', p. 143.
114. Osborne, *Voluntary Recruiting*, p. 115.
115. *Ibid.*, p. 116. Cf. **J. Munson** (ed.), *Echoes of the Great War: The Diary of the Reverend Andrew Clark 1914–1919*, Oxford U.P., 1985, esp. pp. 91–2, 99–101.
116. Cunningham, 'Jingoism', pp. 26–7. Also Price, *Imperial War*; Stedman Jones, 'Working-Class Culture'.
117. Blanch, 'Imperialism', pp. 119–20.
118. **R. Johnson,** 'Three Problematics: Elements of a Theory of Working-Class Culture', in **J. Clarke, C. Critcher** and **R. Johnson** (eds), *Working-Class Culture*, p. 235.
119. Hunt, *Labour History*, p. 334. These issues will be discussed more fully in the following chapter
120. Bristol, Transcript R008, p. 9; R011, p. 14.
121. *Ibid.*, R011, p. 68.
122. *Ibid.*, R011, p. 74.
123. Willmott and Young, *Family and Class*, pp. 130–1. Also Hoggart, *Literacy*, pp. 72+.
124. **W. G. Runciman,** *Relative Deprivation and Social Justice: A Study of Attitudes to Social Inequality in Twentieth-Century England*, Routledge & Kegan Paul, 1966, pp. 223–4; Howkins, *Labouring Men*, pp. 34, 60.
125. **C. Critcher,** 'Sociology, Cultural Studies and the Post-War Working Class', in J. Clarke, C. Critcher and R. Johnson (eds), *Working-Class Culture*, p. 26. Also Runciman, *Relative Deprivation*, p. 9.
126. Lockwood, 'Sources', p. 253. Also Kynaston, *King Labour*, p. 21.
127. Hammerton and Cannadine, 'Diamond Jubilee', p. 120.
128. Howkins, *Labouring Men*, p. 35.
129. Cited **B. Davorn,** 'Women and Shopwork 1875–1925 with Special Reference to Ideology, Conditions and Opportunities', M.A. Thames Polytechnic, 1986, pp. 63–4. Also Bristol R003, p. 10.
130. Bristol, Transcript R011, p. 65.
131. **D. J. V. Jones,** 'The Poacher: A Study in Victorian Crime and Protest', *Historical Journal*, 22, 1979, pp. 827–8, 857–8; Humphries, *Hooligans*, pp. 172–3; White, *Worst Street*, pp. 125–8.
132. **P. Taylor,** 'Daughters and Mothers – Maids and Mistresses: Domestic Service between the Wars', in J. Clarke, C. Critcher and R. Johnson (eds), *Working-Class Culture*, pp. 136–7. Also Manchester, Transcript 21, p. 6; Bristol, Transcript R011, p. 69; R014, p.11.
133. Kynaston, *King Labour*, p. 100. Also Meacham, *Life Apart*, p.

199; Marwick, *Class*, p. 204; Runciman, *Relative Deprivation*, p. 65; Hoggart, *Literacy*, p. 22.

134. Jones, 'Working-Class Culture', p. 493.
135. Roberts, *Classic Slum*, p. 28.

Chapter 7

THE LABOUR MOVEMENT

The first generation of British labour historians concentrated their attention upon the struggles of working-class activists in the two major wings of the organised labour movement: they studied the efforts of the trade unions to protect their members' interests at the workplace; and they examined the attempts of the Labour party to advance the working-class cause in the political arena. So well did they succeed that it sometimes appeared that in certain industries and in certain regions the labour movement assumed such a role in people's lives that the history of the movement became virtually synonymous with the history of the working class.[1] Subsequent generations of labour historians have seen the dangers of such an approach: they have been more concerned to stress the failure of the labour movement to touch the lives of ordinary people; and they have been anxious to explain the inability of the activists, however dedicated and talented, to convert the majority of the working class to their way of thinking.[2] It is the aim of this, the final chapter of the book, to bring together the best of these two contrasting historiographical approaches. Its aim is to stand the striker beside the strike-breaker, the trade-union official alongside the working-class conservative, and so to reveal the role that the labour movement really did play in the lives of ordinary people between 1850 and 1939.

The association between leading-sector employment and trade-union membership is well known. In fact workers in cotton, engineering, coal and the 'new' industries turned to trade unionism in such numbers – and with such apparent enthusiasm – that in these industries the unions certainly did come to play a major role in the day-to-day lives of the working population.

The economic, social and cultural developments discussed in earlier chapters tended to produce in these industries just the sort of conditions in which trade unionism was able to grow and flourish. The increasing concentration of ownership and production brought together large groups of relatively well-paid workers who were in a position to join forces to resist the attempts of the employers to extend their authority and control. It has been found that in coalmining, for example, 'The conditions necessary for the growth of stable trade unionism were much the same as those needed for the development of other kinds of self-help activity. The greater the stability of the population, the greater its homogeneity and the higher its earnings, the more likely were firmly established trade unions to emerge.'[3] It has been found that in 'new' industries such as motor manufacturing neither the heterogeneity nor the individualism of the workforce was sufficient to prevent the growth of trade-union membership. The worker tended 'to join and support his trade union for instrumental rather than class solidaristic reasons. Given his materialistic, home-centred aspirations, the trade union for him is less the symbolic expression of an affective attachment to a working class community than a utilitarian association for achieving his private goal of a rising standard of living.'[4]

Large employers in particular began to perceive the benefits that might be derived from the incorporation, rather than the elimination, of the trade unions. They foresaw considerable advantages in dealing with their employees collectively and in encouraging union leaders to assume a certain disciplinary function. In 1860 the Clitheroe cotton master James Garnett could explain that he had 'put an end to the strike at Low Moor, by having Mr Pinder, the Weavers' secretary. He is much better to do business with than the hands themselves because he can calculate.'[5] Fifty years later many more employers 'had concluded that unions could not be permanently ignored. Moreover to defeat unions was becoming increasingly expensive, and a growing number of employers had realised that there might be advantages in recognising unions and dealing with them, especially if they could do this on a collective basis through their employers' organisations.'[6]

These developments had their effect. For although the collection and interpretation of trade-union statistics is by no means straightforward,[7] Table 10 reveals clearly the speed with which membership spread in the three major leading-sector industries of cotton, engineering and coalmining. It shows that already in 1892 one-third of the workforce in these industries was unionised (with almost a third of engineering workers, nearly a quarter of cotton operatives and 60 per cent of coalminers members of a trade union). Thereafter, membership increased very rapidly so that by 1911 two-thirds of the workforce was unionised (with almost half the country's cotton operatives and nearly three-quarters of its coalminers now trade-union members). Membership peaked at the end of the First World War but declined, as might be expected, in the depression of the late 1920s and early 1930s. But it recovered very substantially so that by 1939 nearly half the workforce was unionised (with 36 per cent of engineering workers, 54 per cent of cotton operatives and more than

TABLE 10. Trade-union membership in cotton (flax and man-made fibres), metals and engineering, and coalmining, 1892–1939

Year	Cotton (flax and man-made fibres)		Metals and engineering		Coalmining		Cotton (flax and man-made fibres), metals and engineering, and coalmining	
	No. (000)	Density %	No. (000)	Density %	No. (000)	Density %	No. (000)	Density %
1892	153	24	310	32	308	60	771	36
1901	178	29	374	26	516	69	1,068	38
1911	337	48	497	29	752	74	1,586	66
1921	484	72	1,255	56	996	77	2,735	66
1931	361	52	633	27	573	51	1,567	37
1939	287	54	994	36	741	81	2,022	48

Source: **G. S. Bain** and **R. Price**, *Profiles of Union Growth: A Comparative Statistical Portrait of Eight Countries*, Blackwell, 1980, pp. 45, 50, 51

80 per cent of coalminers once again members of a trade union). Such expansion meant, not surprisingly, that the unions came to assume a growing and, it will be argued, major role in the lives of the working population.

Yet considerable caution is necessary. For the same statistics that were cited above to indicate the growth of union support can also be used to demonstrate the failure of the unions to recruit more successfully. They show that non-unionism was by no means unknown in coalmining, was common among cotton workers, and virtually endemic in the engineering industry. We still know little enough about the causes and consequences of such non-unionism; but we know enough to see how misleading it would be to think that the history of the unions was synonymous with the history of the workforce, let alone with the history of the wider working-class community.

The survival of non-unionism does not seem so surprising when it is realised how many unions declined to admit either female or unskilled workers to membership. Coalmining unions long resisted the admission of non-hewers. It was not until 1894 that the Denbighshire and Flintshire Miners' Federation accepted surface workers; not until 1900 that the West Bromwich and District Miners' Association decided to admit enginemen and surface workers; and not until 1907 that the rules of the Lanarkshire Miners' County Union were 'altered to make it easier for those employed at the pits aboveground to join' the union.[8] Cotton-spinning unions fought tenaciously to exclude the less skilled. According to one historian, the policy that the Amalgamated Association of Operative Cotton Spinners adopted towards the unionisation of the piecers was 'equivocal to the point of fraudulence'. He explains that because the basis of the spinners' favoured position was 'the continued subalternity of the piecers, opening their union to the piecers on the basis of full membership was out of the question. What the Spinners did – in an apparently sporadic and half-hearted way – was to set up "Piecers' Associations" with low dues which could well have been deducted by the spinners from the piecers' pay packets, as it was the custom in many mills for the spinners to pay the piecers directly.'[9] Engineering unions from the Amalgamated Society of Engineers onwards also wrestled with the problem of unskilled workers. It is instructive to examine, for example, the manoeuvring of the Amalgamated Engineering Union when confronted by an unofficial strike at Oxford's Pressed Steel works in 1934. The national leadership intended originally that all the strikers should be allowed to join the union; but the toolroom workers at Pressed Steel were opposed to the admission of semi-skilled production workers – who responded by enlisting instead in the less exclusive Transport and General Workers' Union. Faced with this loss of new members, the national leadership decided finally that it was prepared to admit any worker – whether skilled or unskilled – on condition only that he was *paid* at the skilled rate.[10]

Even when workers did join a union, they did so with varying degrees of enthusiasm – it was possible after all to 'belong' to a trade union in as many ways as it was to a religious organisation. Membership did not necessarily imply commitment, and commitment itself did not necessarily mean that the union came to occupy a prominent place in the life of the individual member.

Some members were not permitted to play a full part in union affairs. Women unionists found themselves discriminated against in all sorts of ways: even when the Kidderminster Power Loom, Carpet Weavers' and Textile Workers' Association finally brought itself to admit women members during the First World War, it decided that the vote of 25 of its new female members should carry the same weight as that of just one of its existing male members.[11] Many members, of course, had no desire to play a full part in union affairs. According to Elizabeth Roberts, many Preston women belonged to the Weavers, Winders and Warpers Association, 'but most appear to have been concerned only with their wages and their domestic affairs; they simply paid their small subscription as a kind of insurance against the day when they might find themselves in dispute with the management'.[12] Male unionists were not necessarily any more enthusiastic. The historian of the Oxford motor industry believes that in the 1920s 'workers in the Morris factories . . . were not much interested in unions';

'apathy', he suggests, was 'a measured reaction' to exaggerated union claims.[13] Lancashire cotton worker Mr Fairhurst recalls that although he joined the Amalgamated Engineering Union in 1920, he took very little part in its affairs: 'I'm only responsible for all these left-wingers taking charge because I never went to a meeting.'[14]

It seems clear then that even in the industrial sectors of the economy many workers did not join a union; and that of those who did, many remained uninterested in, and largely untouched by, their membership. Yet once again considerable caution is necessary. For there can be no doubt that on the whole unions in the industrial sectors of the economy did come to assume a growing, and in some cases a major, role in the lives both of their members and of the wider working population.

This role derived in part from union involvement in industrial disputes. Even those least acquainted with trade-union and labour history may possibly have heard of the engineering lockout of 1897 or the coalmining disputes of 1893, 1912 and 1921; and even if they have not, they will certainly know something about the largest dispute of them all, the General Strike of 1926. In all events, readers of this book should have by now some general appreciation of the incidence and impact of industrial disputes. They will recall from Chapter 2 that in the decades between 1893 and the outbreak of the Second World War industrial disputes resulted in the loss of over 600 million working days – an average of more than 13 million days a year. They will not be surprised to learn that these disputes occurred overwhelmingly in the unionised industrial sectors of the economy. Thus although mining, building and the whole of manufacturing never employed more than 47 per cent of the workforce, textiles, engineering and mining alone accounted for 59 per cent of all strikes, and 75 per cent of all strikers. Table 11 shows that between 1888 and 1939 textiles accounted for 13 per cent of all strikes and 16 per cent of all strikers; metals, engineering and shipbuilding for 22 per cent of all strikes and 12 per cent of all strikers; and mining and quarrying for 24 per cent of all strikes, 75 per cent of all strikers – and 61 per cent of all the working days that were lost.

These disputes had far-reaching consequences. It was seen in Chapter 2, for example, that they created heavy financial and emotional burdens. Moreover, it is often claimed that strike action served to break down workplace, community and class divisions. 'In a number of instances strikes . . . came to serve as the focal point of community resentment', claims M.J. Haynes. 'The Manningham Mills strike, for example, in Bradford in 1890 had much community support but when the town leadership was seen to be siding with the employer it multiplied. "Riots" took place and attendance at meetings rose at one point to an estimated 60,000 as the issues involved broadened beyond the strike itself.'[15] The trouble is that although such claims

TABLE 11. The share of textiles, mining and quarrying, and metals, engineering and shipbuilding in industrial disputes, 1888–1939

Industry	% of strikes	% of strikers	% of strike-days lost
Textiles	13	16	—
Metals, engineering and shipbuilding	22	12	—
Mining and quarrying	24	47	61
Textiles, metals, engineering and shipbuilding, and mining and quarrying	59	75	—

Source: **J. E. Cronin**, *Industrial Conflict in Modern Britain*, Croom Helm, 1979, pp. 206–10; **B. J. McCormick**, *Industrial Relations in the Coal Industry*, Macmillan, 1979, p. 155.

are easy enough to make, they prove remarkably difficult either to substantiate or to repudiate.

Fortunately it is possible to quantify the incidence and immediate consequences of industrial disputes in a strike-prone industry such as coalmining. The 1893 Lockout lasted from July until November, involved 300,000 men and led to the loss of 21 million working days; the 1912 Minimum Wage Strike affected over a million men and resulted in the loss of 30 million working days; the 1921 Lockout affected over a million men and resulted in the loss of 70 million working days; while the seven-month miners' lockout that followed the General Strike of May 1926 also involved more than a million men, but culminated on this occasion in the loss of more than 145 million working days.[16] This statistical evidence has very obvious limitations. But it is not without its value: it indicates the disruption that strikes and lockouts caused in mining communities, and it reinforces the conclusion that the unions' importance in working-class life derived, to some extent at least, from their involvement in industrial disputes.

In fact the unions' importance in working-class life depended less upon their involvement in industrial disputes than upon their participation in more pacific activities that impinged less intermittently upon the well-being of their members. Union leaders in cotton, engineering and coal organised insurance schemes that were designed to cushion subscribers not just against industrial disputes, but against the everyday vicissitudes of working-class life. From the very beginning of the period the engineers and the spinners both attempted to make comprehensive provision. The Amalgamated Society of Engineers paid six types of benefit – strike, funeral, sickness, accident, unemployment and superannuation; the spinners paid seven – accident, funeral, unemployment, 'breakdown and stoppages', 'leaving trade', emigration and superannuation.[17] It was seen in Chapter 2 that the coalmining unions were more active than is generally realised. During the second half of the nineteenth century nearly two-thirds of English mining unions operated some form of accident insurance. A fifth ran widow and orphan funds, two-fifths insured against injury, and a half organised their own funeral schemes: by 1875 a quarter, and by 1890 a third, of all English coalminers were members of a trade-union organised funeral fund. It is not claimed that these funds provided their subscribers with an adequate source of compensation; and it is certainly not intended to be drawn into the debate as to whether the organisation of such schemes enhanced or impeded the unions' capacity to further the 'true' interests of the working population. But what can be maintained – and with some confidence – is that the organisation of schemes designed to insure against the daily hazards of working-class life enabled the unions to play a part in the lives of even the most uncommitted and apathetic of their members.[18]

Still more important was the fact that union leaders in the high-wage sectors of the economy took over from their members the most fundamental of all industrial relations functions – the negotiation of the pay and conditions under which work was to be undertaken. During the 1860s and 1870s the unions pressed for the peaceful settlement of their differences with the employers: by arbitration (whereby a third party was empowered to impose an agreement on the two sides); by conciliation (whereby a third party was empowered to encourage a settlement between the two sides); and by selling-price sliding scales (whereby the two sides selected a base year for both selling prices and wage rates, and agreed that thereafter changes in the latter should be determined by 'a given percentage change for each change' in the former).[19] Conciliation boards were common in cotton spinning; arbitration, and then selling-price sliding scales, predominated in the iron industry; while in coalmining the pattern was for arbitration to be followed by the establishment of sliding scales. The result was that by 1880, for instance, all the coalminers in Wales, and well over half those in England, had their wage rates determined by union-supported selling-price sliding scales.[20]

During the final two decades of the century the success of the unions, along with the establishment of powerful employers' organisations, led to the abandonment of arbitration, conciliation and sliding scales and paved the way for the development of regional and national systems of collective bargaining. There were several major agreements: the Wages Conciliation Board for coalmining and the Brooklands Agreement for cotton spinning (both in 1893), and the so-called Terms of Settlement for engineering (in 1898). It has been said that by 1910 'almost every . . . well-organised industry, except the railways, had evolved its own system of collective bargaining' with stage-by-stage dispute procedures and joint meetings to discuss grievances and complaints.[21]

It was the First World War that gave the unions a seemingly secure place in the British system of industrial relations. The government 'was forced to recognise the crucial role of labour in an industrial economy at war and the consequent need to secure trade union cooperation. The unions [and their leaders] were soon deeply involved in committees, arbitration and advisory roles on a scale which brought them new rights and status.'[22] It is surprising perhaps that union leaders managed to maintain their agreements so successfully in the years that followed the war. But succeed they did. For despite the hostility of the employers and the decline of coal and cotton, there is no doubt that national collective bargaining agreements and centralised disputes procedures were still firmly in place at the end of the 1930s.[23] The establishment, and maintenance, of these agreements was of the greatest importance to trade-union members in cotton, engineering and coal. For whatever the failings of any particular form of collective bargaining, it was during the period covered by this book that the trade-union leader took over from the individual worker the task of negotiating the terms and conditions on which he or she was employed.

Yet however significant the achievements of the national leadership, it was the local branch secretary who came to assume an immediate, and sometimes commanding, role in the life of the individual member. Nor is this so surprising. For the very success of the national leaders brought them fresh difficulties with which to contend. The more that union leaders assumed new functions, the more their decisions had to be administered and interpreted at the local level.[24] The more that union leaders attained national prominence, the more they tended to become isolated from the rank and file of the membership. One South Wales miner wondered 'why our leaders always hold the conferences at pleasant places like Blackpool and Margate? I have heard men ask one another that question many times. Why not hold them in the Rhondda Valley, or at Landore or Llansamlefar or on the Tyneside?' The explanation, he felt, was all too apparent: 'Every year our leaders spend away from the very heart of the industry makes them feel more contented with the conditions of those they represent.'[25]

Consequently the local branch retained a major role in trade-union affairs. 'Trade union club-houses served as employment exchanges,' recalls engineering worker W.F. Watson. 'When a member knew of a vacancy he put a note in the book, and members discussed who should go after it.'[26] Trade-union branches served an important function too in the administration of insurance benefits; it was at the local level that subscriptions were collected, complaints settled and benefits paid. 'The unions were careful in granting a member donation benefit. Searching inquiries were made as to why he was fired and satisfactory reasons had to be given. If the applicant left of his own accord without good reasons, or if he was discharged for misconduct – either against the firm or his fellow members – benefit was refused, and he would not be again entitled until he had been in employment for eight consecutive weeks.'[27]

The trade-union branch was, if anything, more important still in the negotiation of pay and conditions. Indeed, the authority of the local leadership was sometimes enhanced by grassroots dissatisfaction with the various conciliation, arbitration and collective bargaining agreements that were negotiated at regional and national level.[28]

In coalmining the rift between the leadership and the rank and file manifested itself most visibly in South Wales where the syndicalist Unofficial Reform Committee published *The Miners' Next Step* in 1912. Why was it, demanded the Committee, that the leaders of the South Wales Miners' Federation were so well respected by the colliery owners? The explanation, once again, appeared only too obvious: 'Because they have the men – the real power – in the hollow of their hands. They, the leaders, become "gentlemen"; they become MPs, and have considerable social prestige because of this power.'[29] In engineering the rift between the leadership and the rank and file manifested itself most obviously during the First World War when dissatisfaction with central collective bargaining procedures helped lead to the emergence of the first shop stewards' movement, and 'independent rank-and-file organisation at a local level . . . capable of taking action independently of local and national trade union officials'.[30]

Such dissatisfaction did not always work to the advantage of local officials. But even when they found it difficult to benefit from rank-and-file discontent, they could not help but retain close links with the membership. In the cotton industry the local official always had to 'look downwards to his members' desires and reactions. It is not merely that he is appointed and paid by the local society or its committee,' explains H.A. Turner. 'The limits to his assumption of the members' acquiescence are much narrower. If he exceeds them, he will soon be made aware of the fact by complaining members' visits to his office and by reports of union collectors or mill representatives.'[31] In the coalmining industry the responsibilities of the branch secretary (and his committee) were well established and wide-ranging. It was their duty to 'negotiate with the owner of the colliery a series of piece rates or "prices" for work done'; to ensure that awards made at regional and national level were applied correctly to each individual price list; and to bargain for additional payments whenever geological conditions changed, new working methods were introduced, or a member was required to undertake a task which was not included in the colliery price list.[32]

Clearly then the association between leading-sector employment and trade-union membership was not quite so unambiguous as it sometimes appears. For the majority of trade unionists in cotton, engineering and coalmining it was the branch secretary (and his committee) rather than the nationally known, but rarely seen, general secretary (and his executive) that came to represent the growing power and influence of the union. It was the branch secretary who, together with his committee, collected subscriptions, paid out benefits, organised social functions, haggled with the management, and administered (and interpreted) regionally and nationally negotiated agreements on pay and conditions.

At first sight the history of working-class politics appears much more straightforward. It purports to tell the story of how the working class acquired the vote, and used it to put its own party, the Labour Party, into power. It explains how the franchise was widened so that whereas in 1867 only about 5 per cent of working people had the vote, by 1929 more than 90 per cent of the adult population were entitled to participate in local and parliamentary elections. It explains that in the early years of the period those few working people who had the vote could look for the representation of their interests only to the Liberal Party or, from about 1875, to the so-called Lib-Labs. But the situation, we are told, changed dramatically around the turn of the century: in 1893 the Independent Labour Party was formed to secure the election to parliament of independent Labour candidates, and in 1900 the Labour Representation Committee was established in order to forge an alliance between the trade unions and the nascent socialist movement. Finally, in 1906 the modern Labour Party was born: from modest beginnings (with just 29 seats and 6 per cent of the popular vote in 1906), it replaced the Liberals as the Official Opposition in 1922, and went on to form the two minority governments of 1924 and 1929–31 (when it won 288 seats and 37 per cent of the popular vote). 'For the first time in the history of this country, a party led by working men had gained political power and were able to show their ability to shoulder the responsibilities of government.'[33]

Such an interpretation is not without its complications. It can easily lead one to make two major assumptions: that the parliamentary system became genuinely representative; and that the Labour Party managed to embody the fundamental aspirations of the working class. But if these two assumptions are not accepted, the history of working-class politics appears very different: the establishment of the

Labour Party seems less a solution to working people's problems and more a cause of them; the success of the party seems less a glorious triumph, and more an ignoble betrayal. Thus for scholars such as Ralph Miliband the Labour Party, like the trade unions, acted as a 'safety valve' that assisted the ruling class in its 'management of discontent'. By making only moderate demands, the party allowed those in power to demonstrate their reasonableness and so maintain the survival of an iniquitous system.[34]

The argument here is somewhat different. It will be shown that although working people from the high-wage sectors of the economy did come to support the Labour Party in large, and increasing, numbers, the history of the party never became synonymous with the history of working-class politics; in fact, it will be shown that even those who did vote Labour, often did so from a variety of motives and without a great deal of commitment.

It is easy to assume that virtually all working-class political activity benefited the left in general, and the Labour Party in particular. But such an assumption would be quite erroneous. For psephologists are in no doubt that the proportion of the working-class electorate voting Labour has never exceeded two-thirds, and that in every election working-class voters have supported parties from every part of the political spectrum.[35]

Working-class Fascism is not the stuff of which traditional labour history is made. Yet there can be no doubt that during the 1930s there was a certain amount of working-class support for Sir Oswald Mosley's New Party (of 1931–2) and its successor, the British Union of Fascists (1932–40). It is well known that the latter campaigned hard in the declining cotton towns of Lancashire and in the depressed valleys of the South Wales coalfield.[36] It is well known too that both parties enjoyed a good deal of influential support. It was small wonder, explained a Lancashire employer in the *Daily Mail*, 'if people turn their eyes towards Fascism, seeing what Mussolini and Hitler have done for their countries by sweeping away decadent politicians and supplanting them with a rule of national patriotism'.[37]

It is very difficult to discover the extent to which such propaganda succeeded in attracting working-class – or any other – support. It is clear, however, that the two Fascist parties never mustered as many as 40,000 members and never enjoyed a great deal of electoral success – in the general election of 1931 the New Party contested 24 seats, losing them all with a *total* of less than 37,000 votes.[38] It is less clear to what extent the Fascists exerted a wider, albeit less quantifiable appeal. Carworker Arthur Exell gives some indication of what could be achieved by a single committed activist:

There was a Fascist at [Morris] Radiators, a man named Parsons . . . .
A likeable man in many ways but he really dug his toes in regarding

Fascism, he believed in it, he believed in Hitler . . . . Parsons had a good vocabulary, he could put over an argument well. He more or less convinced a lot of them there that it was the Jews were the problem – because they were so mean and tight. They had to get more money and the only way was by becoming bigger capitalists than anyone. He used to say that there was a Jew at the top of any big firm. He would give names. He'd say, 'Look, Cohen's got that place.'[39]

It remains difficult to know how much weight to accord such evidence. But it does seem that insofar as the Fascists enjoyed popular support, it tended to come, not from highly paid, unionised workers, but from the lower middle class or, as will be seen below, from the poorly paid, non-unionised sections of the working class.[40]

Naturally it was much more common for the better-off, like working people generally, to support one of the two respectable alternatives to Labour: the Liberals or the Conservatives. But it is striking that neither labour historians nor political scientists have ever shown as much interest in working-class liberalism as they have in working-class conservatism. The explanation is not far to seek: for whereas the desire to vote Liberal might seem somewhat surprising, the decision to vote Conservative appears to many to be almost wilfully perverse.

Nonetheless it is well known that during the early years of the period many working people displayed a traditional attachment to the Liberals as the party of social reform. The first two working men elected to parliament were the miners' leaders Thomas Burt and Alexander McDonald who, when they took their seats in 1874, did so as Liberals – and were known as Lib-Labs.[41] Martin Pugh is right to stress the fact that such 'traditional allegiances plainly survived the transition to impersonal and unionised industry for many years'. He cites the way in which a candidate was selected for the mining constituency of Barnsley in 1897: 'the "Liberal 300", of whom two-thirds were apparently working men, picked a mine-owner from Durham who comfortably won the election against both a Conservative and a working-class candidate nominated by the Independent Labour Party.'[42] It is well known too that the Liberals struggled – but failed – to retain support in the years that followed the First World War. But far less is known about the background and motivations of those working people who continued to support the Liberals during their years of decline. It is possible, perhaps, that 'traditional allegiances' to the Liberal Party 'survived the transition to impersonal and unionised industry' rather longer than is commonly supposed.[43]

A great deal more effort has been devoted to trying to understand working-class conservatism. For as McKenzie and Silver have pointed out, it is the 'successful recruitment of considerable working-class support' that 'has made possible the long-term domination of British governments since the late nineteenth century by the Conservatives. Indeed, for most of this period, the Conservative Party has secured about half the total of its votes in general elections from the manual working class.' How can it be, they ask, that 'a party whose leadership has been so consistently and exclusively drawn from the upper strata of society and whose most notable ultimate concern has been to resist any basic transformation of the power structure of society' should 'survive indefinitely as the dominant party in the era of the mass electorate'?[44]

The answers suggested range from good luck to good management.[45] Certainly the Conservative Party has enjoyed more than its share of good luck: from the Liberal Party splitting over Home Rule in the late 1880s, to the Labour Party tearing itself to pieces over the National Government in the early 1930s. No doubt, too, the Conservative Party has had at its disposal a highly efficient party machine, and one that has always directed much of its energy towards the working-class electorate. The 'Primrose Tory League' was founded in 1883 in order to promote 'Tory principles – viz the maintenance of religion, of the estates of the realm, and of the Imperial Ascendancy of Great Britain'. The League accepted (and dramatised) class distinctions, and acquired an enormous membership – many of them women and 90 per cent of them, it was said, members of the working class. The League claimed in 1891 to have a million members (a figure equal to over 15 per cent of the electorate); and it maintained in 1910 that it had two million members (a figure equivalent to more than 25 per cent of the entire electorate).[46]

However the major reason for the success of the Conservative Party with workers in the high-wage sectors of the economy was that it knew how to appeal to the individualism, the patriotism and the unaggressive class consciousness which, as was seen in the last chapter, so distinguished their particular view of the world.[47] The party criticised Gladstone's Liberals for their Irish Home Rule bill and all the other 'iniquities' that they had inflicted upon the 'English race'. It demanded of voters during the Boer War: 'Will you be represented in Parliament by Radicals who take the enemy's side?' It attacked the Labour Party for its internationalism: 'If you value your liberty, your freedom, your Empire, and your country, VOTE CONSERVATIVE.'[48] The rhetoric struck a chord, it seems, with well-off workers across the country: and especially in the Lancashire coalfield; in the munition factories of Woolwich, Newcastle and Sheffield; and in the two great conurbations of Liverpool, and Birmingham and the Black Country.[49]

The success of these centre and right-wing parties must not be allowed to obscure the fact that most working-class political activity did indeed benefit the left. But neither must the fact that most working-class political activity benefited the left be allowed to obscure the fact that by no means all left-wing political activity worked to the advantage of the Labour Party.

Throughout the period, but especially during and immediately after the First World War, the better off formed tenants' associations to resist the imposition of higher rents.[50] Their relationship with the Labour Party varied. 'In some areas, most notably Clydeside, tenants' associations were a simple extension of the labour movement. In Birmingham, by contrast, where deep roots within the community were not struck, it was found mutually convenient for tenants to eschew politics and co-operate with labour as independent allies.'[51] But whatever the associations' political affiliation, they never attracted more than a tiny minority of the better off. The Clydebank Association had 1,000 members; the Birmingham & District Tenants' Federation attained a maximum membership of 33,000 in the early 1930s – a time when the city had a population of more than one million.[52] Their achievements were correspondingly modest. Some, like the Stepney Tenants' Defence League, were successful in recovering illegal rent increases; some, like the Birmingham Federation, 'played an important role in local affairs . . . harassment and intimidation were checked, wrongs redressed, law enforced'.[53] But always, it seems, the associations' achievements were limited by the modesty of their ambitions and the paucity of their support.

It was also the better-off who joined socialist groups like the Social Democratic Federation, the Socialist League, the Independent Labour Party and the Communist Party. As the future Labour Party leader, Ramsay MacDonald, explained in 1911: 'It is the skilled artisan, the trade unionist, the member of the friendly society, the young workman who reads and thinks who are the recruits to the army of socialism.'[54] But the recruits came forward in pitifully small numbers – it has been estimated that there were only some 2,000 socialists in the 1880s and no more than 30,000 by the end of the century.[55]

Neither H.M. Hyndman's Social Democratic Federation nor William Morris's Socialist League ever claimed to have as many as 10,000 members.[56] The Independent Labour Party was no larger but it was very active locally in the years before the First World War. In the cotton town of Nelson, for example, it organised a wide range of social and political activities – it ran a socialist Sunday school and attracted speakers of the standing of Keir Hardie and Ramsay MacDonald.[57] But its membership too was tiny (and was drawn very largely from members of the lower middle class). 'It is a sobering thought', points out Martin Pugh, 'that the total paid membership of the ILP in 1900 has been put at 6,000, a figure equivalent to the paid membership of the Primrose League in Bolton at that time!'[58] Nor was the Communist Party much more successful. It is true that the party exercised a considerable influence over certain trade-union and Labour Party activists and that within two years of its foundation in 1920 it had secured the election of two MPs. But its support among ordinary workers was limited in the extreme: for even at its peak, the party did not manage to attain a membership as high as 20,000.[59] Indeed, it remains one of the most striking features of labour movement historiography that so much attention has been lavished upon socialist groups like the Communist Party (and the Social Democratic Federation and the Independent Labour Party) which recruited such a tiny minority even of the politically active working class.

Paradoxically the one socialist organisation that did develop into a genuinely mass movement, did so at the cost of abandoning its original socialist objectives – and at the cost therefore of losing much of its fascination for historians of the labour movement. The co-operative movement was especially strong in the midlands and north of England: by 1881 it had half a million, and by 1914 more than three million, members – nearly twice as many as belonged to the Labour Party.[60] Yet co-operative ownership of the means of production had given way to co-operative retailing; co-operation had become a means not of abolishing, but of working within the existing capitalist economic and social system. In fact it has been said that by the 1920s a large number of the society's members in a city such as Oxford were conservatives or liberals and that 'there was no wish to be integrated into the Labour movement; on the contrary, it was argued that "co-operation is the very antithesis of socialism. . . .Now the co-operative idea is to make every man or woman a capitalist."'[61]

But of course it was the Labour Party that developed into the only true mass working-class political organisation. Yet even here considerable discrimination is required in order to evaluate the role that it played in working-class life as a whole. For although the party proved consistently successful in persuading working people to vote for it, it was far less effective in encouraging them to participate in its day-to-day activities.

Certainly it is difficult to use the figures of Labour Party membership as evidence of widespread working-class support; for even the party's peak individual membership of 447,000 in 1937 represented less than 1.5 per cent of the country's electorate.[62] It is no easier to interpret what little is known about local Labour Party organisation as evidence of deep-rooted popular support. It is true that by 1924 nearly every constituency had its own constituency Labour Party, and that some were large and active. The constituency Labour Party at Westhoughton near Wigan had an individual membership of 3,000, while that at Woolwich had a membership of somewhere between 3,000 and 5,000. In just one month early in 1926 the Aberavon constituency Labour Party organised 31 separate events: it held a social evening, a supper and several dances; it ran numerous meetings; and it arranged speaking engagements for both A.J. Cook and Emanuel Shinwell.[63] But such enthusiasm and commitment were quite exceptional and were found, it seems, only in the coalfields, on the Clyde, and in west Yorkshire. In most constituencies membership was low and activity correspondingly limited. In Oxford, for instance,

> all that the local Labour party could hope for was to keep itself in existence, maintaining interest and raising funds by various activities. In the West ward, where Labour had its only municipal success in the 1920s, this was always rather difficult. Usually only six or seven members turned up at meetings, and there were often not enough when officers had to be elected. . . . In the East ward there was more activity with a Labour orchestra, choir, and dramatic society in addition to the usual fund-raising gambits. But this vitality was deceptive, there always being some doubt as to whether it served any real purpose.[64]

Although the activists could rarely get leading-sector (or many other) workers to join the party, they did persuade large numbers to vote Labour at the polls. Indeed it seems that from 1922 until the end of the period two-thirds of the working-class electorate voted consistently for the Labour Party. The achievement was startling. At no general election before the First World War did Labour poll more than half a million votes (8 per cent of those cast); yet in 1918 the party polled 2.4 million votes (22 per cent of those cast), and in 1929 and again in 1935 it polled 8.4 million votes (37 per cent of those cast).[65]

The electoral success of the Labour Party owed a good deal to the extension of the franchise, and something perhaps to improvements in the party's organisation.[66] The party's success owed much more to the policies it pursued. To the despair of its socialist critics, the Labour Party developed a series of reformist and class conciliatory policies that appealed to the increasingly prosperous and individualistic, though imperfectly class conscious, workers who were to be found in many industrial sectors of the economy.[67] It is not difficult to find evidence of the party's moderation and rejection of the class struggle. In 1900 delegates at the inaugural conference of the Labour Representation Committee rejected a Social Democratic Federation resolution calling for 'a distinct party . . . based upon a recognition of the class war'. In 1918 the 'Reconstruction Manifesto' *Labour and the New Social Order* stated clearly that 'The first principle of the Labour party . . . is the securing to every member of the community . . . of all the requisites of healthy life and worthy citizenship. This is in no sense a "class" proposal.' The 1927 policy document *Labour and the Nation* affirmed that the party 'speaks not as the agent of this class or that, but as the political organ created to express the needs and voice the aspirations of all those who share in Labour which is the lot of mankind'. As E.F.M. Durbin put it in his book *The Politics of Democratic Socialism* which was published at the very end of the period, it was 'radically false . . . to suppose that the dynamic element of social life is . . . that of class struggle and class warfare'.[68] Such moderation was successful electorally. It proved sufficiently attractive to win the vote of large numbers of the better off, but insufficient to secure either their membership of the party or, very often, their real enthusiasm. 'No dad never got involved with politics,' recalls a Lancashire weaver, 'he was always a Labour man cos he's had to work so hard.'[69]

The history of working-class politics, like the history of trade unionism, is less straightforward than it appears at first sight. But there is no doubt that throughout the period covered by this book workers in the industrial sectors of the economy were the most active politically, and that as time went by the politically active were able to persuade their better-off workmates and neighbours to vote for the Labour Party. There seems no doubt either that this electoral success was achieved because of, rather than in spite of, the moderate, class conciliatory policies that the party espoused.

Having to work hard was no guarantee at all of loyalty to the labour movement. In fact neither the trade unions nor the Labour Party ever played very much part in the lives of the majority of the population who were dependent upon the traditional, low-wage sectors of the economy.

The trade unions were particularly unsuccessful. Indeed, it is well known that at the turn of the century nearly 80 per cent of the male workforce (and practically the entire female workforce outside cotton) were non-unionised; it is less well known perhaps that the majority of the occupied population remained unorganised until well into the twentieth century – as late in fact as 1974.[70]

It is scarcely surprising that labour historians and students of industrial relations have shown more interest in those who accepted, rather then rejected, the overtures of the unions. But they have not been unmindful of the need to explain the failure of the unions to organise those workers who, on the face of it, had most to gain from trade-union membership. They have been able to show that non-unionism resulted from a combination of factors: the union's own policies, the hostility of the employers, and the economic and social circumstances in which so many potential members found themselves.

Union policies themselves could play a part; it was seen earlier in the chapter that even unions recruiting from all sections of an industry's workforce sometimes tended to concentrate their attention upon the most highly paid. The hostility of the employers was much more of a problem; and it is not difficult to imagine the power that a determined individual or company could exercise over an insecure, poorly paid and deferential workforce. Norfolk farming families remember well the discrimination that they faced. 'One girl received a letter from a prospective employer saying that if her "father is a member of the labourers' union she should not engage her".' Another boy recalls 'a childhood of persecution from school teachers and the vicar because of his father's uncompromising stand for the union'.[71] Shop assistant Alice Nugent remembers vividly her first attempt to find out about the union.

> I went to a union meeting because the girls were always grumbling upstairs, off the sales floor, and listening to them I felt I wanted to help. So I did hear that there was going to be a union meeting, so I went along . . .
> So next morning the manager, I was called into his office and he said, 'Miss Ramsbottom, did you go out last night?'
> I said, 'Yes.'
> 'Where did you go?'
> 'I went to the Y.M.C.A.'
> 'What went on?'
> I said, 'A union meeting' and he said, 'Miss Ramsbottom, had you not been one of my best girls you would have been out of here this morning,' and my knees shook and I was scared stiff and I just left the office. I never thought of unions again.[72]

Nonetheless it was the economic and social circumstances of life in the traditional sectors of the economy that militated most strongly against union attempts at organisation. There were so many barriers: the persistence of small units of production; the resilience of casual work, self-employment, begging and petty crime; the competition of the unemployed; the blight of low and uncertain wages; the strength of kinship, neighbourhood and community ties; and the weakness of class consciousness. An East Anglian farm labourer recalls how difficult it was in the years following the First World War: 'An course them days there was a lot of unemployment, them days. When you worked on a farm like, there was always one or two people what was unemployed looking over the gate where you worked.'[73] When Robert Roberts looked back at the Salford slum in which he was brought up in the early years of this century, he concluded that

> general apathy stemmed not from despair at the unions in chains nor the failure of such political action as there was; it sprang from mass ignorance: the millions did not know and did not want to know. At that time one had to work hard to convince the unskilled labourer of the need for trade unions at all. An individualist, he was simply not interested in easing the common lot, but concerned entirely with improving his own, and that not too vigorously. From what little he understood, the aims of trade unionism seemed quite impracticable and those of socialism utterly unreal.[74]

The wonder is that the unions made any headway at all. But progress they did, and gradually trade unionism ceased to be the exclusive preserve of skilled and/or leading-sector workers. Table 12 provides some indication of union recruitment in the low-wage sectors of the economy. It shows that although membership remained stubbornly low in agriculture and distribution, it attained moderately respectable levels in construction and impressively high levels on the railways and in road transport. Indeed, efforts were made in the most unexpected places. In 1920 an attempt was made to extend to London the activities of the Birmingham-based Association of Mistresses and Maids, whose objects included a minimum wage, a regular working day, a uniform allowance, and the right of maids 'to choose by what

TABLE 12. Trade-union membership in agriculture (horticulture and forestry), distribution, construction, railways, and road transport, 1892–1939

Year	Agriculture (horticulture and forestry)		Distribution		Construction	
	No. (000)	Density %	No. (000)	Density %	No. (000)	Density %
1892	34	4	4	1	161	24
1901	0.2	0	20	3	255	25
1911	7	1	62	5	169	18
1921	209	24	155	9	493	68
1931	39	5	152	7	322	27
1939	62	—	276	12	451	30

Year	Railways		Road transport		Agriculture (etc.), distribution, construction, railways, and road transport	
	No. (000)	Density %	No. (000)	Density %	No. (000)	Density %
1892	39	10	33	14	271	10
1901	63	11	41	15	378	—
1911	157	—	103	33	498	—
1921	411	59	197	59	1,465	52
1931	320	55	190	49	1,023	23
1939	373	—	289	68	1,451	—

Source: **G. S. Bain** and **R. Price**, *Prcfiles of Union Growth: A Comparative Statistical Portrait of Eight Countries*, Blackwell, 1980, pp. 43, 63, 67–8.

name they shall be called'.[75] Ten years later it was reported that even London's 'advertising labourers' – the sandwich-board men – had a union of their own.[76]

Yet these are little more than historical curiosities. Such unionisation as there was among the low paid owed much more to the activities of large, single-industry unions such as the National Union of Dock Workers, the National Union of Gasworkers and General Labourers, the National Union of Distributive and Allied Workers (which by 1939 had a membership of 194,000) and the National Union of Railwaymen (which in 1939 had a membership of 350,000). The spread of unionisation among the low paid owed still more to the activities of amalgamated, multi-industry general unions such as the National Union of General and Municipal Workers and the Transport and General Workers' Union. The National Union of General and Municipal Workers was formed in 1924 with Will Thorne as secretary, and a membership of 327,000. For many years the union struggled to retain support and it was not until the economic recovery of the mid-1930s that its membership once again reached 300,000. The Transport and General Workers' Union was created by Ernest Bevin in 1921 and, despite its nickname of the 'Tired and Generally Worthless Union', recruited successfully among dockers, and building and road transport workers. Its membership grew rapidly: from 300,000 at its foundation, to 384,000 in 1930 and 648,000 in 1939. By the end of the period the Transport and General Workers' Union was the largest, and the National Union of General and Municipal Workers the third largest, of all the trade unions in the country. It was a major change. For whereas in 1892 the general unions represented just 13 per cent of trade-union membership, by 1939 the Transport and General Workers' Union and the National Union of General and Municipal Workers alone accounted for 17 per cent of trade-union membership – and 74 per cent of membership in the traditional sectors of the economy.[77]

However, the trade unions were less successful in recruiting the low paid than the preceding discussion might lead one to suppose. For Table 12 reveals the shortcomings, as well as the achievements, of the union movement. It shows that even in the 1930s – after half a century and more of struggle – nearly 50 per cent of railwaymen, 70 per cent of construction workers, 90 per cent of distribution workers and 95 per cent of agricultural workers were still not members of a union. Moreover, Table 12 is misleading insofar as it includes industries (such as construction, railways and road transport) that were relatively easy to unionise, but excludes groups (such as petty criminals, penny capitalists and domestic servants) that were notoriously difficult to organise. Consequently the table does not reveal fully the difficulties, for instance, of recruiting women workers. In 1914 there were less than half a million female trade unionists out of a possible membership of over five million; in 1939 there were fewer than a million female trade unionists out of a potential membership of well over six million.[78] In fact women, the unskilled and the low paid all joined the trade unions in such relatively small numbers as to preclude the latter from playing any direct role in the lives of most of those employed in, or dependent upon, the traditional sectors of the economy.

Even when the unions did manage to recruit successfully among the low paid, it was unusual for them to assume a leading role in the lives of their members. Such a view may seem somewhat surprising, for it is often believed that the industrial militancy of the unskilled unions compensated, to some extent at least, for their numerical weakness. Certainly the historiography of both 'new' and general unionism lays great emphasis upon their propensity to strike. Specialists in labour history will know of the dock strikes of 1911 and 1912, the builders' strike of 1914 and the busmen's 'coronation' strike of 1937; and even non-specialists may well have heard of the 1888 London match girls' strike and the 1889 London dock strike, a dispute that is associated indelibly with the birth of the so-called 'new' unionism. In fact neither the new unions nor their successors, the general unions, were particularly strike-prone – and certainly not when compared to the unions in the industrial sectors of the economy. Table 13 provides

TABLE 13. The share of construction, transport and communication, and agriculture, distribution, finance, public employment and small manufacturing in industrial disputes, 1888–1939

Industry	% of strikes	% of strikers
Construction	12	2
Transport and communication	7	10
Agriculture, distribution, finance, public employment and small manufacturing	16	5
Construction, transport and communication, agriculture, distribution, finance, public employment and small manufacturing	35	17

Source: **J. E. Cronin**, *Industrial Conflict in Modern Britain*, Croom Helm, 1979, pp. 206–10.

strike data for the years from 1888 to 1939. It confirms that although construction, transport and communication, agriculture, distribution, finance, public employment and small manufacturing employed well over a third of all workers, they accounted for only a third of all strikes and involved no more than 17 per cent of all strikers. The conclusion seems inescapable: that insofar as the trade unions did come to exert an influence over low-paid workers, they did not do so by involving them in an endless succession of industrial disputes.

They did so rather by taking over from their members the negotiation of pay and conditions. The unions strengthened their bureaucracies, secured recognition from the employers and worked hard to establish formal systems of collective bargaining. These developments may be seen first in the large single-industry unions that were established around the turn of the century. Their leaders moved their head offices to London and appointed a growing number of full-time officials. The seamen needed a full-time official in every port because their 'lay' officers were so often away at sea. The dockers required a large number of officials to cope with the difficulties of organising a casual workforce; by 1910 Ben Tillett's Dock, Wharf, Riverside and General Labourers' Union had 37 full-time officers – an average of almost 1 to every 400 members.[79] These officials sought to negotiate their members' pay and conditions without involving them in unnecessary industrial action. The Eastern Counties Agricultural and Small Holders' Union provides a typical rural example. Its executive opposed strike action, advocating instead involvement in political activity, the establishment of smallholdings, and the creation of an Agricultural Wages Board where representatives of both sides of the industry could sit down together and settle their differences.[80]

The same conciliatory (and centripetal) tendencies may be discerned later among the amalgamated, multi-industry general unions. Ernest Bevin acquired the leadership of the giant Transport and General Workers' Union by the force both of his personality and of his ability; and although neither he nor his executive wished to abandon the strike weapon, they developed the machinery with which to achieve the peaceful settlement of disputes. 'A pattern of trade union leadership arose out of the turbulent events of the 1920s which was consolidated during the years up to 1940. Trade union leaders became less willing to engage in strikes and to be drawn into them by the precipitate action of their members.'[81]

Yet such a judgement could encourage too sanguine a view of trade unionism's impact upon the low-wage sectors of the economy. Membership remained low, and anti-union feeling was more common than is sometimes supposed. It has been said that even after the Second World War the only unionised workers in the countryside were the railwaymen[82]; it has been found that in poor urban areas like Campbell Bunk 'There was considerable hostility . . . to trade unions. . . .The resistance to trade unionism . . . was well known and had at its back fears of "decasualisation" and its effects on employment chances for those on the industrial margins; and a resentment of the power wielded over workers by trade union officials who seemed to wax fat on members' contributions.'[83]

Even those who did join a union often did so without much enthusiasm. It was difficult for union activists to translate rank-and-file ties of kinship, neighbourhood and community into the work-based trade-union loyalty that they so much desired. It was difficult perhaps for the rank-and-file to feel the same attachment to a giant general union as to a smaller and more intimate organisation. In all events, it seems that trade unionists in the traditional sectors of the economy often displayed only a minimal interest in, and commitment to, the union of which they were a member. J.M. Mogey admitted that his 1956 survey of Oxford life included 'no special investigation of the local trade-union branches as social systems'. But he found that

> There was in many cases a certain amount of hesitation when the drift of conversation approached a point where trade unions should have been mentioned and on occasion it was necessary to ask a direct question; as for example:
> The interviewer reports: 'I had to ask him about the trade union, and he replied "It's doing well . . . now what do they call it?" I suggested in the long pause that it might be the Transport and General Workers. "There's a man comes round every so often for complaints . . . (pause again) . . . no, I don't think it's that, it's just called the General Workers."'

Mogey's final remarks are particularly instructive. He discovered that 'the quality of opinions on the unions . . . covered . . . all shades from the enthusiastic through the vague and accepting to the critical, but it is characteristic even of favourable attitudes to be tinged with resignation. We found', he concluded, 'a general air of acceptance of the unions as something that existed in the background of a job.'[84]

It has been remarked several times already in this chapter that the history of the labour movement is far less straightforward than it appears at first sight. However, what little is known about the political activities of those in the low-wage sectors of the economy does seem reasonably straightforward, and so may be summarised fairly readily. It appears incontrovertible that the least well off participated least fully in all forms of political activity; but that when they did participate, they were more likely than other groups to support 'non-working-class' parties of the centre and right.

The involvement of the poor in the political processes of the country was impeded by two major barriers: the one legal, the other economic and social. The force of the legal impediments is not always sufficiently understood. For it is important to appreciate that the right to vote depended not only upon the possession of the appropriate franchise qualification but also upon the fulfilment of the relevant registration requirements. Neal Blewett has examined the situation in 1911 – more than two-thirds of the way through the period, and five years after the foundation of the Labour Party. He shows how the poor remained doubly disadvantaged: the franchise laws still excluded paupers, live-in domestic servants and, of course, all women; while the registration laws continued to deprive many other groups of the vote to which the franchise laws appeared to entitle them. The difficulty was that the occupation, household, lodger and servant franchises each required the voter to be in possession of his qualification for a year before his name could be entered on the electoral register. This meant, for example, that although a lodger could move to another room in the same house, if he moved to the house next door he would have to wait a full year before qualifying to appear again on the register.[85] A pamphlet written for Labour Party canvassers in 1907 tried desperately to clarify the situation.

> If a man rents a room at 32 More St and pays 4s a week rent for six months and then takes two rooms in the same house and pays 6s per week for another six months and the rent started before July 15, 1905 and continued till July 15, 1906, he would be entitled to claim as a lodger; but if he lived at 32 More St from July 14, 1905 till December 1905 and rented one room at 4s unfurnished or 5s furnished and then moved to 33 More St next door and took two rooms and paid 6s rent, he would lose his vote both as a lodger and a householder; he must either be a lodger and rent rooms in one and the same house for the whole twelve months stated; or a householder and rent the whole of a house, or part of a house that is *separate and complete in itself*, and then he claims for one, two, or more houses, or parts of houses that are dwellings separate and complete in themselves, and the successive houses lived in during the period July 15–July 15 may be in different districts or wards of the same Borough and in the case of County Divisions, in different parts of the same county.[86]

Hard though it may be to believe, the major barrier to the participation of the poor lay not in the intricacies of electoral law but in the never-ending struggles of day-to-day existence. The poor had neither the time, the money, the energy, nor the inclination for political struggle. Indeed, many viewed politics as a form of recreation rather than as a means of obtaining power. 'We voted for the chappie that came around,' recalls a Bristol man of elections in the late 1920s; 'and I suppose who shouted loudest we'd go and vote for him especially if they took the old people to the voting place in his motor car!'[87] Others regarded the entire labour movement with weary cynicism. 'Frank W . . . twenty-nine, says he is disillusioned about politics and thinks trade unionism a farce; he knows about it from the inside through his father (a docker's delegate at many conferences), and through his own experience at the docks.'[88] Standish Meacham, as so often, perceives the situation with great clarity:

> . . . the poorer the family, the less its concern with problems beyond those of its immediate survival. Political commitment demands a consciousness that change is both desirable and possible – a consciousness foreign to most men and women trapped at the level of 25 shillings a week. Concern seldom tended to move beyond the immediate and the concrete: 'Ah understands nowt about politics and nowt Ah want to understand. But Ah do understand a load o' coal.' The attitude bred the maxims: 'Politics never did anybody any good'; 'Of course, all politics are crooked'; 'There's nowt to choose between 'em'.[89]

It was seen earlier in the chapter that one way in which the history of working-class politics can prove misleading is by perpetuating the belief that popular politics necessarily furthered the cause of the left in general and of the Labour Party in particular. It is a warning that needs to be kept constantly in mind when considering the attitudes of those dependent upon the traditional sectors of the economy; for when the poor did participate in the political process, they did so quite often by supporting parties of the centre and the right.

Some supported nationalist parties – between 1885 and 1918 the Irish Nationalists alone won 745 parliamentary seats and attracted 12 per cent of all the votes cast in general elections.[90] Others supported the Fascists. For although the British Union of Fascists drew the bulk of its support from the lower middle class, it also managed to exploit the grievances of groups such as 'shop assistants, cinema usherettes, barmaids, servants, etc., particularly where these could be shown to be exploited by big Jewish employers'. Indeed, the one place that the Fascists succeeded in attracting a mass following was in that centre of marginal trades, the east end of London, where the party's virulent anti-semitism resulted in a 19 per cent poll in the local elections of 1937.[91]

But the poor, like the better off, were far less likely to support the Nationalists or the Fascists than they were the Liberals or the Conservatives. Unfortunately the liberalism of the poor has attracted very little interest indeed. However, it does seem clear that the Liberals managed to retain a certain following; indeed the strength of the Conservatives and the growth of Labour meant that the early twentieth-century Liberals came to rely more and more upon the votes of the rural poor.[92] Yet even in the towns some Liberals knew how to root out the popular vote: Frank Gray ran an unashamedly populist campaign at Oxford in the general election of 1922. 'To get at this vote in the lower half of the social structure Gray attempted to place himself in people's lives, although in a non-political way. It was all a matter of flower shows, sport, and the avoidance of political opinion.'[93]

The conservatism of the poor has received a great deal more attention. It is well known that the Conservatives attracted votes in the countryside and exerted a considerable popular appeal in poor areas such as the east end of London.[94] It was suggested above that the Conservative Party's electoral success derived from a combination of luck, organisation and policy. Its policy was to appeal both to self-interest and to what have been called the 'traditional emotions'; the Conservatives claimed to have legislated in the working-class interest on such matters as health, factory reform and workmen's compensation. Moreover, they knew very well how to appeal to the deference which, as was explained in the last chapter, remained common among workers in agriculture, retailing, domestic service and other jobs that brought the worker 'into direct association with his employer or other middle class influentials'. Political activists were well aware of the crucial role that deference could play; they believed that on the railways, for instance, there was a clear distinction between on the one hand 'the goods side and drivers and firemen not brought into touch with the public [who] are Radicals, [and on the other hand] passenger guards and porters who are also under-paid but with funds augmented by tips and the patronage of the rich [who] are Conservatives'.[95]

Accordingly it may not seem so surprising to find that the disadvantaged were much less likely than their better-off workmates and neighbours to exhibit any sympathy for the growing number of left-wing organisations that came into existence during the final decades of the nineteenth century. It will be recalled from earlier in the chapter that tenants' associations, the co-operative movement and socialist groups (like the Social Democratic Federation, the Independent Labour Party and the Communist Party) proved even less attractive to the poorly paid than to workers in the leading sectors of the economy.

In fact the disadvantaged were reluctant to join even the pressure groups that were set up specifically to meet their needs. It is well known that the unemployed were a particularly difficult group to organise.[96] In early twentieth-century Birmingham the Right to Work Committee drew its members chiefly from the ranks of skilled trade-union activists.[97] In Oxford the unemployed of the 1920s 'were no sort of threat to stability: local working-class leaders found them difficult to organise, lacking in any sense of cohesion, and always vulnerable to key men in their organisations leaving when they found work elsewhere'.[98] Only the National Unemployed Workers' Movement achieved any real success in mobilising the unemployed. Established in 1921, and organised largely under the Communist Party leadership of Wal Hannington, the movement claimed in the early 1930s to have a membership of between 50,000 and 100,000. But this was clearly an exaggeration; it is unlikely, in fact, if it ever had as many as 40,000 members – well below 2 per cent of those registered officially as unemployed.[99]

Even the Labour Party found it hard to make much headway. In all events it was never very successful in persuading the poor to become members of the party. The rural areas proved persistently intractable. It is true that during and immediately after the First World War the party made some progress in constituencies that had been thought of as unwinnable; but thereafter it floundered on its inability to draw the agricultural population into membership and so involve them in the routine burdens of organisation.[100] The poorer areas of the towns and cities proved little more amenable to Labour Party attempts to extend recruitment. Indeed, it is striking how greatly local constituency Labour parties remained dominated by the skilled and/or uniformed working class, and how little part was played by women, the poor, the unskilled and the unemployed.[101]

Nor were the activists able to persuade the poor to vote Labour on the same scale as the better off. Quantification is impossible, but it is clear that the Labour vote lagged badly in rural areas. It was seen earlier in the chapter that by the late 1920s Labour nationally was polling some two-thirds of the working-class vote and well over one-third of all the votes that were cast. Yet in the general election of 1929 the Labour vote in the rural heartland of East Anglia was substantially lower, ranging from 22 per cent in Suffolk, to 27 per cent in Cambridgeshire and the Isle of Ely, 30 per cent in Lincolnshire, 31 per cent in north and east Essex, and a maximum of 35 per cent in Norfolk.[102] The urban poor seemed little more enthusiastic. Two reports published just after the end of the period reveal how far the Labour Party still had to go in persuading the disadvantaged to support it electorally. In 1943 the Carnegie Trust published a study that had been conducted in Liverpool, Cardiff and Glasgow between 1936 and 1939. It found that:

> Out of a total of 1490 young unemployed men for whom information was available, only 20 . . . were attached in membership to one or other of the political organisations. . . .At least 10 per cent of the young men did not even know the names of the various political parties. . . .The overwhelming majority of the men had no political convictions whatsoever. When asked why, they invariably replied, 'What does it matter?'[103]

A decade later Ferdynand Zweig published the results of the investigation into British working-class life that he had carried out during the late 1940s. He concluded in *The British Worker* that the popularity of socialist (in which he included Labour Party) ideas differed 'according to the industrial group, age, status, education, and upbringing'.

In the coal-mines almost everyone is a socialist of one brand or the other. . . .

Hotel workers, shop assistants, hairdressers, and many other workers in distributive trades – judging from those I met – form the other extreme. Among them you find a much greater tolerance for what is called capitalism and they often think of socialism as quite impracticable. A shop assistant will tell you: 'Socialism is an ideal. Ideals are all very well but you can't buy a loaf of bread or a joint of meat with them. People want cash.'[104]

Zweig is right. Such attitudes were not uncommon in the traditional sectors of the economy and always proved most difficult for the Labour Party to dislodge.

It is only in this final chapter, a study of the labour movement, that there can be any real justification for devoting more attention to the minority of workers in the high-wage sectors of the economy than to the majority who were dependent on the traditional, low-wage sectors. Yet even here caution is necessary, for it would be easy to be misled into believing that in certain industries at least the history of the labour movement became synonymous with the history of the workforce as a whole. Nothing, it should now be clear, was further from the truth. It has been seen that even in leading-sector industries such as cotton, engineering, coal and motor manufacturing it was only the trade unions – and not the Labour Party – that could make any claim at all to assuming an everyday role in the lives of ordinary people. It has been seen too that in other parts of the economy, in industries such as farming, retailing, transport and domestic service, neither the trade unions not the Labour Party ever managed to play anything approaching a comparable role in the lives of working people. For a surprisingly large minority of the working-class population the labour movement ended the period very much as it had begun it: as an irrelevance that intruded only intermittently into the routine of day-to-day life.

NOTES AND REFERENCES

1. **J. Winter,** 'Introduction: Labour history and Labour historians', in **J. Winter** (ed.), *The Working Class in Modern British History: Essays in Honour of Henry Pelling*, Cambridge U.P., 1983, p. vii; **H. Perkin,** 'Social History in Britain', *Journal of Social History*, 10, 1976, p. 133.
2. **R. J. Morris,** 'Whatever Happened to the British Working Class, 1750–1850', *Bulletin of the Society for the Study of Labour History*, 41, 1980.

3. **J. Benson,** *British Coalminers in the Nineteenth Century: A Social History*, Gill & Macmillan, 1980, p. 196.
4. **D. Lockwood,** 'Sources of Variation in Working Class Images of Society', *Sociological Review*, 14, 1966.
5. Cited **W. H. Fraser,** *Trade Unions and Society: The Struggle for Acceptance 1850–1880*, Allen & Unwin, 1974, p. 101. Also pp. 100, 102–3.
6. **W. R. Garside** and **H. F. Gospel,** 'Employers and Managers: Their Organizational Structure and Changing Industrial Strategies', in **C. J. Wrigley** (ed.), *A History of British Industrial Relations 1875–1914*, Harvester, 1982, p. 112. Also **R.C. Whiting,** *The View from Cowley: The Impact of Industrialization upon Oxford, 1918–1939*, Clarendon Press, 1983, p. 105. Cf. Manchester Polytechnic, Manchester Studies, Transcript 664, p. 16.
7. **G. S. Bain** and **R. Price,** *Profiles of Union Growth: A Comparative Statistical Portrait of Eight Countries*, Blackwell, 1980, pp. 1–9, 13–21.
8. Benson, *British Coalminers*, p. 197.
9. **J. L. White,** 'Lancashire Cotton Textiles', in Wrigley (ed.), *Industrial Relations*, pp. 216–17. Also **H. A. Clegg, A. Fox** and **A. F. T. Thompson,** *A History of British Trade Unions since 1889: Volume 1, 1889–1910*, Clarendon Press, 1964, p. 429.
10. Whiting, *View*, pp. 65, 82.
11. **J. Benson,** 'Work', in **J. Benson** (ed.), *The Working Class in England, 1875–1914*, Croom Helm, 1984, pp. 78–9. Also **G. Braybon,** *Women Workers in the First World War: The British Experience*, Croom Helm, 1981, pp. 30–3, 69, 72, 79–80, 82, 101.
12. **E. Roberts,** *A Woman's Place: An Oral History of Working-Class Women 1890–1940*, Blackwell, 1984, p. 147.
13. Whiting, *View*, pp. 45, 111. Also pp. 81, 106.
14. Manchester Studies, Transcript 126, p. 4.
15. **M. J. Haynes,** 'Strikes', in Benson, *Working Class*, pp. 119–20. Also **H. I. Dutton** and **J. E. King,** *'Ten Per Cent and No Surrender': The Preston Strike, 1853–1854*, Cambridge U.P., 1981, ch. 3.
16. **J. Benson,** 'Coalmining', in Wrigley (ed.), *Industrial Relations*, pp. 200–1; **D. Butler** and **A. Sloman,** *British Political Facts 1900–1975*, Macmillan, 1975, pp. 296–7.
17. **C. G. Hanson,** 'Craft Unions, Welfare Benefits, and the Case for Trade Union Law Reform, 1867–75', *Economic History Review*, xxviii, 1975, p. 248; **H. A. Turner,** *Trade Union Growth Structure and Policy: A Comparative Study of the Cotton Industry*, Allen & Unwin, 1962, p. 139.
18. Clegg, Fox and Thompson, *Trade Unions*, p. 7.
19. Benson, 'Coalmining', p. 195. Also **J. H. Porter,** 'Wage Bargaining under Conciliation Agreements', *Economic History Review*, xxiii, 1970; **S. Webb** and **B. Webb,** *Industrial Democracy*, The authors, 1913, pp. 223, 239.
20. Porter, 'Wage Bargaining', p. 470; Benson, 'Coalmining', p. 191.
21. Garside and Gospel, 'Employers and Managers', p. 105; **A. McIvor,** 'Employers' Organisations and Labour Relations Strategy in Lanca-

The labour movement

shire: General Trends and Developments', Paper read to Economic History Society, University of Loughborough, 1981.

22. **J. F. C. Harrison,** *The Common People: A History from the Norman Conquest to the Present,* Fontana, 1984, p. 358.
23. Whiting, *View,* p. 76; McCormick, *Industrial Relations,* p. 42.
24. **V. Gore,** 'Rank-and-File Dissent', in Wrigley (ed.), *Industrial Relations,* p. 65; Whiting, *View,* p. 69.
25. Cited Benson, *British Coalminers,* p. 206.
26. **W. F. Watson,** *Machines and Men: An Autobiography of an Itinerant Mechanic,* Allen & Unwin, 1935, pp. 29–30. Also pp. 73, 84, 100, 112.
27. *Ibid.,* p. 30; Benson, *British Coalminers,* p. 203.
28. Porter, 'Wage Bargaining', pp. 470, 472. But cf. **A. Reid,** 'Dilution, Trade Unionism and the State in Britain during the First World War', in **S. Tolliday** and **J. Zeitlin** (eds), *Shop Floor Bargaining and the State,* Cambridge U.P., 1985.
29. **H. Francis** and **D. Smith,** *The Fed: A History of the South Wales Miners in the Twentieth Century,* Lawrence and Wishart, 1980, pp. 14–15. See also **B. Holton,** *British Syndicalism 1900–1914: Myths and Realities,* Pluto Press, 1976.
30. **J. Hinton,** *The First Shop Stewards' Movement,* Allen & Unwin, 1973, p. 331. Also **J. Zeitlin,** 'The Emergence of Shop Steward Organization and Job Control in the British Car Industry: A Review Essay', *History Workshop,* 10, 1980, p. 124.
31. Turner, *Cotton Industry,* p. 310.
32. Benson, *British Coalminers,* pp. 210–13.
33. **E. Hopkins,** *A Social History of the English Working Classes 1815–1945,* Arnold, 1979, p. 245. A valuable overview of most of the period is provided by **M. Pugh,** *The Making of Modern British Politics 1867–1939,* Blackwell, 1982.
34. **T. Forester,** *The Labour Party and the Working Class,* Heinemann, 1976, p. 66.
35. **J. Hinton,** *Labour and Socialism: a History of the British Labour Movement 1867–1974,* Wheatsheaf, 1983, p. vii.
36. **R. Skidelsky,** 'Great Britain', in **S. J. Woolf** (ed.), *Fascism in Europe,* Methuen, 1968, p. 269; **J. D. Brewer,** 'The British Union of Fascists: Some Tentative Conclusions on its Membership', in **S. U. Larsen, B. Hagtvet** and **J. P. Myklebust** (eds), *Who Were the Fascists: Social Roots of European Fascism,* Universitetsforlaget, 1980, p. 545.
37. *Daily Mail,* 8 January 1935.
38. Skidelsky, 'Great Britain', p. 257; Butler and Sloman, *Political Facts,* p. 183; **R. Thurlow,** *Fascism in Britain: A History, 1918–1985,* Blackwell, 1987.
39. **A. Exell,** 'Morris Motors in the 1930s. Part II: Politics and Trade Unionism', *History Workshop,* 7, 1979, pp. 49–50.
40. Skidelsky, 'Great Britain', p. 269; Brewer, 'British Union of Fascists'.
41. Pugh, *Politics,* p. 77.
42. *Ibid.,* p. 76.
43. **R. Gregory,** *The Miners and British Politics 1906–1914,* Oxford U.P., 1968, pp. 178, 191.

44. **R. MacKenzie** and **A. Silver,** *Angels in Marble: Working Class Conservatives in Urban England,* Heinemann, 1968, pp. 14, 240.

45. For a brief guide, see **F. Parkin,** 'Working-class Conservatives: A Theory of Political Deviance', *British Journal of Sociology,* 18, 1967, esp. pp. 278–9.

46. McKenzie and Silver, *Angels,* pp. 37–9, 43–4; Pugh, *Politics,* pp. 6, 46–51, 249–51.

47. McKenzie and Silver, *Angels,* pp. 19, 28, 48–9. In Lancashire religion was also a major factor: see **R.L. Greenall,** 'Popular Conservatism in Salford 1868–1886', *Northern History,* 9, 1974.

48. McKenzie and Silver, *Angels,* pp. 54–6, 66.

49. Pugh, *Politics,* pp. 83, 86–7; Greenall, 'Salford'.

50. **D. Englander,** *Landlord and Tenant in Urban Britain 1838–1918,* Clarendon Press, 1983, pp. 98, 185–8.

51. *Ibid.,* p. 316.

52. *Ibid.,* pp. 126–7, 171; **A. Sutcliffe** and **R. Smith,** *Birmingham 1839–1970,* Oxford U.P., 1974, p. 179.

53. **D. Englander,** 'Tenants and Politics: The Birmingham Tenants' Federation During and After the First World War', *Midland History,* vi, 1981, p. 136. Also Englander, *Landlord,* p. 311.

54. Pugh, *Politics,* p. 77.

55. Harrison, *Common People,* p. 338; **H. Pelling,** *The Origins of the Labour Party 1880–1900,* Clarendon Press, 1965, p. 229.

56. Pugh, *Politics,* p. 79; Forester, *Labour Party,* p. 31.

57. Manchester Studies, Transcript 679, pp. 2, 22. See **D. Howell,** *British Workers and the Independent Labour Party 1888–1906,* Manchester U.P., 1983.

58. **M. Pugh,** *The Tories and the People 1880–1935,* Blackwell, 1985, p. 2. Pelling, *Labour Party,* p. 229.

59. Butler and Sloman, *Facts,* p. 143; Whiting, *View,* pp. 95, 125, 167; Stevenson, *British Society,* p. 292.

60. **P. H. J. H. Gosden,** *Self-Help: Voluntary Associations in the 19th Century,* Batsford, 1973, pp. 186, 196.

61. Whiting, *View,* p. 149. Also Gosden, *Self-Help,* p. 185; **S. Pollard,** 'Nineteenth-Century Co-operation: From Community Building to Shopkeeping', in **A. Briggs** and **J. Saville** (eds), *Essays in Labour History,* Macmillan, 1967.

62. Butler and Sloman, *Facts,* pp. 135, 200. By no means all activists were working-class. See **A. Reid,** 'Class and Organization', *Historical Journal,* 30, 1987, pp. 236–7.

63. **C. Howard,** 'Expectations Born to Death: Local Labour Party Expansion in the 1920s', in **J. Winter** (ed.), *The Working Class in Modern British History: Essays in Honour of Henry Pelling,* Cambridge U.P., 1983, pp. 73–4; Pugh, *Politics,* p. 251.

64. Whiting, *View,* p. 148. Also p. 176; Howard, 'Expectations', pp. 78–81; Forester, *Labour,* p. 91; Pugh, *Politics,* pp. 251–2.

65. Butler and Sloman, *Facts,* pp. 182–4.

66. **C. Chamberlain,** 'The Growth of Support for the Labour Party in Britain', *Political Studies,* 24, 1973.

67. Forester, *Labour,* pp. 22–3, 42–3, 47; Pugh, *Politics,* p. 261. Also

S. **MacIntyre**, 'British Labour, Marxism and Working Class Apathy in the Nineteen Twenties', *Historical Journal*, 20, 1977.

68. L. V. **Panitch,** 'Ideology and Integration: The Case of the British Labour Party', *Political Studies*, 19, 1971, pp. 189, 191, 193, 195. Also **R. Barker,** 'Political Myth: Ramsay MacDonald and the Labour Party', *History*, 61, 1976.

69. Manchester Studies, Transcript 708, NP. Also Forester, *Labour*, pp. 6, 35, 54.

70. R. **McKibbin**, 'Why Was There no Marxism in Great Britain?', *English Historical Review*, xcic, 1984, p. 298; Hinton, *Labour*, p. vii.

71. A. **Howkins**, *Poor Labouring Men: Rural Radicalism in Norfolk 1872–1923*, Routledge & Kegan Paul, 1985, p. 103.

72. B. **Davorn**, 'Women and Shopwork 1875–1925 with Special Reference to Ideology, Conditions and Opportunities', M.A. Thames Polytechnic, 1986, p. 71.

73. Howkins, *Poor Labouring Men*, p. 137; **D. Martin,** 'Women Without Work: Textile Weavers in North-East Lancashire 1919–1939', M.A. University of Lancaster, 1985, p. 41.

74. R. **Roberts,** *The Classic Slum: Salford Life in the First Quarter of the Century*, Manchester U.P., 1971, p. 90. Also White, *Worst Street*, pp. 108–9.

75. *Labour Leader*, 5 February 1920.

76. White, *Worst Street*, p. 42.

77. Kynaston, *King Labour*, pp. 142–3; Butler and Sloman, *Facts*, p. 294. Cf. **V. L. Allen,** *Trade Union Leadership: Based on a Study of Arthur Deakin*, Longman, Green & Co., 1957, pp. 224–5.

78. Bain and Price, *Union Growth*, p. 39.

79. Clegg, Fox and Thompson, *Trade Unions*, p. 478; Howkins, *Poor Labouring Men*, p. 144; Hinton, *Shop Stewards*, pp. 49–50.

80. Howkins, *Poor Labouring Men*, pp. 13, 37, 95, 104, 178.

81. Allen, *Leadership*, p. 103. Also pp. 77, 90.

82. Howkins, *Poor Labouring Men*, p. 111.

83. White, *Worst Street*, p. 108.

84. J. M. **Mogey**, *Family and Neighbourhood: Two Studies in Oxford*, Oxford U.P., 1956, pp. 135–6.

85. N. **Blewett**, 'The Franchise in the United Kingdom 1885–1918', *Past and Present*, 32, 1965, pp. 33–6.

86. Meacham, *Life Apart*, p. 204. Also Englander, *Landlord*, p. 8.

87. Avon County Reference Library, Bristol People's Oral History Project, Transcript RO56, p. 37. Also RO11, pp. 61–2; Meacham, *Life Apart*, pp. 202–3.

88. E. **Slater** and M. **Woodside**, *Patterns of Marriage: A Study of Marriage Relationships in the Urban Working Classes*, Cassell, 1951, pp. 249–52.

89. Meacham, *Life Apart*, p. 204. Also **R. Hoggart**, *The Uses of Literacy: Aspects of Working-Class Life with Special Reference to Publications and Entertainments*, Penguin, 1957, pp. 103, 279–80.

90. McKenzie and Silver, *Angels*, p. 11; Butler and Sloman, *Facts*, pp. 144–5.

91. Skidelsky, 'Great Britain', pp. 269–71; Brewer, 'British Union of Fascists', pp. 545–6.

92. Howkins, *Poor Labouring Men*, p. 85.
93. Whiting, *View*, p. 133. On populism generally, see Harrison, *Common People*, pp. 334–5.
94. Pugh, *Politics*, pp. 83, 86–7.
95. *Ibid.*, p. 75. Also MacKenzie and Silver, *Angels*, pp. 37, 47, 242–3, 256.
96. S. Constantine, *Unemployment in Britain between the Wars*, Longman, 1980, p. 42. But cf. K. Mourby, 'The Social Effects of Unemployment on Teesside 1919–1939', Ph.D. Teesside Polytechnic, 1982, p. 165.
97. C. Collard, 'Unemployment Agitation in Birmingham, 1905– 1910', in A. Wright and R. Shackelton (eds), *Worlds of Labour: Essays in Birmingham Labour History*, University of Birmingham, 1983, p. 41.
98. Whiting, *View*, pp. 144–5.
99. Harrison, *Common People*, p. 373; Stevenson, *British Society*, p. 290; W. G. Runciman, *Relative Deprivation and Social Justice: A Study of Attitudes to Social Inequality in Twentieth-Century England*, Routledge & Kegan Paul, 1966, p. 63; K. D. Brown, *The English Labour Movement 1700–1951*, Gill & Macmillan, 1982, p. 275.
100. Howard, 'Labour Party', pp. 69, 71; Howkins, *Poor Labouring Men*, pp. 126–7.
101. Slater and Woodside, *Patterns of Marriage*, p. 252. Also White, *Worst Street*, pp. 107–8.
102. Howard, 'Labour Party', p. 69.
103. Constantine *Unemployment*, p. 97. Also Mourby, 'Social Effects', p. 158.
104. F. Zweig, *The British Worker*, Pelican, 1952, p. 187.

CONCLUSION

Any attempt to encapsulate 90 years of working-class history in a single volume may well seem unduly ambitious; and any attempt to summarise the results of that undertaking in a few hundred words will no doubt seem foolhardy in the extreme. Yet it is believed that certain important conclusions have emerged from the evidence presented in this book and that they are worthy of brief recapitulation.

It will be recalled that one of the specific objectives of the book was to show that class existed, and that class mattered. This, it is believed, has been accomplished. Indeed, as Mike Savage and Andrew Miles explain at the end of their 1994 study of the working class between 1840 and 1940, 'although the particular working class whose development we have examined in this book may today be undergoing a further process of remaking, this does not constitute an adequate basis for questioning the continued significance of class in general.'[1]

It will be recalled too that the second specific objective of the book was to examine the view that during the years between 1850 and 1939, 'working people were slowly but assuredly being moulded into a homogeneous working class which enjoyed a common work experience and outlook'.[2] It must be perfectly clear by now that such a proposition simply cannot be sustained; it is apparent that the working class never became the homogeneous mass that certain commentators appear to imagine. For despite the profound, and often centripetal, changes that took place during this period, working people continued to be divided in very many ways: by their age and their gender; by the ways in which they made their living; by the amount of money they earned; by the type of accommodation in which they lived; and by the strength of the ties that bound them to their family, their neighbourhood and their community. The skilled worker toiled next to the unskilled; the prosperous home-owning family lived near the poverty-stricken slum-dweller; the class-conscious, trade-union Labour Party member coexisted alongside the deferential, apolitical, non-unionist who remained supremely indifferent to the efforts that the labour movement was making on his or her behalf. Neither group was typical, but neither should be forgotten.

It will be recalled finally that the third specific objective of the book was to examine the proposition that material circumstances determined the social and cultural aspects of working-class life, and in particular the apparent readiness of working people to accept the economic and social system in which they lived. These are large and difficult issues. But the conclusion appears inescapable; it seems plain that in seeking to understand the social and cultural developments that took place between 1850 and 1939 primacy should normally be afforded to the material circumstances of working-class life. It has been seen time and time again that there existed a close correlation between material, demographic, ideological and organisational developments, and that these developments tended to be mutually reinforcing. In the industrial sectors of the economy, changes at the workplace, growing prosperity, and improved accommodation combined together to encourage the emergence of a smaller, healthier and more ambitious family, its declining neighbourhood and community ties counterbalanced by its growing class consciousness and its increasing commitment to the labour movement.

The correlation between material, demographic, ideological and organisational developments meant that in the 'traditional' sectors of the economy the combination of established work practices, lower incomes, and inferior accommodation impeded the changes that were taking place among the better off: family life changed less quickly; kinship, neighbourhood and community ties remained more resilient; and both class consciousness and commitment to the labour movement proved a great deal slower to emerge. Yet it is important to appreciate that even here the economic, social and cultural changes that took place did tend, on balance, to improve the lot of the working population, and so reconcile them to the capitalist system in which they found themselves. This is a plea then, not for the reinstatement of some crude economic determinism, but for the recognition that during this period occupation and income (and to a lesser extent housing) were generally the most important determinants of working-class experience.

It has been the fundamental purpose of this book to reflect, and develop, the attempts that have been made to study the social, as well as the labour, history of the working class. It is believed that the attempt to identify , and synthesise, material, demographic, ideological and organisational developments has proved of considerable value. It has confirmed the interdependence of what have been regarded too often as distinct aspects of working-class experience; and it has suggested once again that the day-to-day lives of ordinary working people were a great deal more varied, creative and complex than is commonly supposed.[3]

REFERENCES

1. **M. Savage and A. Miles,** *The Remaking of the British Working Class 1840–1940*, Routledge, 1994, p. 90.
2. **J. A. Schmiechen,** 'State Reform and the Local Economy: An Aspect of Industrialization in Late Victorian and Edwardian London', *Economic History Review*, xxviii, 1975, p. 413.
3. **J. Benson,** 'Introduction', in **J. Benson** (ed.), *The Working Class in England 1875–1914*, Croom Helm, 1984.

SELECT BIBLIOGRAPHY

INTRODUCTION

Bourke, J., *Working Class Cultures in Britain, 1890–1960: Gender, Class and Ethnicity*, Routledge, 1994.

Brown, K. D., *The English Labour Movement 1700–1951*, Gill & Macmillan, 1982.

Harrison, J. F. C., *The Common People: A History from the Norman Conquest to the Present*, Fontana, 1984.

Hopkins, E., *A Social History of the English Working Classes 1815–1945*, Arnold, 1979.

Hopkins, E., *The Rise and Decline of the English Working Classes 1918–1990: A Social History*, Wedenfeld and Nicolson, 1991.

Meacham, S., *A Life Apart: The English Working Class, 1890–1914*, Thames & Hudson, 1977.

Smith, D., 'Social History and Sociology – More Than Just Good Friends', *Sociological Review*, 30, 1982.

Winter, J., 'Introduction: Labour History and Labour Historians', in **Winter, J.** (ed.), *The Working Class in Modern British History: Essays in Honour of Henry Pelling*, Cambridge U.P., 1983.

CHAPTER 1. WORK

Benson, J., *The Penny Capitalists: A Study of Nineteenth-Century Working-Class Entrepreneurs*, Gill & Macmillan, 1983.

Benson, J., 'Work', in **Benson, J.** (ed.), *The Working Class in England 1875–1914*, Croom Helm, 1984.

Coombes, B. L., *These Poor Hands: The Autobiography of a Miner Working in South Wales*, Gollancz, 1939.

Exell, A., 'Morris Motors in the 1930s. Part I', *History Workshop*, 6, 1978.

Howkins, A., *Poor Labouring Men: Rural Radicalism in Norfolk 1872–1923*, Routledge & Kegan Paul, 1985.

Joyce, P., *Work, Society and Politics: The Culture of the Factory in Later Victorian England*, Methuen, 1982

McIvor, A. J., *A History of Work in Britain, 1880–1950*, Palgrave, 2001.

McKenna, F., *The Railway Workers 1840–1970*, Faber & Faber, 1980.

Roberts, E., *Women's Work 1840–1940*, Macmillan, 1988.

Taylor, P., 'Daughters and Mothers – Maids and Mistresses: Domestic Service between the Wars', in Clarke, J., Critcher, C. and Johnson, R. (eds), *Working-Class Culture: Studies in History and Theory*, Hutchinson, 1979.

White, J., *The Worst Street in North London: Campbell Bunk, Islington Between The Wars*, Routledge & Kegan Paul, 1986.

Whiting, R. C., *The View from Cowley: The Impact of Industrialization upon Oxford, 1918–1939*, Clarendon Press, 1983.

CHAPTER 2. WAGES, INCOMES AND THE COST OF LIVING

Benjamin, D. K. and Kochin, L. A., 'Searching for an Explanation of Unemployment in Interwar Britain', *Journal of Political Economy*, 87, 1979.

Benson, J., *The Rise of Consumer Society in Britain, 1880–1980*, Longman, 1994.

Booth, A. E. and Glynn, S., 'Unemployment in the Interwar Period: A Multiple Problem', *Journal of Contemporary History*, 10, 1975.

Bowley, A. L., *Wages and Income in the United Kingdom since 1860*, Cambridge U.P., 1937.

Burnett, J., *A History of the Cost of Living*, Penguin, 1969.

Constantine, S., *Unemployment in Britain between the Wars*, Longman, 1980.

Fraser, D., *The Evolution of the British Welfare State: A History of Social Policy since the Industrial Revolution*, Macmillan, 1973.

Reid, G. L. and Robertson, D. J. (eds), *Fringe Benefits, Labour Costs and Social Security*, Allen & Unwin, 1965.

Rowe, J. W. F., *Wages in Practice and Theory*, Routledge & Kegan Paul, 1928.

Rowntree, B. S., *Poverty: A Study of Town Life*, Macmillan, 1902.

Webb, A. L. and Sieve, J. E. B., *Income Redistribution and the Welfare State*, Bell, 1971.

CHAPTER 3. HOUSING

Burnett, J., *A Social History of Housing 1815–1985*, Methuen, 1986.

Chapman, S. D. (ed.), *The History of Working-Class Housing: A Symposium*, David & Charles, 1971.

Daunton, M. J., *House and Home in the Victorian City: Working-Class Housing 1850–1914*, Arnold, 1983.

Englander, D., *Landlord and Tenant in Urban Britain 1838–1918*, Clarendon Press, 1983.

Jevons, R. and Madge, J., *Housing Estates: A Study of Bristol Corporation Policy and Practice between the Wars*, University of Bristol, 1946.

Swenarton, M., *Homes Fit For Heroes: The Politics and Architecture of Early State Housing in Britain*, Heinemann, 1981.

Swenarton, M. and **Taylor, S.**, 'The Scale and Nature of the Growth of Owner-Occupation in Britain between the Wars', *Economic History Review*, xxxviii, 1985.

White, J., *Rothschild Buildings: Life in an East End Tenement Block 1887–1920*, Routledge & Kegan Paul, 1980.

Young, T., *Becontree and Dagenham: A Report Made for the Pilgrim Trust by Terence Young*, Becontree Social Survey Committee, 1934.

CHAPTER 4. FAMILY

Anderson, M., *Approaches to the History of the Western Family 1500–1914*, Macmillan, 1980.

Benson, J., *Prime Time: A History of the Middle Aged in Twentieth-Century Britain*, Longman, 1997.

Chinn, C., *They Worked all their Lives: Women of the Urban Poor in England, 1880–1939*, Manchester U.P., 1988.

Davies, A. and **Fielding, S.** (eds), *Workers' Worlds: Culture and Communities in Manchester and Salford, 1880–1939*, Manchester U.P., 1992.

Gillis, J. R., 'Servants, Sexual Relations, and the Risks of Illegitimacy in London, 1801–1900', *Feminist Studies*, 5, 1979.

Jones, S. G., *Sport, Politics and the Working Class: Organised Labour and Sport in Interwar Britain*, Manchester U.P., 1988.

McKibbin, R., 'Work and Hobbies in Britain, 1880—1950', in **Winter, J.** (ed.), *The Working Class in Modern British History: Essays in Honour of Henry Pelling*, Cambridge U.P., 1983.

Oddy, D. J., 'Working-Class Diets in Late Nineteenth-Century Britain', *Economic History Review*, xxiii, 1970

Outhwaite, R. B., 'Age of Marriage in England from the late Seventeenth to the Nineteenth Century', *Transactions of the Royal Historical Society*, xxiii, 1973.

Roberts, E., 'The Family', in **Benson, J.** (ed.), *The Working Class in England 1875–1914*, Croom Helm, 1984.

Roberts, E., *A Woman's Place: An Oral History of Working-Class Women 1890–1940*, Blackwell, 1984.

Shorter, E., *The Making of the Modern Family*, Fontana, 1977.

Slater, E. and **Woodside, M.**, *Patterns of Marriage: A Study of Marriage Relationships in the Urban Working Classes*, Cassell, 1951.

Smith, F. B., 'Health', in **Benson, J.** (ed.), *The Working Class in England 1875–1914*, Croom Helm, 1984.

Vincent, D., 'Love and Death and the Nineteenth-Century Working Class', *Social History*, 5, 1980.

Walton, J. K., 'The Demand for Working-Class Seaside Holidays in Victorian England', *Economic History Review*, xxxiv, 1981.

Walton, J. K., *Fish & Chips and the British Working Class, 1870–1940*, Leicester U.P., 1992.

Weeks, J., *Sex, Politics and Society: The Regulation of Sexuality since 1800*, Longman, 1989.

CHAPTER 5. KINSHIP, NEIGHBOURHOOD AND COMMUNITY

Dennis, R., *English Industrial Cities of the Nineteenth Century: A Social Geography*, Cambridge U.P., 1984.

Duncan, R., 'Case Studies in Emigration: Cornwall, Gloucestershire and New South Wales, 1877–1886', *Economic History Review*, xvi, 1963–4.

Durant, R., *Watling: A Survey of Social Life on a New Housing Estate*, King, 1959.

Frankenberg, R., *Communities in Britain: Social Life in Town and Country*, Penguin, 1966.

Jeavons, R. and **Madge, J.**, *Housing Estates: A Study of Bristol Corporation Policy and Practice between the Wars*, University of Bristol, 1946.

Lewis, G. J., 'Mobility, Locality and Demographic Change: The Case of North Cardiganshire, 1851–71', *Welsh History Review*, 9, 1979.

Mogey, J. M., *Family and Neighbourhood: Two Studies in Oxford*, Oxford U.P., 1956.

Perry, P. J., 'Working-Class Isolation and Mobility in Rural Dorset, 1837–1936: A Study of Marriage Distances', *Transactions of the Institute of British Geographers*, 46, 1969.

Williams, W. M., *The Sociology of an English Village: Gosforth*, Routledge & Kegan Paul, 1956.

Young, M. and **Willmott, P.**, *Family and Kinship in East London*, Penguin, 1957.

Young, T., *Becontree and Dagenham: A Report Made for the Pilgrim Trust by Terence Young*, Becontree Social Survey Committee, 1934.

CHAPTER 6. INDIVIDUAL, NATION AND CLASS

Cannadine, D., 'The Context, Performance and Meaning of Ritual: The British Monarchy and the "Invention of Tradition", c. 1820–1977', in **Hobsbawm, E.** and **Ranger, T.** (eds), *The Invention of Tradition*, Cambridge U.P., 1983.

Cunningham, H., 'The Language of Patriotism, 1750–1914', *History Workshop*, 12, 1981.

Cunningham, H., *The Volunteer Force: A Social and Political History 1859–1908*, Croom Helm, 1975.

Fraser, W. H., *The Coming of the Mass Market, 1850–1914*, Macmillan, 1981.

Hammerton, E. and **Cannadine, D.**, 'Conflict and Consensus on a Ceremonial Occasion: The Diamond Jubilee in Cambridge in 1897', *Historical Journal*, 24, 1981.

Humphries, S., *Hooligans or Rebels? An Oral History of Working-Class Childhood 1889–1939*, Blackwell, 1981.

Jones, G. S., 'Working-Class Culture and Working-Class Politics in London, 1870–1900: Notes on the Remaking of a Working Class', *Journal of Social History*, 7,1974.

McLeod, H.., *Religion and the Working Class in Nineteenth-Century Britain*, Macmillan, 1984.

McLeod, H., *Class and Religion in the Late Victorian City*, Croom Helm, 1974.

Mann, M., *Consciousness and Action Among the Western Working Class*, Macmillan, 1973.

Marwick, A., *Class: Image and Reality in Britain, France and the USA since 1930*, Fontana, 1981.

Moorhouse, H. F., 'The Marxist Theory of the Labour Aristocracy', *Social History*, 3, 1978.

Price, R., *An Imperial War and the British Working Class: Working-Class Attitudes and Reactions to the Boer War 1899–1902*, Routledge & Kegan Paul, 1972.

Savage, M. and Miles, A., *The Remaking of the British Working Class, 1840–1940*, Routledge, 1994.

Springhall, J., *Youth, Empire and Society: British Youth Movements, 1883–1940*, Croom Helm, 1977.

CHAPTER 7. THE LABOUR MOVEMENT

Bain, G. S. and Price, R., *Profiles of Union Growth: A Comparative Statistical Portrait of Eight Countries*, Blackwell, 1980.

Chamberlain, C., 'The Growth of Support for the Labour Party in Britain', *Political Studies*, 24, 1973.

Clegg, H. A., Fox, A., and Thompson, A. F. T., *A History of British Trade Unions since 1889: Volume I, 1889–1910*, Clarendon Press, 1964.

Clegg, H. A., *A History of Trade Unions since 1889: Volume 11, 1911–1933*, Clarendon Press, 1985.

Forester, T., *The Labour Party and the Working Class*, Heinemann, 1976.

Haynes, M. J., 'Strikes', in Benson, J. (ed.), *The Working Class in England 1875–1914*, Croom Helm, 1984.

Laybourn, K., *The General Strike of 1926*, Manchester U.P., 1993.

McKenzie, R. and Silver, A., *Angels in Marble: Working Class Conservatives in Urban England*, Heinemann, 1968.

Mansfield, N., *English Farmworkers and Local Patriotism, 1900–1930*, Ashgate, 2001.

Panitch, L. V., 'Ideology and Integration: The Case of the British Labour Party', *Political Studies*, 19, 1971.

Pugh, M., *The Making of Modern British Politics 1867–1939*, Blackwell, 1993.

Pugh, M., *The Tories and the People 1880–1935*, Blackwell, 1985.

Wrigley, C. J. (ed.), *A History of British Industrial Relations 1875–1914*, Harvester, 1982.

Wrigley C. J. (ed.), *A History of British Industrial Relations: Volume II, 1914–1939*, Harvester, 1986.

INDEX